A History

of

Greek Religion

A History

of

Greek Religion

by

MARTIN P. NILSSON

Professor Emeritus of Classical Archaeology and
Ancient History and sometime Rector of
the University of Lund

Translated from the Swedish

by

F. J. FIELDEN

Formerly Lecturer in the University of Lund

Second Edition

GREENWOOD PRESS, PUBLISHERS
WESTPORT, CONNECTICUT

Library of Congress Cataloging in Publication Data

Nilsson, Martin Persson, 1874-1967.
  A history of Greek religion.

    Translation of Den grekiska religionens historia.
    Reprint of the 2d ed. published by Clarendon Press,
Oxford.
    Includes bibliographical references and index.
    1. Greece--Religion. 2. Mythology, Greek.
3. Crete--Antiquities. 4. Greece, Modern--Antiquities.
I. Title.
[BL781.N5313   1980]   292'.08   80-13430
ISBN 0-313-22466-8 (lib. bdg.)

Copyright Oxford University Press 1949.

This reprint has been authorized by The Oxford University Press.

Reprinted in 1980 by Greenwood Press,
A division of Congressional Information Service, Inc.
88 Post Road West, Westport, Connecticut 06881

Printed in the United States of America

10 9 8 7 6 5 4 3 2 1

PREFACE TO THE SECOND EDITION

SINCE the first edition of this book appeared in 1925 Greek religion has been treated in many papers and in some larger works: I mention, for example, O. Kern, *Die Religion der Griechen*, 3 vols., 1926–38; U. v. Wilamowitz, *Der Glaube der Hellenen*, 2 vols., 1931–2; H. J. Rose, *Primitive Culture in Greece*, 1925, and *A Handbook of Greek Mythology*, 1928. But unfortunately the stresses of the time have prevented any major alteration of the text from the first edition. I think, however, that the views expressed hold good still except for minor changes and modifications. A full documentation and discussion will be found in my *Geschichte der griechischen Religion* (in *Handbuch der Altertumswissenschaft*), of which the first volume to the time of Alexander the Great appeared in 1941 and the second to the end of Antiquity is in the press. Here I must ask the reader to peruse this preface and call his attention to the notes appended at the end of the book in which addenda, corrections, and references to ancient authors will be found.

The chapter on the prehistoric religion of Greece was based on the materials collected for my *Minoan-Mycenaean Religion and its Survival in Greek Religion*, which was published two years later in 1927. Since then this age has been treated in many papers and books, and new finds have been made. I need refer here only to Sir Arthur Evans's *Palace of Minos*, vols. ii–iv. I reworked the subject briefly in my *Gesch. d. griech. Rel.*, i, pp. 237 et seqq. In the earlier book, since the evidence is monumental, I treated the Minoan and the Mycenaean religion as essentially one, but I pointed also to some differences. Hades, the realm of the shadows, is not Minoan; the shield-carrying goddess on the limestone tablet from Mycenae (p. 26), a forerunner of Athena, is a Mycenaean remodelling of the Minoan house-goddess; the lavish funeral cult of the Mycenaeans contrasts with the poorness of the tombs from the great age of Crete. A fresh example is

provided by the splendid finds at Midea.[1] The Swedish
excavations at Asine revealed a ledge with idols and vessels,
just as in the Minoan house chapels, but to these were
added a great head and a stone axe, perhaps Zeus and his
thunderbolt. The ledge was placed, not in a small chapel, but
in a corner of the megaron, the great living-room.[2] The cult
was open to the public.

A renewed examination of the relations of the religion of
the Mycenaeans, on the one hand to the Minoan religion and
on the other to Homer, raised new problems. The Mycenaeans
were Greeks and, unlike the peaceful Minoans, they were a
warlike people. Many heroic myths and especially the great
mythical cycles come down from the Mycenaean age,[3] and
with them those gods who are so closely associated with the
myths that they cannot be separated from them. The State
of the gods, Olympus, is modelled after the pattern of the
Mycenaean kingdom, a mighty king ruling over sometimes
recalcitrant vassals. The question arose whether the Minoan
garb does not cover Mycenaean ideas which were very different
in character. Such problems are very likely to arise when
a less-civilized people takes over the artistic forms of a highly
developed culture—the representation of Ahuramazda in
the guise of the god Assur provides a typical example. Homer
preserves a heritage from the Mycenaean age.[4] More important than the archaeological details is the fact that Homer
knows only a pre-Dorian Greece and depicts a feudal society
under the rule of a war-king. He may have preserved some
elements of Mycenaean religious belief as well. In my *Gesch.
d. griech. Rel.*, i, pp. 338 et seqq., I pointed to two such
elements: the fatalism fitting to a warring age, and the divine
apparatus whose origin is partly to be found in the belief in
a personal relation between god and man. The sharp contrast between burial in the Mycenaean age and cremation in
Homer has now been diminished. At Midea the dead were

[1] A. W. Persson, *The Royal Tombs at Dendra near Midea*, 1931.
[2] See my *Min.-Myc. Rel.*, p. xx et seq. and plates iii and iv.
[3] The subject is treated fully in my *Mycenaean Origin of Greek Mythology*, 1932.
[4] I gave an account in my book, *Homer and Mycenae*, 1933.

laid down in sarcophagi but the tomb offerings partly burned. Traces of fire are found in many Mycenaean tombs and burnt bones in late sub-Mycenaean graves. Homer knows only the mound. The top of the tholos tomb projected above the ground and was covered by a mound and a tholos tomb on flat ground was likewise covered.[1] It seems that sometimes a stone was erected on the top. The Mycenaeans were Greeks, the ancestors of the historical Greeks, and there is no dividing them into watertight compartments. We are therefore justified in searching for Mycenaean traces in Homer.

Some modern anthropologists blame classical scholars for not noticing the use of myths as ritual texts or their social importance.[2] This proves only the anthropologists' ignorance of Greek myths and of their characteristic peculiarities. It is no less wrong to judge Greek myths by the standard of certain primitive peoples than it is to judge the myths of primitive peoples by Greek standards, as was done earlier. We have some few extremely scanty remains of Greek ritual texts; myths are hardly referred to in them. At the festivals of the gods myths were chanted; but they were poetical, not liturgical, compositions. A myth rarely affected ritual.[3] The social importance of the myths was great and it is referred to on p. 60; their political importance is discussed on pp. 237 et seqq. The statement 'that myth is essentially an explanation, a sort of primitive science', is incorrect. The *aitia* cannot be compared with science. The desire of man to find an explanation for everything which strikes his attention is universal and often takes fantastic forms. Such *aitia* are current among all peoples.

The most difficult and obscure problem of the archaic age, Orphism, has been treated variously,[4] since Professor Kern

---

[1] N. Valmin, 'Tholos Tombs and Tumuli' in *Corolla archaeologica* (*Acta Instituti Romani Regni Sueciae*, ii), 1932, pp. 216 et seqq.

[2] E. g. B. Malinowski, *Myth in Primitive Psychology*, 1926. For a judicious view on the question see E. Ehnmark, 'Anthropomorphism and Miracle', *Uppsala universitetets årsskrift*, 1939, fasc. 12, pp. 136 et seqq.

[3] See the excellent treatise by H. J. Rose, *Modern Methods in Classical Mythology*, 1930.

[4] My paper, 'Early Orphism and Kindred Religious Movements',

prepared the ground, collecting the testimonies and fragments. Professor Linforth tries in a learned and searching
analysis almost to wipe out Orphism. He acknowledges as
Orphic only what is 'sealed with the name of Orpheus'. But
this seal is a fake, all Orphic writings are pseudepigrapha.
He overlooks the fact that Orphism is a conventional name
for the main branch of various religious movements and
cannot be separated from them. He remarks justly (pp. 327
et seqq.) that according to Olympiodorus man was not
created from the ashes of the Titans but from the soot in the
smoke which rose from their smouldering bodies. Olympiodorus is a late author and so are others who relate that the
Titans ate the torn limbs of the child Dionysos. But this is
implied already; the Orphics remodelled the Dionysiac rite
of tearing asunder an animal (in the myth a child) and eating
its flesh into the myth that the Titans dismembered the child
Dionysos. The origin of man from the Titans is implied in
the saying, quoted by Plato, about the titanic nature of man.
For man is not wholly evil; there is also something divine
in him. As to the transmigration of the souls the words of
Pindar, Olympians, ii, vv. 56 et seqq., which precede the
words quoted here (p. 222), are important, for, rightly
understood, they say that just as a man may do wrong in
this world and be punished in the Underworld, so he may do
wrong in the Underworld and be punished in this world.
Man alternates between this and the other world.

Certain parts of the subject-matter of the third and the
fourth chapters have been treated more amply in my *Greek
Popular Religion*[1] where I tried to describe Greek religion
from the point of view of the farmer and the man in the
street. It contains also a chapter on the Eleusinian religion.
In my interpretation of the myth which is at the bottom of
the Eleusinian cult (cf. p. 211),[2] I take the four months

Harvard Theol. Rev., xxviii, 1935, pp. 181 et seqq.; W. K. C. Guthrie,
Orpheus and Greek Religion, 1935; I. M. Linforth, *The Arts of Orpheus*,
1941.

[1] New York, Columbia Press, 1940, reprinted 1947, with illustrations.

[2] I treated the religion of Eleusis at greater length in my paper,
'Die eleusinischen Gottheiten', *ARw*, xxxii, 1935, pp. 79 et seqq.

during which Kore is absent as the summer months and this has been contested; but, if one takes seriously into account, first, that Demeter is not a goddess of vegetation in general but of cereals especially, and second, the climate of Greece and the agricultural calendar, my interpretation is irrefutable. After the harvest in June the corn was stored in subterranean silos. It was not brought up again till the seed-time approached in October (cf. p. 123); and it was only then that Kore was reunited with her mother. During these four months the fields are barren and desolate, burnt by the scorching sun. No green is seen on them, and Kore is absent.

The clash between religion and its critics, which culminated in the famous trials for atheism in Athens, is mentioned but briefly, pp. 266 and 275. In the last instance it depended on the revolutionizing ideas propagated by the natural philosophers and the sophists, but in my *Greek Popular Religion* I tried to show that the conflict was promoted by the seers who became aware that Natural philosophy was a danger to their art. For if such phenomena as eclipses, abnormalities in the organs of animals, and so on depended on natural causes, they were not omens, and the art of the seers was worthless. Trials of this kind, moreover, were staged for political ends, and the anger of the ordinary men against the sophists whom they accused of being the originators of the wantonness and dissoluteness of the young men came into play. It is conspicuous in the accusation of Socrates.

In a recently published book, *Greek Piety*,[1] I viewed Greek religion from another angle, trying to set out the main lines of the ideas of the Greeks concerning the world, the universe, the vicissitudes of human life, and its dependence on higher powers, ideas which derived from the educated classes and penetrated to the people too. In the archaic age the cry for justice was raised in religion as well as in the State. Justice was the great problem of this age. The demand for justice led, on the social plane, to a demand for the equal distribution of the good things of life and, on the religious plane, to the idea of equalization of men's fates in such a way that a given

[1] Clarendon Press, 1948.

amount of good luck was counterbalanced by an equal amount of ill luck. This idea found expression in the doctrine of *hybris* and *nemesis*, man's frowardness and the gods' smiting down of. the froward. The power which brought about such a levelling was not to be found in individual gods, but only in a general conception of deity, the divine. This religion of resignation gave neither the support and hope in tribulation nor the comfort in sorrow which man looks for from a higher power. It could not stand up against criticism.

The present book is devoted to an account of Greek national religion and its decay. There was no room to treat of the rebuilding which was begun after the fall of the old religion. This rebuilding is called syncretism, *viz.* a blending of various religions, and the major part is ascribed to Oriental religions, including astrology. It is often said that Greece was suffocated in the grip of the Orient. This is only partly true. Greek thought made an important contribution: a new conception of the Universe and its rule, of which astrology is but a secondary element; the conception of power and the belief in daemons which degenerated into sorcery and superstition; a strong monotheistic tendency; transcendentalism on which dualism and asceticism depended; certain propensities to mysticism and spiritualism—all reinforced by Oriental influence. A new religion was built up of these elements embodying as much as possible of the old Greek myths and of Oriental cults. I have tried to set out these factors in the last part of my *Greek Piety*, which is a summary of the evidence and the discussions in the relevant parts of my *Gesch. d. griech. Rel.*, vol. ii.

I hope that the reader who in addition to the present book takes notice of the two small books already mentioned will attain to an understanding of what Greek religion was and what became of it.

M. P. N.

LUND,
January 1948.

CONTENTS

ABBREVIATIONS

AJ.   *Jahrbuch des Deutschen archäologischen Instituts.*
AJA. *American Journal of Archaeology.*
AM.   *Mitteilungen des Deutschen archäologischen Instituts zu Athen.*
ARw. *Archiv für Religionswissenschaft.*
BSA. *Annual of the British School at Athens.*
EA.   Ἐφημερὶς ἀρχαιολογική.
IG.   *Inscriptiones Graecae.*
JHS. *Journal of Hellenic Studies.*
NJb. *Neue Jahrbücher für das klassische Altertum.*
MA.   *Monumenti antichi della R. Accademia dei Lincei.*
RGVV. *Religionsgeschichtliche Versuche und Vorarbeiten.*
RHR. *Revue de l'histoire des religions.*
TPC. A. J. Evans, *Mycenaean Tree and Pillar Cult, JHS*, xxi, 1901,
        pp. 99 et seq.

I

MINOAN-MYCENAEAN RELIGION AND ITS SURVIVAL IN GREEK RELIGION

THE principal tendencies in the study of Greek religion in recent times seem to take us back to the methods adopted in the early days of archaeological research. Either the attention was allowed to dwell upon the ruins and inscriptions which were scattered about in the neighbourhood of an ancient site, or else the intervening layers were impatiently broken through for the purpose of arriving at the oldest and most primitive evidences of human life. Similarly, the study of religion has either preferred to concern itself with the downfall of the religion of antiquity at the great crisis which ended the classical period, or has endeavoured to lay bare the primitive foundation upon which the Greek religion, like others, was built up. There is undeniably some justice in the complaint that the Greek religion of the period when the prosperity and culture of Greece were at their height has been neglected. And when attempts are made to penetrate to the deepest and most primitive foundations, it is only too easily forgotten that a people with a highly and richly developed culture lived in Greece before the Greeks.

The Bronze Age of Greece has emerged in wonderful freshness and splendour from the protecting bosom of the earth, in which it had lain hidden for more than three thousand years. The culture of that age originated in Crete, but it put forth magnificent off-shoots upon the mainland, especially in Eastern Greece. It is now an established fact that the people who created it were not of Grecian nor on the whole of Aryan race. A change of religion therefore took place in Greece in prehistoric times, and the first step towards an understanding of the history of the Greek religion is to seek to explain what this change involved. We must therefore begin by trying to form a conception of the religion of the Bronze Age, the Minoan-Mycenaean religion.[1]

Material is not lacking. Of the numerous archaeological finds a great many are clearly of religious import. But the Minoan-Mycenaean religion is a picture-book without text. If we wish to compel the pictures to speak, the most obvious method is to make use of analogies from other religions. Since the racial origins of the people are unknown, none of the religions of the world has in fact greater pretensions than another to supply the text, but it lies in the nature of things that it should have been first sought in Greece itself and among the neighbouring peoples. Before the distinction of race was established, inferences were freely drawn from the religion of classical Greece ; nowadays this is only done with due precaution. Before we argue for the historical continuity of the Minoan-Mycenaean and the Greek religions we must first know what the Minoan-Mycenaean religion was in itself. Some students of the question have sought to connect it with the ancient religions of the East—of the Semitic world and of Egypt. Traces of Semitic and Babylonian influence upon Minoan-Mycenaean culture are vague and difficult to detect. Not so with the influence of Egypt. It can be shown that active relationships existed between

[1] The chief work on the Minoan-Mycenaean religion is still Evans, *The Mycenaean Tree and Pillar Cult*, *JHS*, xxi, 1901, pp. 99 et seq. Later works are concerned only with the explanation of separate monument groups, or with the developing of a special point of view. Summaries by R. Dussaud, *Les Civilisations préhelléniques*, ch. 7 ; Blanche Williams in *Gournia*, App. A, p. 51 ; and G. Glotz, *La Civilisation égéenne*, livre iii. Compare also my essay, *Die Anfänge der Göttin Athene* (*Det Kong. Danske Videnskabernes Selskab. Hist.-filol. Meddelelser*, iv. 7, 1921).

Crete and Egypt ; the first efflorescence of Minoan culture in the Early Minoan Age seems to have been due to Egyptian impetus ; Cretan art sometimes follows Egyptian models, and even adopts two elements of the Egyptian cult (the sistrum and the ankh). But all this is far from proving that Egyptian influence was the foundation of Cretan art and religion. On the contrary the evidence points to the independence and originality of the Minoan-Mycenaean religion, just as Minoan-Mycenaean art is original and independent, and even when it follows Egyptian models, breathes its own spirit into them.

Far greater weight is now attached to the connexions between the Minoan-Mycenaean religion and the religions of Asia Minor, for there are philological indications that the pre-Grecian population of Greece and the primitive population of Asia Minor belonged to the same race. But these indications concern Western Asia Minor only. The position of the Hittites in regard to race and language has not yet been definitely determined, and until this has been done the comparisons which are often made between their religion and that of other peoples ought to be treated with caution.

It is necessary, in the first place, to form an idea of the Minoan-Mycenaean religion from the relics themselves, and as far as possible without using foreign analogies for their explanation. Only when this foundation has been laid can we venture to go farther. But here it must not be forgotten that the monuments are of two different kinds and contribute in different degrees to our conception of the religion. One kind is composed of idols and actual objects of the cult, the other of sculptured, painted, or engraved representations of objects and scenes connected with the cult. In the latter the creative imagination of the artist plays a part, and this is especially so in representations of the gods. They are depicted as the eye of imagination sees them, seldom in the form taken by their images in the cult ; indeed it is even conceivable that the cult knew no images, although the artist has represented the epiphany of a god. It is therefore advisable to begin by looking at the Minoan-Mycenaean religion not as depicted by the creative imagination, but through the actual relics of the cult.

The earliest inhabitants of Crete, like many other neolithic peoples, lived in caves. When the caves were abandoned for better dwelling-places, they continued to be used as burial-grounds and as centres of the cult. Here we have an instance of that religious conservatism of which other traces are to be found in the Minoan religion, e. g. in the roughly moulded bell-shaped idols which were worshipped at a date when art had long since left these primitive figures behind it, and in the garment of hides worn by the officiating priests at the ceremonies of the cult, as seen on the H. Triada sarcophagus and on gems. On Mount Ida there are two cult-caves, at Kamares and at Patso (the famous cave of Idaean Zeus on the top of the mountain, on the other hand, has only yielded finds from post-Minoan times) ; the finds from the cave at Psychro in Eastern Crete are particularly abundant, though this is not the Diktaean cave but the cave at Lyktos to which Hesiod makes Rhea carry the new-born Zeus.[1] An important cave exists in the neighbourhood of Knossos, and at its seaport town of Amnisos is the cave of Ilithyia. There are also open-air places of the cult, e. g. at Petsofà on the eastern coast, which has yielded numerous finds, and again on the top of Mount Juktas near Knossos, where there is also a smaller cave.

The finds give no information as to the nature of the cult or as to the god who was worshipped at these places, but it is otherwise with the numerous objects belonging to the cult found in houses and palaces. At Gournia [2] and in the so-called Sanctuary of Double Axes at Knossos [3] these

---

[1] J. Toutain, *RHR*, 1911, ii, pp. 277 et seq.
[2] *Gournia*, p. 47 and pl. 11.   [3] *BSA*, viii, 1902, pp. 93 et seq.

objects were still in their ancient places. The finds are so numerous that we may probably assume that every palace and at least every good-sized house had its cult, though the rooms devoted to the cult were very small. Among the articles discovered are tables of libation, horns of consecration, and bell-shaped idols. The Gournia idol had a snake wound round it, and various fragments of similar idols with snakes have been found at other places. The snake-goddess is the most in evidence of the Minoan divinities. In two stone cists under the floor of a room in the palace of Knossos objects from a sanctuary of the palace had been packed, including a snake-goddess in faience, another statuette of a woman with snakes in her hands, presumably a priestess, and models of the garments comprised in the wardrobe of the goddess.[1] The most remarkable single find is an ivory statuette (now in Boston) of the snake-goddess ; the snakes and the edges of the skirt are of gold.[2]

It has been thought that the snake represents the soul of the deceased, and consequently that we have here a goddess who rules over the lower world, like Persephone. But it is not explained why the goddess of the lower world should have taken her place in the domestic cult. However, the snake is not always the representative of the dead ; both ancient and modern folk-lore know it as the protector of the household who brings luck to the house, and in the Greece of our day it is still called ' the lord of the house ' and receives offerings. There is no need to look any farther for an explanation of the Minoan domestic snake-goddess.

Bell-shaped idols have only been discovered among burial offerings upon one occasion, and in this case a room in an old house had been used for the burial, so that it is not absolutely certain that these idols were burial gifts. Other idols—apart from votive ones—have been found in graves or separately. The former is the case with the well-known

[1] *BSA*, ix, 1903, pp. 35 et seq.   [2] *AJA*, xix, 1915, pls. 10–16.

Mycenaean idols and with the naked female idols which are often regarded as images of a goddess and are compared with the Oriental Goddess of Fecundity. Images of gods are not as a rule placed in graves, although the two gold plates from the IIIrd shaft-grave at Mycenae, representing a naked woman with birds, are an undoubted example of the practice. The simplest explanation is to consider these female images in the same light as images of animals and other burial gifts : they were to serve the dead in another world. In regard to the representation of the gods no conclusions can be drawn from them.

Among the objects discovered at the places of the cult mentioned above the so-called horns of consecration, the double axe, and tables of offerings of various forms are especially prominent. A form of the last-named, resembling a small round table with three very short legs and a shallow depression on the surface, was found on several sites in Crete and at Mycenae also. At Mycenae a stepped base of a kind similar to that upon which the double axe was erected was recently found. These finds are important because they show that the cult was carried on upon the Mycenaean main-land in the same manner as in Minoan Crete.

The horns of consecration and the double axes occur very often in representations of scenes belonging to the cult. The former are two horn-shaped projections pointing up-wards and connected by a staff-like base. Their origin is unknown. They have been compared with the ' horns of the altar ' in the Semitic cult. They often occur upon altars but are placed as a detached implement upon them. It has been supposed that they are an abbreviated and conven-tionalized imitation of the boukranion. It is certain, at least, that the horns are the place of consecration : the holy objects were placed between them.

The double axe is the symbol of the Minoan religion, a symbol just as characteristic and omnipresent as the

Christian Cross or the Mohammedan Crescent Numerous
examples have been found which could have served no
practical but only a sacral end—richly ornamented double
axes of thin sheeted bronze, miniature axes of different
materials ; very often they occur on vases and gems and
carved on the stones of the walls and pillars of the palace
of Knossos. But not every double axe, any more than
every cross, has significance as an object of the cult. Its
purpose is to place the building or the object under a higher
protection or to preserve it from desecration, just as the
cross painted on a wall often does in modern Italy.

There is a Carian word, *labrys*, which means ' double axe '.
At Labranda in Caria, Zeus Labrandeus, the god with the
double axe, was worshipped in historical times. Since the
original population of Crete and that of Caria were undoubtedly related, it is a natural supposition that the god
with the double axe was worshipped also in Crete. His
nature is determined more closely by comparison with the
Hittite god of the sky, Teshub, who is represented with the
double axe and the lightning. The double axe is therefore
supposed to be the thunderbolt, like Thor's hammer. But
before adopting this generally accepted opinion, we must
test it in the light of the native Minoan material.

The double axe occurs often in scenes relating to the cult.
The most important representations are those on the
sarcophagus from H. Triada.[1] On one side stand two
double axes on high pillars wrapped round with green. On
each double axe a bird has alighted. The sacrifice goes on
underneath—a sacrifice to the gods, not an offering to the
dead, apparently. It is undoubtedly tempting to see in the
double axes objects of the cult, fetishes, symbols of divinity,
or whatever they may be called. But this is not certain,
for on one side the figure of the god also stands before his
shrine. Some seal-impressions show the double axe in the

[1] Published by Paribeni, *MA*, xix. 1

hands of ministers of the cult[1] and the moulding form from Palaikastro represents a woman holding a double axe in each of her uplifted hands.[2] She is perhaps a goddess, but may also be a priestess. The double axe therefore never occurs in the hands of any male god, and this is very remarkable if it represents the thunderbolt, for the god of the lightning is always a male deity. Under these circumstances the possibility of another explanation must be considered.

The double axe is sometimes represented as standing between the horns of consecration, but the common assumption that the small double axe found in the so-called Sanctuary of Double Axes in the palace of Knossos stood between the horns of consecration cannot be proved. It is still more often depicted between the horns of the boucranion. The boucranion is the skull of the animal sacrificed which was left on the spot as a memento of the sacrifice and became a well-known ornamental motif in Greek art. The connexion reminds us that the double axe may be the sacrificial axe with which the animal was killed, as in later times. It is conceivable that the principal implement used in the sacrifice acquired an increased importance for the cult. This was the case, e. g., with the double axe with which the Tenedians sacrificed their victims to Dionysos ; they placed it on their coins as the emblem of the city. In this way the axe may have become a symbol, even an object, of the cult.

A characteristic feature of Minoan art is to be observed as regards both the double axe and the horns of consecration. When a motif has become common, it spreads and is widely used without any deeper meaning. And so we can neither be sure that all the objects and parts of buildings which are decorated with the double axe are really of sacral

[1] JHS, xxii, 1902, p. 78, fig. 5 ; MA, xiii, p. 39, fig. 33, compared with BSA, ix, 1903, p. 60 ; BSA, viii, 1902, fig. 59.

[2] EA, 1900, pl. 4a.

importance nor that all the buildings which bear the horns of consecration are really temples. But that several of them are temples and altars is shown plainly enough by the votaries standing in front of them ; on gems it is not always possible to distinguish with certainty between temple and altar.

In these representations of scenes pertaining to the cult the tree takes a prominent place. It stands behind the altar or behind something which is more like an enclosure and is reminiscent of the walls with gateways that surround sacred trees on certain reliefs belonging to the Alexandrian period. The cult rises to a violent, ecstatic dance, during which the tree is shaken or a branch is broken from it. That we have here to do with a genuine tree-cult is shown by other gems on which the branches are placed between the horns of consecration ; daemons water them from libation jugs and the characteristic high-spouted libation jugs often occur surrounded by branches.[1] On the other hand, it is no longer a pure, primitive tree-cult, but one which is connected with the anthropomorphic gods. Thus, in such scenes of the tree-cult, a bell-shaped idol is seen floating down through the air,[2] or a god with spear or shield, or a bird, which last is also the form of the gods' appearing. On the famous ring from the Acropolis treasure of Mycenae sits a woman under a tree —clearly a goddess, since she is receiving the adoration of other women approaching her. Another gem shows a priestess before the altar with the sacred branches, invoking the divinity by blowing into a shell.

We now come to the subject of the representations of the epiphany of the gods. They are not few in number, but the undeniable gain for our understanding of the Minoan divinities is less than might be expected. One thing is clear : it was supposed that the gods appeared in the shape

---

[1] Most of them reproduced in *TPC*.

[2] *JHS*, xii, 1892, p. 77, fig. 1.

of birds. A bird sits on each of the double axes under which the sacrifice on the H. Triada sarcophagus is proceeding. On a terra-cotta from Knossos, representing three columns, a bird sits on each column.[1] A temple model from the IIIrd shaft-grave at Mycenae is crowned with the horns of consecration and birds flock around it. The bird is added to the figures representing the gods to denote their epiphany. Two gold plates from the same tomb represent a woman surrounded by birds. The idol from the so-called Sanctuary of Double Axes at Knossos has a bird on its head. It is useless labour to try to determine the species of the birds, and the interpretation of the gold-foil from the IIIrd shaft-grave as Aphrodite with her doves is open to grave doubt. Probably a manifestation of the god was seen in any and every bird which happened to fly near at the time of sacrifice.

Most commonly the gods are represented as the eye of imagination sees them, in ordinary human form and dress and with no distinguishing attributes, and even when the figure does show certain peculiarities their interpretation is uncertain. A ring from Knossos shows a goddess with a mirror in her hand, another from Mochlos [2] has in the foreground a large ship and behind this a sitting woman, doubtless a goddess, since behind her appears the sacred tree within its enclosure. A striking feature, and one to which attention has often been called, is the predominance of the female divinities ; the male occur far less often and are distinguished by a spear or a shield.

There is a tendency to explain these figures along one particular line. Evans finds everywhere the great Nature-goddess with her paramour ; Dussaud the chthonic goddess, Earth the Mother.[3] It is tempting thus to reduce the explanation of the figures to a single formula, but in this

---

[1] *BSA*, viii, 1902, p. 28, fig. 15.

[2] *Revue archéologique*, 1910, ii, p. 32.

[3] Dussaud, *op. cit.*, pp. 250 et seq.

simplification there is a risk of doing violence to the evidence. For it is very possible that the Minoans had a multitude of gods—indeed this is likely, to judge by other peoples with a similar or somewhat less developed culture. It is therefore necessary to keep the types of divinity separate. The representations of the gods in general are not as a rule very characteristic, but two types can be distinguished from the rest. One of these is represented on a painted limestone slab from the Acropolis of Mycenae.[1] It is a goddess whose body is almost entirely hidden by the great Mycenaean shield : the rigid position reminds one of an idol. The other is a seal-impression from Knossos, showing a goddess with a spear in her hand standing on a heap of stones or a mountain and guarded by two lions disposed heraldically ; on one side is a worshipper, on the other a temple.[2] The resemblance to the Great Mother from Asia Minor, who haunts the mountains and is accompanied by lions, is obvious.

In connexion with this important figure stands a whole series of images on gems and seal-impressions.[3] The heraldic arrangement is prominent, two animals being symmetrically placed on either side of a central figure, sometimes rising on their hind-legs, sometimes in another position, lying, standing, or carried. Much more rarely do we find a single animal in combination with a human figure, an unsymmetrical arrangement. therefore. The animals are of all kinds —lions, bulls, goats, birds, and imaginary creatures, sphinxes and griffins. The central figure is very often a human being, man or woman, shown grasping the necks or legs of the animals to express power over them ; this is the type that was later called ' Mistress of Animals ' (Πότνια

[1] The best reproduction in *AM*, xxxvii, 1912, pl. 8.

[2] *BSA*, vii, 1901, p. 29, fig. 9.

[3] Mostly reproduced in *TPC* and Furtwängler, *Antike Gemmen*, vol. iii, pls. 2 and 3.

Θηρῶν), of which the best examples are two seal-stones recently found during the excavations of the British School at Mycenae. On either side of the goddess is a rampant lion, and above her head is a curious object composed of three wavy lines (snakes?) and the double axe. But in the Minoan-Mycenaean world there also appears a 'Master of Animals'. Quite often the central figure is not a human being but a tree or a pillar or merely an altar upon which the animals rest their fore-feet. These instances are adduced as proof of a tree- and pillar-cult, but the evidence is not convincing. Just as the beasts guard the goddess, so they may guard and defend her sacred tree, her temple, or altar. For the pillar has an architectural use and upholds the beams of the roof—the best-known example is the relief above the Lion Gate at Mycenae—and the same is true of the pillars of the cult which are supposed to exist in the palace of Knossos. We may compare the winged genii and fabulous creatures which guard the entrances to the Assyrian palaces.

In place of the animals animal-shaped genii (*daimones*) now and again appear, but the central figure may also be one of these daemons subjugating the beasts. The figure is animal-shaped although upright like a man; there can be no question of its being a human figure disguised as an animal. The head and legs are those of an animal, though of what species it is impossible to say. It is safer to refrain from the description 'lion daemons' frequently adopted. A typical and curious feature is what appears to be a loose skin or other covering extending over the back from the crown of the head downwards, and below the waist suggesting the body of a wasp. It is often provided with patterns and has a dorsal comb of bristles or globule-tipped hairs. Apart from small and unimportant variations, the type is fixed. These daemons appear as servants of the gods with libation jugs and other vessels in their hands; they water the sacred branches. Sometimes they are dragging dead animals, presumably sacrificial animals.

The uniformity of the type is apparent upon comparison with the few representations of other animal-shaped genii. A sculptured shell-plate from Phaistos,[1] which undoubtedly reveals Babylonian influence,[2] shows a procession of four animal-headed figures in long garments; the first three have heads of mammals, the last has a bird's head. A seal-impression from Zakro is of interest.[3] A woman with up-lifted arms is standing opposite an animal-shaped figure which is sitting on the ground like a dog and also has uplifted arms. The difficulty is to say which is the worshipper and which the worshipped. Still more interesting is the so-called Minotaur seal-impression from Knossos.[4] On a folding-stool sits a creature with human legs and trunk but with hoofs, tail, and the hornless head of (apparently) a calf; facing him stands a man with lowered arms and therefore not a worshipper. Upon this mysterious image really depends the question whether there actually was a bull-cult in Crete, as is often stated under the influence of the stories of Europa and the Minotaur. For, often though bull-fights and hunts are represented, there is not the slightest indication that these had any religious significance. We must require more definite evidence.

The above-mentioned purely formal extension of the carved or painted motif is nowhere so strongly shown as in relation to the fantastic hybrid creatures. Starting with these daemons and with the figures of the sphinx and griffin borrowed from the East, Minoan art created a whole series

[1] *MA*, xii, pl. 8, 1.

[2] Compare, for instance, the so-called Hades relief, often repro-duced, e. g. in Jeremias, *Handbuch der altorientalischen Geisteskultur*, p. 68, or the amulet, Roscher, *Lexikon der Mythologie*, iv, p. 1494, fig. 55. [3] *JHS*, xxii, 1902, p. 78, fig. 4.

[4] *BSA*, vii, 1901, p. 18, fig. 7 a.

of fantastic combinations of human and animal limbs and parts of the body. Seal-impressions from Zakro [1] show a motley collection of these products of an absolutely unbridled fancy, which have no counterpart anywhere in the world and seem to be due to the fevered imagination of an over-heated brain. They have naturally no religious significance.

In the second millennium the Greeks migrated into the country that was to be theirs and settled down among the native population. The latter did not vanish, but became merged in the Greek people. It is disputed whether the masters of the Mycenaean fortresses of the mainland were colonists from Crete or, as I consider certain, Greeks who had adopted the Minoan culture.[2] In the latter case, with the Minoan culture they adopted to a very wide extent the Minoan religion; if the former supposition be true, the Cretan overlords must still more strongly have influenced the subordinate, undeveloped Grecian people, not least in religious matters.

Natural religion is associated with the soil. Lands may change in respect of population and language, but the immigrants do not refuse their homage to the old gods of the country. The latter do not entirely disappear, even though they are supplanted and transformed. This was in all probability what occurred in the change of religion which took place in Greece in prehistoric times, and it is therefore our duty to seek for traces of the Minoan-Mycenaean religion in the Greek, even though the circumstances are such as to oblige us to make considerable assumptions. The change of religion did not, however, take place without conflicts between the old and the new gods. It has been

---

[1] *JHS*, xxii, 1902, pls. 6–10.

[2] Compare my essay on the great migrations of the peoples in the second millennium B.C. in the Swedish periodical *Ymer*, 1912, pp. 188 et seq.

supposed that the myth of the struggle of the Titans and Kronos with Zeus and the Olympic deities reflects this battle of the cults.[1] This is possible but not demonstrable. Except for Kronos, the Titans are abstractions or empty names of whose significance we cannot judge, and even the significance of Kronos in religion and cult has faded. Probably he was an ancient harvest deity.

The continuity can sometimes be shown. Two well-known mythological figures even bear obviously pre-Greek names, Hyakinthos and Rhadamanthys. Hyakinthos is the name both of a flower and of an ancient god whom Apollo supplanted : he made him his favourite and appropriated his festival. Rhadamanthys belongs to the south of Crete. With him is associated the idea of Elysium, the ' Isles of the Blessed ' far away to the west. The idea is in irreconcilable opposition to the ordinary Greek conception of the future life, and this peculiarity finds its explanation in the fact that we have here a pre-Grecian picture of another world.[2]

Far more important is the continuity of the centres of the cult. In Crete the cave-cult continued. In the cave of Idaean Zeus the cult did not begin till after Minoan times, in the cave of Psychro it ceased at the end of that period, but the memory of it still survived in the myth ; the cave of Patso was dedicated in Grecian times to Hermes Kranaios.[3] At Amnisos, the port of Knossos, Ilithyia had a cave which is mentioned in the *Odyssey* and by Strabo.[4] On the top of Mount Juktas there is a shrine in the open air with votive terra-cottas and sherds dating from Middle Minoan down to Grecian times. Modern popular tradition points it out as

[1] M. Mayer, *Giganten und Titanen* (1887) ; M. Pohlenz, *Kronos und die Titanen, NJb*, xxxvii, 1916, pp. 549 et seq.

[2] L. Malten, *Elysion und Rhadamanthys, AJ*, xxviii, 1913, pp. 35 et seq.

[3] *Museo italiano di antichità classica*, ii, 1888, pp. 913 et seq.

[4] See the periodical Παρνασσός, x, 1886–7, pp. 339 et seq.; but the identification is uncertain.

the grave of Zeus.[1] On the ruins of the Minoan town at Palaikastro was built the temple of Zeus Diktaios, where the remarkable hymn to Zeus was found ; [2] near the palace of H. Triada Zeus Velchanos had his temple,[3] the young beardless Zeus peculiar to Crete. At Prinias were found fragments of an archaic statue of a goddess, but a still more illuminating fact is that the entirely Minoan fragments of an idol and vessels of the cult, with snakes, that were also found, must, from their technique and the circumstances of their discovery, belong to the geometrical period.[4] Thus the cult of the snake-goddess was continued in the geometrical period under its ancient form.

Where Greek inhabitants had succeeded pre-Greek, it is only natural that Greek temples should have succeeded the Minoan, for example at Phaistos and at many places on the mainland. No definite proof that there was continuity also in the cult can be drawn from this fact, although such continuity is probable. But many famous centres of Greek religion have yielded undoubted relics of Mycenaean times : Delphi, Delos, Eleusis, Kalaureia (whose temple of Poseidon was the meeting-place of a council of Amphictyons), the temple of Aphaia on Aegina, the Menelaïon (Helen's shrine at Sparta), and so on. At Eleusis, Delos, and at Delphi the excavations have given direct proof that the cult had its origin in Mycenaean times. Under the *cella* of the temple at Delphi and before its eastern front, where afterwards the great altar stood, were found layers of earth mixed with remains of sacrifices and numerous Mycenaean sherds and idols.[5]

Still more important is the evidence supplied by the chief

[1] A. J. Evans, *The Palace of Minos*, i, pp. 151 et seq.

[2] *BSA*, vii, 1901, pp. 298 et seq.

[3] *Rendi conti della R. Accademia dei Lincei*, xiv, 1905, pp. 380 et seq.

[4] *Bollettino d'arte*, ii, 1908, pp. 456 et seq.

[5] *Fouilles de Delphes*, v. 1 (P. Perdrizet, *Monuments figurés*), pp. 3 et seq.

centres of Mycenaean culture on the mainland. On the ruins of the Mycenaean palace at Mycenae a temple of Athena was built. Under the foundations of the so-called old Temple of Athena on the Acropolis at Athens lie the remnants of the Mycenaean royal palace. The megaron of the palace of Tiryns was converted into a temple to Hera, and the ancient altar, which had stood in the court-yard of the Mycenaean prince, was transformed into an altar to the Greek goddess.[1] The famous temple of Hera at Argolis, the Heraion, lies on a hill where a Mycenaean palace was once situated.[2] The connexion is clear. With the cessation of the monarchy—perhaps even earlier, as it weakened—the cult which had formerly been the king's domestic cult became public. Finally the royal palace became the seat of the goddess and the chief temple of the free state. There are therefore serious reasons for considering the question of the continuity of the cult. Do Hera and Athena go back to Mycenaean times ?

In regard to Hera, the matter would be easy to decide if Schliemann were right in recognizing the cow-headed Hera (βοῶπις) in certain idols found in Mycenae, for the cow plays an important part in certain Argive legends relating to Hera. We often hear of the cow-headed female idols from Mycenae, but in reality not a single such idol has been discovered. All the animal heads with horns rest upon an animal's body, or else are broken off just below the neck.[3] However tempting the association may be, it is without any basis in fact. On the other hand, the domain of the worship of Hera (apart from Olympia and younger cults) is remarkably limited. She belongs to districts which are or were once Ionian (Argolis, Euboea, Samos). Thus a clearer

---

[1] *Tiryns*, ii, pp. 2 et seq., recently contested by C. W. Blegen, *Korakou*, pp. 130 et seq.

[2] *Tiryns*, i, pp. 114 et seq.

[3] Schliemann, *Mykene*, pp. 118 et seq.

light is thrown upon her passionate partisanship of the Argives in Homer. She was their national goddess.

In regard to Athena we may go farther. Mention has already been made of a painting from Mycenae representing a goddess bearing a shield. With some justification this goddess has been called Athena : at any rate she is her predecessor. The tutelary goddess of the house is not a warlike divinity, but amid a martial people like the Mycenaean population of the mainland the household goddess of the prince would necessarily become a martial goddess. This explains the curious circumstance that the Greek divinity of war is a goddess; above all, she protects the citadel and the town and in older times the person of the king. Therefore in Homer Athena is the personal tutelary goddess of the heroes. In the myth the image of the goddess, the palladium, is a pledge upon which the existence of the city depends ; it is inaccessible, concealed in the heart of the citadel. This feature is explained by the fact that the cult was the domestic cult of the prince, and the goddess his household goddess, hidden in the heart of the palace.

The *Odyssey* makes Athena retire to the strong-house of Erechtheus at Athens. Here the old idea clearly persists ; the goddess has her dwelling in the palace of the prince. Erechtheus is a mythical reflex of the king who in the Mycenaean age resided on the Acropolis of Athens : in historical times he was worshipped as a hero. Already in the Catalogue of Ships the conditions are reversed and Athena is made to receive Erechtheus into her temple. A temple has taken the place of the royal palace. This is the later conception. Herodotus tells how the ' house-protecting snake ' (οἰκουρὸς ὄφις) which lived in Athena's temple left the Acropolis at the approach of the Persians. Under the shield of Phidias' statue of Athena a great snake wreathed itself. It can be understood why Athena is associated with the guardian snake of the home if she originated in Mycenaean times. The goddess worshipped in the Minoan domestic shrines was a snake-goddess.

This is not the only connexion of Athena with the Minoan-Mycenaean religion. By her temple grew her sacred olive which, when burned down by the Persians, in one night put out a shoot a yard long. The tree-cult appears very prominently in the Minoan religion, although it is found all over the world and is especially widespread in European and Teutonic folk-lore. With one exception, Homer has no gods in the form of animals : Athena, however, sometimes transforms herself, along with some other god, into a bird, and it is by this very transformation that the aged Nestor recognizes her. In Homer she appears in the form of birds of different kinds ; in later times the owl, which lives among the stones and crevices of the citadel, is her constant companion. This is the Minoan epiphany of the god in the form of a bird. Both the snake and the bird are creatures sacred to Athena. The Minoan house-goddess appears sometimes with the snake, as at Gournia, sometimes with a bird, as at Knossos ; but in the chapel at Gournia too, as well as in other places, small terra-cotta birds have been found with the house-goddess. She protected house and town, and where a warlike spirit prevailed, as on the mainland, she had consequently to be a warlike armed goddess.

If Athena herself originated in Mycenaean times, it may be asked if her name also is not Mycenaean. This is quite possible. No even approximately satisfactory etymology has been found. The ending -ήνη (Doric -άνα) is common enough in place-names which cannot be explained through Greek.[1] Like -νθος and -σσος it may represent a pre-Grecian element. The name Mykenai is probably also pre-Grecian, for it has the same ending and is related to the names

[1] This view is shared, according to information communicated in a letter, by Professor Wackernagel, who has suggested the connexion Mycene—Mycale—Mycalessus.

Dionysos. We have probably here a reflection of the
conflict between the cult of Dionysos and the worship of the
old Nature-goddess. Sometimes it led to a struggle, sometimes to a union between the two. The outstanding feature
is the death of Ariadne. In Argos she lay buried in the
temple of the Cretan Dionysos. On Naxos she had died, and
the inhabitants celebrated in her honour a festival which
was partly ' a feast of sorrow and gloom ' and partly a
festival of joy. A similar festival is mentioned for Locris.
In Cyprus she is said to have died in childbed and been
buried. At her festival a youth represented a woman in
childbed. In Crete she is said to have hanged herself in
despair. The same fate was shared by another obsolete
goddess, Helena,[1] whose temple in Sparta rests upon
Mycenaean remains.[2] In Rhodes Helena was supposed to
have hanged herself on a tree and was afterwards worshipped
as δενδρῖτις, the tree-goddess. In other ways also both
she and her husband Menelaos have connexions with the
tree-cult.

Ilithyia is known in Greek myth as the goddess who
assists women in the pangs of child-birth. The derivation
of her name from a Greek root is now generally abandoned ;
it appears in varying forms, Eleutho, Eleusinia, &c., and is
apparently connected with Eleusis, the mysteries of which
are of pre-Greek origin,[3] and with Elysium, the Minoan
conception of the other world. She is closely allied with
Artemis, who herself appears in the function of Ilithyia, and
we have traced Artemis back to the Minoan age. All these
circumstances may be explained if Ilithyia was a name of
the Minoan Nature-goddess who protected the birth of men
and animals, but in the Greek religion survived only as the
divine midwife.

[1] Nilsson, op. cit., pp. 426 et seq.
[2] BSA, xiv, 1908, pp. 108 et seq.
[3] A. W. Persson, Der Ursprung der eleusinischen Mysterien,
ARw. xxi, 1922, pp. 287 et seq.

On the strength of the comparison with Magna Mater, at whose side her youthful lover Attis stands, it is generally believed that the Minoan Nature-goddess too had a youthful paramour. But certain indications seem to me to point to quite another and a peculiar idea. No Greek myth is so curious as the story of the birth of Zeus. This myth is especially Cretan and the Zeus of the story is very unlike the 'king of heaven' of Greek mythology. Its peculiarities are probably a Minoan heritage. An outstanding feature is that the child is not nursed by its mother—she passes out of the story when it is born—but is brought up by wild animals or nymphs, by the goat Amaltheia according to the common myth, by bees and an eagle according to another myth, by a sow according to a tradition from the town of Praisos, by a bitch according to the coins of Cydonia.[1] The fable of the suckling of the child by an animal is told in many countries about legendary heroes (Cyrus, Romulus and Remus, &c.); that it was applied to Zeus in Crete proves that he was there thought of as an infant child abandoned by its mother. And this infant was born annually. There is a curious tale that Zeus was born in a cave in Crete and that at a certain time every year a fire was seen flashing forth from this cave, 'when the blood from the birth of Zeus streamed forth'.[2] This child is the year-god, the ἐνιαυτὸς δαίμων of Miss Harrison, the spirit of fertility, the new life of spring.

The same idea appears in a cult whose name proves it to have been of Minoan origin, that of Artemis Hyakintho-trophos. The epithet shows that Hyakinthos was thought of as nursed by Artemis, the Minoan Nature-goddess. His name is also the name of a flower and the myth relates that he died and was buried, just as Zeus died and was buried in Crete.

If we seek for further traces of the divine child which is

---

[1] Svoronos, *EA*, 1892, pp. 1 et seq., especially for the coin images.
[2] The so-called Boios, in Antoninus Liberalis. ch. 19.

not reared by its mother and which is the spirit of fertility, we shall find them in that religious centre of pre-Greek origin, Eleusis. It is related that the hierophant cried out the sacred formula : ' The Mighty and Strong One has brought forth a strong son ',[1] and this statement is borne out by two vase paintings which show Ge emerging from the ground and holding out the child Ploutos—' wealth ', in the old sense of the fruit of the fields—to Athena.[2] The same representation is more commonly applied to the birth of Erichthonios, whose name is derived from χθών, ' earth ' ; Erichthonios may originally be a spirit of the fertility of the fields, although mythology has converted him into a legendary ancestral king of Athens.

The same idea recurs in the Dionysiac religion. The Thyiades of Delphi performed a ceremony of the awakening of the child in the winnowing-basket (λικνίτης) ; the baby's cradle was the agricultural instrument in which the corn, called ' Ploutos ' by the Eleusinians, was placed to be cleaned. The common myth relates that Semele, the mother of Dionysos, was killed before his birth, and Homer already speaks of the nurses of Dionysos. As nurses they must have a child to nurse ; consequently the conception of Dionysos as a new-born child not reared by its mother is old.

Etymologically Semele signifies ' Earth ' and Dionysos ' Son of Zeus '.[3] This has been proved by the aid of Phrygian inscriptions. Now we know of Mater Hipta and Zeus Sabazios through inscriptions from the borderland of Phrygia, and an Orphic hymn invokes her as the nurse of Bacchus.[4] The Phrygian invaders took over the cults of the old inhabitants, chief of which is the cult of the Great

[1] ἱερὸν ἔτεκεν πότνια κοῦρον βριμὼ βριμόν, Hippolytus, Refutatio haereseon, v. 8.

[2] S. Reinach, Cultes, Mythes et Religions, ii, p. 270 ; Répertoire des vases peints, i, p. 1.

[3] P. Kretschmer in Aus der Anomia (1890), pp. 17 et seq.

[4] J. Keil in Wiener Eranos (1909), pp. 102 et seq.

Mother of the Mountains, who is related to the Minoan Nature-goddess : and the indigenous population of Western Asia Minor was akin to the Minoans.

The god who is born annually dies annually. Accordingly Dionysos died and was buried at Delphi, and Zeus in Crete, and the tomb of Hyakinthos was shown at Sparta and at Tarentum. This type of god is well known : the annually dying and re-born deity is a vegetation spirit. It acquires a deep emotional value as the divine prototype of the inexorable fate of man, whose birth and decay form so salient a feature of the mysteries. The idea would seem more natural if it originated in the Minoan religion, in which the tree-cult seems to find ecstatic expression in sacred dances and to which belongs the goddess Ariadne, who dies in childbed. But it is a unique feature that the spirit of vegetation should be imagined as a little child. We have reason to think that this is a Minoan peculiarity.

If these suggestions are to be regarded as well founded, they are of primary importance for the understanding of the deep religious movement which the spreading of the Dionysiac religion caused in the older historic age of Greece. I venture to think that the strength of this movement may be better understood if it is regarded as involving not the importation of an entirely foreign deity, but only the revival of ancient Minoan religious ideas which had for a time fallen into the background. And if this be so it may be possible to account for the old tradition of the Cretan origin of the Delphic cult.

Another well-known feature of the myths concerning vegetation spirits is the holy marriage, which in the Greek myth is that of Zeus and Hera. This marriage was celebrated at Knossos and was also said to have taken place at Gortyn beneath an evergreen plane-tree. The bride of Zeus at Gortyn is commonly called Europa ; the coins of the town represent her as seated in a tree with Zeus approaching her in the guise of an eagle. This Minoan bird-epiphany recurs in other myths ; as a cuckoo Zeus won the love of Hera in Argos, and as a swan he deceived Leda. The youthful, beardless Cretan type of Zeus, in Phaistos surnamed Ϝελχανός, must be the bridegroom of the holy marriage. On Mount Dikte there was an image of this youthful Zeus, and accordingly the famous hymn found in the temple of Zeus Diktaios at Palaikastro[1] celebrates this god, whom it beseeches to come annually, conferring good-luck and fertility on fields, men, and cities.

It is surely astonishing that the name of Zeus, the god of the heavens, should have been applied to the divine child of Crete. But there seems to be a connecting link. Child-gods are found in several places in Greece ; they are both mentioned in literature and represented by images. They are often called ἄνακες, ‘ the rulers’. The Dioskouroi also are κοῦροι, ‘ boys’, and sons of Zeus. They have become gallant young men, but they also appear under the similitude of children. A host of Minoan traditions remain attached to them. Zeus begot them in the guise of a bird ; their sister Helena is a Mycenaean tree-goddess. Their cult is a domestic cult. The snake is their sacred animal and representative ; their symbol on Spartan monuments—two upright beams united by a cross-beam—is nothing but an abbreviated representation of the half-timber work of a house. They are the domestic and tutelary deities of the Spartan kings, whom they accompany even to the battle-field.

Both the Zeus-child and the sons of Zeus show relationship with the Minoan religion, but with different sides of it. The Zeus-child was worshipped in caves; he was not a domestic god like the Dioskouroi. Nevertheless it is remarkable that the name of the god of the heavens and launcher of the thunderbolt should have been given to the Cretan child-god, for there can be no doubt that the latter is the original. The

[1] *BSA*, xv, 1909, pp. 357 et seq.

Greek gods in the form of children constitute, as has been said, the connecting link. The immigrating Greeks knew Zeus as the protector of the storehouse and home (ἑρκεῖος, κτήσιος).[1] The household snake, which had the same function, therefore lent to Zeus his shape. Zeus Ktesios and kindred forms appear in the likeness of a snake. Further, the Greeks had tutelary household daemons in the form of dwarfs, or learned to know them. These became, not Zeus, certainly, but his sons, Διὸς κοῦροι, and ' rulers, lords ', ἄνακες. When, finally, a divine child was found in Crete, this too became Zeus, although it was not a household deity. The transition had far-reaching consequences. Old legends becoming implicated, there arose the myth of the birth of Zeus, the story of the swallowing and rescue of the child, and of his being suckled by wild beasts.

Alongside the cult of the gods stands that of the dead and of the heroes. The magnificence of the funeral-cult in Mycenaean times is often spoken of, but from the point of view of the history of religion a still more important fact is that the continuity of a cult by the grave-side can be directly traced from Mycenaean to classical times. This appears from finds in the entrance to the bee-hive tomb at Menidi in Attica.[2] After the tomb had been closed during the period when vases of the so-called third Mycenaean style were in use, the cult went on uninterruptedly before the entrance until some time in the fifth century B. C. The votive gifts are those that are characteristic of the hero-cult —shields and horses of terra-cotta, drinking-vessels and vessels for perfumes, &c. When sherds and figures which cannot have got there by accident, and are not such as were employed in the interment, are found at the entrance to a bee-hive tomb, the natural explanation is that their

[1] M. P. Nilsson, *Zeus Ktesios, A M*, xxxiii, 1908, pp. 279 et seq.
[2] Furtwängler und Löschcke, *Mykenische Vasen*, p. xi ; P. Wolters, *A J*, xiv, 1899, pp. 103 et seq.

presence is due to the cult of some hero. This is the case with the so-called Tomb of Clytaimestra at Mycenae.[1] In the entrance were found fragments of large geometrical vessels, roughly modelled figures of horsemen, and pearls that had once belonged to a necklace. That a cult took place upon the shaft-graves in Mycenae is also to be presumed, since the site had been levelled and the familiar monuments erected on it in late Mycenaean times. There is a trace from a later period, though it is of itself insufficient for us to build with certainty upon it. At a depth of six feet Schliemann found a sherd of a black-figured vase from the end of the sixth century, bearing an inscription according to which the vessel had been dedicated to ' the hero '.[2] Only a very extra-ordinary circumstance could have brought this unimportant sherd here from some other place ; at most it can but have been swept down from somewhat higher ground. But if that is so, then at the end of the sixth century a hero was still worshipped on the burial-ground of the old Mycenaean kings.

This immediate continuity of the cult of the dead from Mycenaean down to classical times is essentially of the very greatest importance. The cults of the dead and of the heroes are carried on under the same forms : the latter must therefore have arisen from the former. The difference is only that the cult of the dead belongs to a certain family, whereas the cult of the heroes has broken away from the family and become the property of the people. Against this it has been objected that if the heroes' graves were opened no bones would be found in them, for the heroes, it is said, are originally not dead men but fallen deities. Such deities are certainly found among them : local gods, for instance the Mycenaean god Hyakinthos, have been forced to take a subordinate position by the greater gods who usurped their functions. But in principle the cult of the heroes arises

[1] Schliemann, *Mykene*, pp. 114 et seq. and 135.
[2] *Ibid.*, p. 129 ; *IG*, iv. 495.

from that of the dead. Since the cult goes back to Mycenaean times it is not difficult to understand why most graves of heroes contain no physical remains. How many graves must have been robbed in the dark ages between the fall of the Mycenaean culture and the advance of the new ! And when the outlines of the hero-cult had once been conceived, it was transferred to places which contained no grave. Half-forgotten local cults and their centres were appropriated to the cult of heroes and received well-known names from the myths.

The border-line between heroes and gods is unstable, and we have a remarkable example from Delos which shows how the cult of heroes might be transformed.[1] Within the sacred area was found a Mycenaean grave distinguished by two upright stones emerging above the surface of the ground ; in the Alexandrian age the place was surrounded by a wall into which an altar was built. The remarkable thing is that this grave was left undisturbed in the great purification of Delos undertaken by the Athenians in the year 426, when all the graves were taken up and their contents removed to Rheneia. In all probability it is the grave that was later known as the grave of the Hyperborean Virgins, Laodike and Hyperoche, of which Herodotus speaks. This hypothesis has quite recently received valuable confirmation from the discovery of what appears to be a second Mycenaean grave close to the temple of Artemis ; it is presumably the grave of the two other Hyperborean Virgins, Opis and Arge, which is also mentioned by Herodotus.[2] The Hyperborean Virgins are closely connected with the tree-cult, with Artemis and Apollo. Thus the cult at the old Mycenaean grave lived on for more than a thousand years, but acquired a new significance. For the Hyperborean Virgins do not belong to the circle of the heroes.

[1] *Compte rendu de l'Acad. des Inscriptions*, 1907, p. 338 ; 1909, p. 544.　　　　[2] *Ibid.*, 1923, pp. 238 et seq.

II

ORIGINS OF GREEK MYTHOLOGY

It was the Greek myths that led to the discovery of the glories of the Bronze Age. Schliemann had a fanatical belief in Homer. He set out to find the Troy around whose walls Hector and Achilles ran their race, and the wealthy city of Mycenae where Agamemnon ruled, and his divining-rod brought unsuspected things to light. The same rod was used by Sir Arthur Evans. He followed the legends of the Labyrinth, King Minos, and his dominion of the seas. Thence was first revealed the full extent and importance of the Minoan-Mycenaean civilization. Only in one case have results been wanting, when Dörpfeld sought for the palace of Odysseus upon Ithaca-Leucas. What was found there that is certainly Mycenaean is no more than has been found even outside Greece—mostly sherds. And a moment's thought reveals the cause. The Odysseus myth is young, it is not a genuine heroic legend but a romance, built up on the common motif of the faithful wife who waits for her absent husband and in spite of everything is finally reunited to him.

Traces of the Mycenaean culture have been eagerly sought in Homer, but remarkably little attention has been paid to the Mycenaean connexions of the mythology. At most a general remark has been made, as by Professor Wide, to the effect that the formation of the legends took place in the main in Mycenaean times.[1] It must be so, if so much else in Homer goes back to the same period. For already in Homer the mythology has reached a fully developed stage, even if it does not in all respects appear in the form most familiar

[1] Wide, in Gercke und Norden, *Einleitung in die klassische Altertumswissenschaft*, 3rd edition, ii, p. 217.

to us. Its further development, its humanizing, has even proceeded very far.

The myths, as has been mentioned, afforded a clue to the discovery of some of the principal centres of Mycenaean civilization, but, curiously enough, the relation between the places of mythology and the Mycenaean centres which is proved hereby has never been followed up. No one has ever put the question, and by a systematic inquiry endeavoured to answer it : Is there a persistent connexion between the centres of Mycenaean culture and the myths, in particular the great cycles of the myths ? In other words, are the chief centres of Mycenaean civilization also the centres referred to in the myths ? If they are, it is proved that in the main the development and localizing of the cycles of the myths falls within the Mycenaean period, with important consequences for our investigation of the myths. An inquiry of this kind is very simple and can be made in a brief survey.

Tiryns is the home of Heracles and to that town belong the central legends of his exploits, although the incidents of his birth are connected with Thebes. To the former town, and not to Mycenae, he drives Geryon's oxen, according to Hesiod. From its walls he treacherously hurls down Iphitus. There he lives as a vassal under Eurystheus, king of Mycenae. Herein is reflected the fact that Tiryns is the older town, which was later ousted by Mycenae. This is the meaning of the legend, and archaeology corroborates it. To Tiryns also belongs the myth of the Proitides, which in its present form belongs to a younger type. With this city, too, the Bellerophon story is properly connected, for the intrigue which gives occasion to the exploits of the hero is carried on at the royal court of Tiryns, although he is genealogically referred to Corinth.

The famous Heraion, the chief temple of Argolis, succeeded a Mycenaean royal fortress. In this place belongs the story of Io and Argos.

In regard to Mycenae itself a simple reference to the myths of the houses of Perseus and Atreus is sufficient.

Argos, which afterwards became the capital, was in Mycenaean times an inconsiderable place, and this fact is reflected in the myth. The legends located there—that of the Danaides, for instance—are not of the same importance as those mentioned above. But the predominant position of Argos in later days is shown in the systematizing and genealogical character of the myths attaching to it.

In Sparta there is the temple of Helen, which comes down from Mycenaean times, and a little to the south the rich bee-hive tomb of Vaphio. To this locality belong the myths of Helen and her brothers, the Tyndaridae, who had become confused with the Dioskouroi (cp. above, pp. 34 et seq.), and of their fight with another pair of brothers, the Apharetidae, who are attached to Laconia and Messenia. According to one version they fought about the daughters of Leukippos, and the shrine of Leukippos was in Sparta.

Pylos is celebrated in the legends as the home of the Nelidae. Modern Pylos has considerable Mycenaean remains, but Dörpfeld is undoubtedly right in locating the Homeric Pylos at Kakovatos, a little farther up the west coast. The assumption was brilliantly confirmed by the finding of three bee-hive tombs, once rich, although now plundered and destroyed, and the remains of a palace.

Attica in earlier times does not take that dominating position in mythology which it holds later, but is rich enough in legends. The most important is that of Theseus, which has grown in historical times at the expense of the Herakles stories, and next to this the legends of the mythical kings. Attica, too, is full of Mycenaean remains. The myths, there-fore, do not belong solely to Athens, but are spread all over the country-side. Theseus seems to have his home in north-eastern Attica. Eleusis, with its Demeter myth, takes a separate position of its own, and this, too, is a Mycenaean town.

Boeotia rivals Argolis in mythological fame. It was the second chief province of Mycenaean culture in Greece. Thebes is celebrated through the myths of Kadmos, Amphion and Zethus, Oedipus, and the Seven. This is in harmony with the importance of the town in Mycenaean times, which is borne out by the discovery of considerable remains of a Mycenaean palace; unfortunately it has not been possible to dig this out completely because it lies right in the middle of the modern town.

The rival of Thebes in mythical times was Orchomenos. According to the Herakles legends this town had compelled Thebes to pay tribute to it. There are ruins there of a magnificent bee-hive tomb which vies with those of Mycenae. The palace itself has not been discovered, but there are fragments of its wall-paintings. There dwelt the celebrated tribe of the Minyans. The story of the daughters of Minyas is of the common later Dionysiac type, but to this town, too, belong Athamas and his family.

Athamas, through the cult, has also connexions with Halos, and this lies in Thessaly, near Iolkos, on the Pagasaean Gulf. With Iolkos is associated another of the great cycles of myths, that of the Argonauts. It is natural that this particular story should have been considerably transformed with increasing knowledge of foreign lands. Iolkos is the most northerly Mycenaean site, and in the neighbourhood have been found a couple of ill-built but quite rich bee-hive tombs.

The above list exhausts all the more important cycles of myths except one, that of the Calydonian hunt. Calydon has not yet been excavated, but numerous Mycenaean sherds have been picked up on the surface and there are walls which may be Mycenaean.[1] This is the most promising of the Greek sites which have not been explored. I am sure that it would yield not only the ruins of the famous temple of

[1] Πρακτικὰ τῆς ἀρχαιολογικῆς ἑταιρείας, 1908, pp. 99 et seq.

Artemis Laphria but also considerable remains from the Mycenaean age. The hunting of the wild boar was a favourite sport in Mycenaean times; it is represented, for instance, on a wall-painting at Tiryns.

The great cycles of myths, then, belong to the main centres of Mycenaean culture, and—what is more significant —their richness and fame are in direct correspondence with the importance of the towns in Mycenaean times. The most splendid of the Mycenaean sites is Mycenae: it is also the most famous city of the mythology. Next follow Thebes, Tiryns, and at some distance Attica, Lacônia, Pylos, Orchomenos, and so on.

That this easy and obvious comparison has never been made can only be due to the one-sidedness of all the principal lines of mythological research.[1] K. O. Müller placed the historical point of view in the foreground; from the geographical distribution of the cults and the myths he and his followers sought to draw conclusions as to the migrations and early history of the Greek tribes. But the grounds for such conclusions proved to be inadequate. The historical school

[1] No literature has so quickly gone out of date as the numerous writings on mythology. K. O. Müller laid down his principles in his important *Prolegomena zu einer wissenschaftlichen Mythologie* (1825). The most distinguished representative of the neo-historical school is Wilamowitz and its weaknesses become apparent in his pupils, most characteristically in P. Friedländer's *Herakles*. The natural-mythological school, whose best-known representative was Max Müller, dominated the literature of some decades ago. Its views are set forth with particular clearness in the earlier portions of the mythological work of reference, Roscher's *Lexikon der Mythologie*, where unfortunately the hypotheses are too often allowed to overshadow the facts. The most distinguished mythographer of our time, the late C. Robert, has recently published three parts of his great work, *Die griechische Heldensage* (the fourth is forthcoming), a fresh treatment of the material designed to supersede Preller's *Griechische Mythologie*, vol. ii. His *Oidipus* (1915), in which he investigates the development of a single legend in literature and art, is a model piece of research; so far as it deals with the origin of the myth, I am, however, not able to agree with him.

became the neo-historical, which discarded most of the tribe-mythology and devoted itself above all to establishing, by means of a study of literary and artistic traditions, the older form of the myths and their development through the ages. One branch of this study is the mythology of art, the other and wider branch is the history of the myths in literature : the two go hand in hand. This mythological research is a necessary preliminary to the interpretation of the myths and the understanding of their origin, but it has its limitations, a fact of which not all the devotees of the method have been conscious. The results are therefore anything but consistent and sure.

So long as we are dealing with later literature, including tragedy, the question of the age in which Greek mythology originated need not concern us, for the origin obviously belongs to a much earlier period. But it is otherwise in a more remote age, where the myths are met in their oldest known form. For it is principally this oldest form that must be used as the foundation for our understanding of the myths and their origin. The literature in question is principally the post-Homeric epic—the cyclical epics, dealing with all the extensive cycle of myths associated with the Trojan war, and the others, dealing with different cycles. It seems to be imagined that, after the fashion of the tragedies, these post-Homeric epics refashioned the myths, and indeed created new ones. In tragedy the poet, urged by his desire for dramatic effect, sought to draw something new from a constant rehandling of the myths. But can we credit the post-Homeric epic poets with anything of the kind ? In regard to Homer, it is not said that he remodelled the myths ; he deals in the traditional material, but his greatness lies in his humanizing of it. It is a recognized fact that the difference between Homer and the later epic poets lies in the interest which the latter take in the material as such, and the question is whether this interest was that of the creative imagination or not rather the systematizing passion of the collector. Judging by the total character of the later epic one is more inclined to believe the latter. This does not of course exclude the utilization of less-known myths or the insertion of minor changes in the details and localization of the stories, more particularly in the genealogical padding, in which the minstrel made alterations in order to flatter his patron or his audience. The composition also made certain demands which had to be complied with. To give an example, it may be true, as has been assumed, that a lost and never-mentioned epic created the familiar cycle of the twelve labours of Herakles. But, if so, the process consisted in a selection from existing motifs, and not in a new creation of legends. This hypothetical poem is therefore of more importance for literary history than for the history of the myths.

The firm ground on which the neo-historical school desires to place the history of the myths has begun to quake suspiciously. In reality the literature from which the oldest forms of the myths are deduced is a more or less unknown quantity. The old epics must first be reconstructed from few and often scanty fragments and from dry synopses compiled by later writers, whose sources have, moreover, first to be hypothetically determined. Thus subjectivity and hypothesis are present from the very beginning. The attempt to connect the epics with particular places is attended with no less difficulty, for the minstrels were wandering singers, one of the intellectual connecting-links in the disintegrated Greece of the archaic period. The materials for the legends were in great measure traditionally handed down in the singing-schools, other points were picked up by the minstrels in their wanderings. They may have introduced episodes and carried out minor alterations in order to please a patron or a certain audience, but it does not seem likely that the national interests and aspirations of a city would set their

stamp upon the poems as a whole. The evidence for anything of this kind is presented from an extremely arbitrary
and subjective point of view, and we must undoubtedly
estimate the influence of the post-Homeric epic upon the
formation of the myths considerably lower than is done by
the neo-historical school. The method in question can take
us no farther than to the oldest known form of the myths,
which is not necessarily the same as the original form : this
latter may appear in a later record. To make use of the
study of the myths in drawing conclusions as to history and
literature is another matter. There we are far from the
origins. In order to reach these, at least hypothetically,
other methods—internal criteria—are obviously required,
and these will shortly be discussed in detail.

I need not dwell upon the so-called comparative mythology
which was at one time the dominating tendency in the study
of religion, but it is worth while considering for a moment
how it was possible to attempt, as did the supporters of the
method, to trace back the heroic legends to divine origins,
to seek expression in every myth for some representation of
the gods. This leads us to the fundamental question : What
is mythology ? As we read it in a modern or ancient handbook it is divided into two parts : divine and heroic myths.
But in reality the border-line does not fall where this
division would suggest, but within the domain of the divine
myths themselves. The divine mythology consists of two
parts, separate in principle, but connected by a thousand
interwoven threads. The one is of sacral and religious origin,
the other of mythical.

The mythological representation of a god begins by
describing his nature, activity, and sphere of action, the
forms in which he appears, his attributes. Thus Zeus is
represented as the cloud-gatherer, the sender of rain and
hurler of the thunderbolt, as the patron of the house and
of social and ethical customs and regulations. Artemis is the

mistress of the wild beasts and the fosterer of the coming
race ; Athena the protectress of the royal line and later of
the city, and therefore also the leader in ordered warfare
and the bestower of all the accomplishments required in
a civilized community ; and so on. The peculiar attribute
of Zeus is the lightning, of Apollo the bow, &c. The form
of the epiphany is determined in the anthropomorphic
period by the god's activity and character. The animal
form is rare (e. g. Zeus Ktesios in the guise of a snake). The
animals are generally attributes, sacred creatures such as
Athena's owl and the hind of Artemis.

Even from these brief indications it is evident how
numerous are the points of contact and departure for
mythological themes, but all that is due to religious belief in
the gods and their activities must be clearly and sharply
distinguished from the mythical in the proper sense of the
term—the adventures of the gods, their life-history, which
begins with their birth but really has no end, since they do
not die. Professor Wundt has rightly pointed out that the
divine myths are in this respect modelled upon the heroic.

The combination of both these parts into the biography
of a god was achieved spontaneously at a very early date.
This is the reason why the comparative study of religion
was for so long but comparative mythology. From the
beginning religion was included under mythology, and then
mythology in its entirety was given a religious implication.
Thus the religious was allowed to become absorbed in the
mythological, and this of necessity led to error. The great
advance of the study of religion depends upon the fundamental conception of the religious and sacral as such, and
the adopting of this conception as the basis of investigation.

These principles are now recognized and applied even to
the study of antique religion, but the purely mythical—that
part of mythology which is not connected with the religious
and the sacral—and above all the heroic myth, has had to

take a subordinate place or has been dealt with along special lines as was mentioned above, without much connexion with the study of religion. But mythology in the traditional sense is a complete whole into which both religious and mythical conceptions enter, and the tangle must be unravelled as a whole. This has its importance for the study of religion also, but we must now begin from the other end, the mythical, and endeavour to distinguish the threads in the many-coloured skein.

It is a generally recognized fact that folk-tale motifs form an important element in the Greek myths, in fact almost every study of modern folk-lore points out in passing that corresponding motifs occur in the mythology of Greece. Hartland has given the title *The Legend of Perseus* to a voluminous investigation of a group of folk-tales represented in Greek mythology by the Perseus story. Andrew Lang has brilliantly brought out the resemblance between the Greek divine myths and cosmogony and those of primitive peoples.[1] Wundt in his great work has emphasized the development from the folk-tale, or perhaps more properly the primitive tale, to the myth.[2] But there has hitherto been no systematic attempt to apply the results of the study of folk-tale to the understanding of Greek mythology. This is due to a one-sided tendency, in respect of both method and material, in the different schools of research. Greek mythology lends itself neither to the attempt of the Scandinavian school to determine the geographical extension and home of the different legends—local variants are practically non-existent—nor yet, though somewhat better, to the

[1] A. Lang, *Myth, Ritual, and Religion*. Frazer has collected old and modern parallels of the Greek myths in his edition of Apollodorus.

[2] W. Wundt, *Völkerpsychologie*, vols. v and vi, *Mythus und Religion*. The fragments of antique folk-tales are collected by L. Friedländer in an appendix to his work : *Darstellungen aus der Sittengeschichte Roms : Das Märchen von Amor und Psyche und andere Volksmärchen im Altertum*, 9th edition, iv, pp. 89 et seq.

tracking out of the vestiges of the world of primitive ideas. Both methods, often in conflict or ignoring one another, seek before everything to maintain their positions. When we stand before material of a special character, we must attack it by the aid of any methods and inferences of proved reliability, wherever they may be found.

I shall here make a brief attempt to do this. In the first place it is of fundamental importance to distinguish between the two broad tendencies in folk-tale and myth, which I shall call the inventing and the explanatory or aetiological tendencies. The latter has a definite end in view; its purpose is to explain the origin of living creatures, things, customs and institutions, and peculiarities in them, in fact, of everything which surrounds man and arouses his attention. Aetiological tales are found in all ages and at all stages of culture and have been known from of old. Callimachus wrote a whole work with the title *Aitia*. In the study of religion they take an important place. Here I shall only point out that the aetiological tale has a far wider range than is generally admitted. We shall return to it towards the end of the present chapter.

The other main group is composed of folk-tale motifs in the proper sense of the term. I have called them ' invented ', not, of course, in the sense that these tales are a free creation of the imagination independently of any pre-existing basis. On the contrary we shall see that culture and religious and social ideas set their stamp upon them. But they are invented in the sense that, unlike the aetiological tale, they have no definite end in view, but are related merely for the pleasure of telling stories. Naturally, amalgamations and doubtful cases are not wanting. It is, for instance, often impossible to decide whether a Greek animal-transformation tale is really an explanatory tale or belongs to the invented variety.

The invented tale embraces a great though not unlimited number of motifs which are combined in various ways. It is one of the most important results of the study of folk-tales to have demonstrated this and to have resolved the tales into their different motifs. But it is wrong to believe that the tales have thereby been turned into a confused and inorganic mosaic. Among many primitive peoples, it is true, the motifs are loosely strung, one after the other, without any clear beginning or end. But the European folk-tale, like the Greek myth, is an artistically finished composition, although within the frame-work of the whole the motifs may be interchanged and vary. Folk-tale motifs enter into the Greek myths in greater number than is commonly supposed, and the demonstration of this fact is of fundamental importance. Motifs may vary according to the nature of the culture and new ones are added with its advance, but even in the tales of the most highly developed peoples there is a fundamental stock, the peculiar nature of which betrays its origin in the childhood of the human race. It is principally this which proves to be common to Greek myth, European folk-tale, and the tales of ancient times and of primitive peoples.

I call these motifs simply ' folk-tale motifs ', and shall endeavour as far as possible to undertake a systematic analysis of them in order to make clear the part they play in Greek mythology, and at the same time to show how the distinguishing feature of the Greek mind, its rationalism, led to a selection, a purification, and a remodelling of the too fantastic elements in the folk-tale material ; the Greek myth has arisen from the folk-tale through a process of humanization.

I begin with the motifs which, at least on a superficial acquaintance, would seem to be the most characteristic of the folk-tale : they may be called ' adventure motifs '. The hero of the tale has often a whole series of battles and trials to go through, from fights with monsters of every kind down to the cleansing of an unswept stable. The Augeas motif

recurs in modern folk-tales, and of the fights with monsters
I need hardly speak. Greek mythology abounds in real and
fabulous beasts—lions, bulls, horses, dragons, sphinxes, sea-
monsters, the Chimaera, the Minotaur. Sometimes the fight
takes place in a more imaginative fashion—the hero is
devoured by the monster and hews his way out from within.[1]
But this version lives only in remote regions of the mythology; it was too extravagant for the rationalistic Greeks.
The motif of man swallowed by other creatures and returning uninjured is extremely common in primitive tales, and
the folk-tale and the divine myth also know it. Kronos
devoured his offspring, and Zeus Metis.

Motifs of this kind are usually held together by the frame-
work of the story. The struggles or the trials are imposed
by some enemy of the hero, who has him in his power.
Hera's enmity, or in the common version the jealousy of
Eurystheus, drives Herakles from labour to labour, and the
same idea is seen in the Psyche story, when Venus lays upon
Psyche almost impossible tasks. Bellerophon is sent from
one adventure to another. In modern tales the same part is
often played by the cruel step-mother. According to the
often profound logic of the tales, the struggle and victory
merit their reward. The princess and half the kingdom is
the familiar formula. Greek heroes also, Bias, for instance,
demand half the kingdom as a reward, and when it is refused,
two-thirds, but the Greeks were strangers to our romantic
sentimentality, which also colours the folk-tale, as well as to
the idea of female succession. The princess is the reward of
the victor who has delivered her from the monster (Andro-
meda, Hesione) ; this is natural and indeed obvious. The
kingdom is bestowed together with the hand of the queen,
when she is a widow : this is familiar from the *Odyssey*.

[1] Cleostratus of Thespiae, Paus. ix. 26. 3 ; Herakles in a version
of the Hesione myth, Schol. to Lycophron, v. 33 ; possibly Jason
in a vase-painting, Roscher, *Lex. der Mythol.* ii, p. 85.

A similar idea is the simplest basis of the Oedipus story :
Oedipus, having overcome the Sphinx, receives as a reward
the hand of the queen. The hand of the fair princess is
announced as the prize for any who can undergo a certain
test. Many try and fail, until at last the right man comes
along. In the Greek myth this motif has been somewhat
altered in accordance with the innate love of the Greeks for
agonistic contests. Eurytos offers the hand of his daughter
Iole as a prize to any one who can beat him in shooting with
the bow, Oinomaos the hand of Hippodameia to any one
who defeats him in the chariot-race, but, with the evil
cunning which is usually practised in these ordeals, he stabs
the unlucky suitor from behind as he overtakes him. This
tale has been associated with the Olympic games as one of
the many explanations of their founding. The contest motif
became a usual device, as when the suitors of Penelope
or Pallene or the Danaides have to run races. Similarly,
the sons of Endymion decide at Olympia who shall have the
kingdom. It is less common for the maiden herself to
impose the contest upon her lovers, but a famous instance
is that of Atalanta, who runs a race with her suitors and
kills those whom she defeats, until at last she is overcome
by Milanion through the familiar ruse of the apple which he
throws down upon the course.

Envious foes who try to rob the hero of the fruits of
victory are also found in the Greek myths. When, for
instance, the hero has slain the monster, the courtiers gain
possession of the body and give out that they have done the
deed, but the hero has cut out the monster's tongue, shows
it, and puts them to shame. This is a wide-spread folk-tale,
which in Greece is told about Alkathoös and Peleus. The
flight amid dangers is often combined with special difficulties.
The hero, like Theseus in the Labyrinth, cannot find the
way. Then the beloved princess is at hand with her Ariadne
thread. This occurs in modern folk-tales also, but more

commonly a line of pebbles is laid on the way in, or else grains of corn or crumbs of bread are thrown down which the birds come and devour, whereby the difficulties are increased. Often the fugitives save themselves by casting behind them objects which the pursuer stops to pick up— a somewhat similar device is put to another use in the Atalanta story—or else the objects cast down are transformed into mountains, woods, lakes, &c., which hinder the pursuer. The last motif is not found in Greek mythology, it is again too fantastic for the Greek rationalistic habit of mind ; but a rationalized form of it is seen when Medea cuts up her brother Apsyrtos and drops the body, limb by limb. Her father stops to pick up the limbs and is thereby prevented from overtaking the fugitives.

We have here a peculiarity of the folk-tale which is almost more characteristic than the pure adventure motif, namely, its extremely primitive ideas of life and the universe. In the modern folk-tale these ideas stubbornly persist, proving the origin of the folk-tale in the primitive tale. But in the Greek myths they were in a considerable measure eliminated —this is one of the great points of difference—owing chiefly to the rationalizing tendency already mentioned ; and the process of elimination was carried farther when the tale became a myth, was associated with the gods, was related before highly civilized audiences of warriors and princes, and was admitted into literature. Such ideas may be conveniently described as possessing a magical character. Just as the Greek gods, unlike those of many other peoples, are not concerned with magic, so the Greek myth, unlike the folk-tale, has no magical ingredients. Magic first returns when the genuine Greek spirit vanishes in the great transformation of philosophy and religion which began during the Hellenistic period.

And so we miss the witch who is so common in our own folk-tales. There are two exceptions, Medea and Circe, but significantly enough they are foreign women. Medea at least is Asiatic, from Colchis, but Circe too is genealogically connected with the same country. It is suggestive that Circe appears in the *Odyssey*. This epic, reflecting life and legends from the Ionian merchant-cities, has much more of the folk-tale in our sense of the term than the chivalric *Iliad*, which moves within the circles of the royal courts. The ideas of taboo, which play so great a part in folk-tales, are also rare in the Greek myth. A certain word must not be mentioned, a room must not be entered, and the transgression of this command forms the turning-point of the tale. There is an example, however, in the Psyche story, where Psyche must not look upon her bridegroom by daylight. No less common in the folk-tale are the magical objects, wishing-objects, such as the table ' Serve-up ', or the donkey ' Kick-out ', wonderful rings, weapons, clothes, and numerous other articles whose magical power is able to rescue in time of greatest need. These have at least left traces in the Greek myth. When Perseus set out to slay the Gorgon, he had from the gods his magical equipment—the helmet of Hades which made the wearer invisible, the winged sandals which bore him through the air, and the wallet. ' The knife of Peleus ' was a proverbial expression denoting rescue from the direst peril. The myth only says that Peleus had his knife from Hephaistos and with it defended himself against the wild beasts, when he was treacherously abandoned in the forests of Pelion. The proverb seems to show that this is a rationalized adaptation of a more primitive tale.

The folk-tale reveals extremely curious and fantastic ideas about life or, as we might say, at least with partial justification, about the soul, naturally under an entirely material conception. The life or the soul can be parted from its owner and deposited in some inaccessible place, and until it is discovered the owner cannot be killed. This is the 'external soul' so often referred to in ethnological research.

The idea is found, for instance, in the Egyptian tale of the two brothers.[1] The date of this tale—it is found in a record from the middle of the second millennium B.C.—has brought about a revolution in our conception of the history of the folk-tale the extent of which can hardly be exaggerated. One of the brothers, Bata, has deposited his heart in an acacia tree and left his brother a pot of ale ; when he gets into danger, the ale will begin to froth. His faithless wife, who has become Pharaoh's consort, has the tree cut down, and Bata dies. Then the ale in the pot froths and the brother sets out to seek Bata. He comes upon the dead body, and after some difficulty also succeeds in finding the heart, which he puts into water and gives the dead man to drink, whereupon the latter returns to life. Bata is now transformed into a bull of Apis, which is taken to Pharaoh. The woman has the bull killed, but some drops of blood fall on the ground. From them two trees spring up which say : ' I am Bata '. The woman has them cut down but two chips fly into her mouth and she becomes pregnant. Her son is once more Bata, who now becomes the heir-apparent and Pharaoh, and kills his faithless former wife.

In this tale the most important of the motifs under discussion are found united : the separable or external soul, the life-tokens, the primitive ' migration of souls ', and the miraculous birth. These motifs were too fantastic for the rationalistic Greeks. The life-tokens, which play so prominent a part in the modern variations of the Perseus group, hardly occur, but the external soul has at least left traces. The purple lock which must be cut from the head of Nisos before his town can be taken (the tale of Scylla, the same motif in the tale of Komaitho) is something differ-

---

[1] G. Maspéro, *Les contes populaires de l'Égypte ancienne*, 4th edition, pp. 1 et seq.

ent from the Samson motif. There the hero's strength dwells in his hair, here it is upon a single lock that his well-being depends. It is the ' external soul ' idea combined with the belief in the significance of the hair. Still clearer is the Meleager story. The hero will live as long as the brand which is snatched from the hearth at his birth is not consumed. His death was brought about when his mother in anger casts it upon the fire.

We find in the folk-tales the dismemberment motif. In the Medea story it is combined with another folk-tale motif, that of rejuvenation. Medea first cuts up a ram or Jason's father Aison, boils the pieces, and out of the cauldron the dismembered animal or mortal rises up in rejuvenated form. But when Pelias is to be rejuvenated, the sorceress omits to put the proper charm into the cauldron and Pelias remains dead. The variation is expressive of the dramatic tendency which characterizes the Greek tales. In another group of tales the dismemberment takes place in association with a cannibalistic banquet—the stories of Tantalos, Thyestes, and Lycaon. Pelops, the son of Tantalos, is brought to life again by the gods ; a shoulder-blade, which the sorrowing Demeter has absentmindedly devoured, is replaced by a new one of ivory. This is typical Greek rationalism amid the fancifulness of the folk-tale.

The miraculous birth from the severed limbs or the blood is more common, although the identity with the dismembered victim, the primitive ' soul migration ' so characteristic of the folk-tale, is lacking in the Greek myths, and its absence is no less characteristic of them. From the teeth of the slaughtered dragon armed men spring up in the Kadmos and Jasion stories. The motif occurs still more baldly in the tales of the cosmogony, which have preserved more of their primitive crudity than the heroic tales. They were not, like the latter, rationalized and refined in courtly circles, but were first related by the meditative peasant-poet, Hesiod. From the drops of blood of the mutilated Uranos the earth gives birth to the creatures for which mythology had no father ready to hand—furies, giants, the nymphs, and the wood-nymphs, the Meliae. From the foam which formed when his genitalia were cast into the sea, Aphrodite arises. The myth is here associated with an etymology (ἀφρός, ' foam ').

There is also a miraculous birth of another kind. Helen is born from Leda's egg, Athena from the forehead of Zeus, Dionysos from his thigh. Parallels from Scandinavian and Indian mythology are often adduced ; there are others in the primitive folk-tales.

The relationship to animals is no less primitively fantastic in the folk-tale. The animals stand, as among totemistic peoples, on the same level as human beings ; they talk, marry, and act like men and women. Hence arose both the moralizing animal fable of antiquity and the medieval animal tale. The animals are often wiser and stronger than men, and the helpful animals, who succour the hero in his need, are a common motif.[1] It is seen in the Psyche story, that finest of the few examples of the antique folk-tale. The ants sort out the heaps of corn, the task which Venus has imposed on Psyche, and Zeus' eagle fetches Proserpine's salve of beauty from the lower world. To judge by the many modern parallels, an animal-transformation tale lies behind the central motif according to which the bridegroom takes on his human shape only at night. But commonly in antiquity the animal fable went its own way and ceased to belong to mythology.

Metamorphosis into the form of some animal is common in the folk-tale and still more so in the tales of primitive peoples. The hero alternates between man and beast, so that one hardly knows which he is. Such transformations also occur very often in antique mythology, but in divine,

[1] A. Marx, *Griechische Märchen von dankbaren Tieren* (1889).

not heroic, myths. We shall see later that they may have another origin, in the aetiological tale, and very often it is difficult if not impossible to decide to which of the two varieties they belong. This is in great measure due to the fact that the mythology has undergone a literary revision, and the tales of metamorphosis in particular chiefly appear in later writers, who have remodelled them according to an established scheme. The folk-tale often makes an evil witch transform men into animals. There is an example of this in the Circe story, one of the many folk-tale motifs in the *Odyssey*.

Here may suitably be included some mention of those supernatural beings which we are accustomed to classify among the lower figures of popular belief, although they have sprung from religious ideas. Elves, wood- and sea-nymphs, and so on, play a great part in the folk-tale. A common type of story deals with a marriage with a female creature of this species, a fairy or a sea-nymph. She is usually won through battle or guile and is subject to her human lord as long as he observes a certain taboo. But when he utters the forbidden word or does the forbidden thing, she departs once again to her element and returns at most once or twice to see her children. Greek mythology furnishes a typical example in the Thetis story. Thetis was a sea-nymph whom Peleus won in battle. He kept hold of her although she changed herself into different forms, and compelled her to accompany him to his house. This power of transformation, which is also familiar from the folk-tale, was in Greece the special attribute of the creatures of the sea. Proteus transforms himself in the same way when Menelaos tries to draw knowledge from him by force, and so does Nereus, when Herakles wishes to learn the way to Erytheia. Only if they are held tight in spite of everything do they submit. In the Thetis story the taboo motif is lacking, but the story betrays its relationship to the folk-tale in that

Thetis returns to her element shortly after the birth of her son, though she comes back at times to help and comfort him. The special character of the Greek myth is shown in the fact that this more original version is ousted by that more widely known, according to which Thetis was given away in marriage by contrivance of the king of the gods.

Traces of primitive social conditions have also been eagerly sought in the folk-tale. Thus man-eating witches and giants have been explained by the cannibalism of primitive ages. In Greek legend we have the Cyclops, Thyestes, and Tantalos. But we may have here an aetiological tale, as is almost certainly the case with the Lykaon story. Human sacrifices formed part of the cult of Zeus on Mount Lykaion even in historic times. Social conditions, too, are often said to be reflected in the preference of the folk-tale for the youngest son. In the common myth Zeus is the youngest brother, while in Homer he rules in virtue of his right as the first-born. Among certain peoples it is the legal custom for the right of inheritance to rest preferably upon the youngest brother, not the eldest. But the motif may also be attributed to the fondness of the folk-tale for the Cinderella, the poor weak creature who is raised to power or splendour.

Motifs of this kind are, however, liable to a greater degree of alteration and revision than those previously mentioned. Every age and culture unconsciously adapts the tale to contemporary conditions. Our own tales, for instance, constantly speak of kingdoms, kings, and princesses, those of the primitive peoples of tribes and chiefs. Social conditions colour the folk-tale. When we find in the Greek myths, just as in the Indian, such frequent reference to the carrying off of women and the stealing of cattle, no profound natural mythology underlies the story but merely the simple fact that in the days of our Aryan ancestors these things were common and were most usual causes of disputes and wars. There would be a certain plausibility in seeing in these motifs an inheritance from the invading Greeks rather than from the peaceful Minoans, but so long as we know so little about the conditions of the Minoan age this is an uncertain guess. In the Minoan period also women and cattle played a very important part.

Equally characteristic is the great importance attached to murder in Greek mythology—murder often committed without premeditation or still more often led up to by trifling causes—but the idea of vengeance for blood is not prominent, as it is, for instance, in Scandinavia. There is no vendetta, no series of murders, but the murderer simply goes into exile. This, therefore, becomes a most convenient device for moving a hero from one place to another, when it is desired to harmonize conflicting variants of the myths.

If we search for them, we may find in the myths various relics of an earlier age, such, for instance, as the practice known from Scandinavian and Roman law of transferring land by symbolically handing over a sod.[1] It had vanished from practical use without leaving a trace. Still more is it so with religious rites, such as the human sacrifice, which are of rare occurrence in the actual cult but a common motif in the myth. The custom of purifying the army by causing it to march between the bleeding members of the victim lived on in backward Boeotia and in Macedonia ; otherwise the myth has appropriated it.[2]

It has been said that the folk-tale has no connexion with morals. This may be true to-day of the folk-tale which has remained as a residuum of primitive times, but not of the folk-tale in a stage of living development. Primitive people tell stories about the origin of their customs and institutions

[1] *A Rw*, xx, 1920, pp. 232 et seq.
[2] For the lustration rite see my *Griech. Feste*, pp. 404 et seq. ; in the myths Apollodorus, iii. 13. 7, with the note of Frazer, and transferred to Xerxes, Herodotus, vii. 39. 3.

and the punishments incurred by any neglect or breach of them. These motifs, which may be called ethical provided that no philosophical meaning be attached to the term, are more closely connected than others with social conditions. In a people with a markedly patriarchal system such as the Greeks originally possessed these motifs naturally centre in the family and its laws. We have here an important series of stock motifs which are especially concentrated in the Oedipus story, the incestuous union of mother and son and of father and daughter (Pelopia, Tydeus), the struggle between father and son, which recurs in Teutonic legend (Hildebrand and Hadubrand), the hostile brothers (Eteokles and Polynikes, Akrisios and Proitos, Atreus and Thyestes), the problem of vengeance for blood when the murderer belongs to the same family as the victim (Orestes, Alkmaion). Here, as we shall see, Delphi stepped in and re-modelled the myths in her own interests.

One of the family motifs is very common in our folk-tales, namely, that of the wicked step-mother. She is found also in the Greek myth (Ino, Sidero), but since among the ruling classes polygamy may be said to have been practised, another motif is added, that of the new and jealous wife (Dirke, Ino). Nor is the Potiphar's wife motif uncommon in the Greek myth (Bellerophon and Stheneboia, Peleus and the wife of Akastos).

With these motifs, reflecting the social conditions of an earlier period, we approach a much disputed question, viz. the historical element in the myth. And if it is true, as I tried to show at the beginning of this chapter, that the great cycles of the myths are associated with the famous centres of Mycenaean times, the question becomes of increased importance. Will it not then become more probable that historical reminiscences of these towns and of their princely houses enter into the myths ? The mere putting of such a question was for a time regarded as unscientific. The so-called euhemeristic mode of interpretation has sinned much, but the method of reducing all myths to divine myths has no less to answer for. The proscription of the method of historical interpretation was a measure of defence against a dangerous rival. That the method has its justification can now hardly be disputed, in view of the brilliant corroboration it has received from archaeological discoveries. An historical basis certainly underlies the description of the Trojan wars in the *Iliad*, the march of the Argive princes against Thebes which forms the background to the War of the Seven, and the accounts of the lordship of Minos over the Aegean Sea. Whatever the name Agamemnon may imply, there is reflected in his figure the power of the king of Mycenae as the mightiest ruler in Greece.[1]

But when Schliemann and Dörpfeld see in the shaft-graves of Mycenae the graves of the elder royal house, the Perseids, and in the bee-hive tombs the resting-place of the younger, the Atreidae, we are justified in doubting their conclusions. For nothing is more dangerous than to try to extract history from the myths : to lay bare the historical element is only possible when we have access to some external means of verification, independently of the story.

[1] Concerning the historic element of the Homeric epic compare H. M. Chadwick, *The Heroic Age*. Quite recently Dr. Forrer has published readings of certain tablets from Boghaz-köi, which seem to prove that some kings of the Greek myth were real historical personages of the Mycenaean age. In these tablets there appears about 1325 B. C. a king of a country Ahhijava, called Tavagalavas, who was equal in power to the Hittite king and also ruled over Pamphylia ; his father was probably a certain Antaravaas. These names are identified with Eteokles (original form Etevokleves) and Andreus, according to Pausanias, x. 34, mythical kings of Orchomenos in Boeotia, and Ahhijava with Achaivoi, the Achaeans. From a linguistical point of view there is no objection to the identification. About 1250–1225 B. C. another king of Ahhijava, Attarissijas, attacks Caria and devastates Cyprus ; he is identified with Atreus of Mycenae. See *Mitteilungen der deutschen Orient-Gesellschaft zu Berlin*, no. 63, March 1924.

Legend acts with sovereign freedom in dealing with persons, times, and places, and blends them all together, mingling with them purely mythical elements. An instructive example is the Nibelungenlied, where we happen to have a means of control and can observe how freely and capriciously the story handles historical personages and events and their dates.

We turn instead to the other main group, the explanatory tale and myth, or more simply the *aition*, as it is often called, from the Greek word *αἴτιον* meaning ' cause '. These tales, which seek to give a reason for everything which arouses man's attention in surrounding Nature, in customs and institutions, going so far back even as the creation of the world, are at least as popular among the people as the folk-tale. From the time of my childhood in a country district of Sweden I remember hardly any folk-tales proper, but a great many explanatory tales. The old ones are refashioned and new ones are constantly appearing, invented on the model of the old. An interchange goes on between folk-tale and explanatory tale. The former may be converted into the latter by having an aetiological conclusion tacked on to it, or the purpose of an aetiological tale may have been lost, so that only the story is left, and the tale can then not be distinguished from an ordinary folk-tale, unless parallels reveal its true character. We shall meet examples of both kinds.

It will probably be best to begin with the explanatory tales which are most obvious and whose importance has long since been duly appreciated—the cult *aitia*, the purpose of which is to explain the origin of some peculiar practice belonging to the cult. The explanation is to this effect : It was done thus on a particular occasion, and thus must it therefore always be done. Of the sacrificial victim the gods receive only the bones and a few scanty morsels enveloped in the adipose membrane. Why is this ? Because, when

gods and men contended with each other at Mekone,
Prometheus collected the pieces of the sacrificial victim into
two heaps and bade Zeus choose. He chose the worse of
the two, and therefore the gods still receive it. When
Orestes the matricide came a fugitive to Athens, King
Pandion had a separate pitcher of wine brought out for every
guest, so that none should be contaminated by drinking
wine ladled from the same vessel as the wine of the murderer ;
and therefore at the feast of Pitchers (χόες) wine was never
drawn from a common mixing-bowl, but every one poured
wine into his cup from his separate pitcher.

In the historical introduction to his description of the
province of Phokis, Pausanias relates that the Phocians,
on the occasion of a desperate struggle with the Thessalians,
piled up all their property upon a huge pyre, collected their
women and children together, and commanded the soldiers
left in charge, if the Phocians should be defeated, to kill
them, lay their bodies upon the pyre, and burn up everything
together. This looks like an historical anecdote, perhaps even
history. ' Phocian desperation' (Φωκικὴ ἀπόνοια) had become
a proverb. But Plutarch makes an addition which betrays
the connexion. The Phocians were victorious, and in
memory of their victory a great feast, the Elaphebolia, was
celebrated at Hyampolis. At this a great pyre was erected,
on it were laid property and figures in the likeness of human
beings, and the whole was set on fire.[1] The custom is well
known, the annual bonfire in which all kinds of things,
even living animals and sometimes human beings, are
burned. What we might have thought to be an historical
incident proves to be an aetiological tale invented to explain
the peculiar customs at the annual bonfire.

This fire was customary in ancient Greece and was lit,
as is still sometimes the case to-day, upon the top of a
mountain. The myth of the self-cremation of Herakles

[1] M. P. Nilsson, *Griech. Feste*, pp. 221 et seq.

upon Mt. Oeta has arisen from this custom, which on that particular mountain was associated with the worship of the hero. When it was asked why human figures were laid upon the pyre, the explanatory myth replied that Herakles himself was once cremated on the pyre and that the custom was annually repeated in memory of him.[1]

More rarely a tale of this type takes the form of an explanation of certain changes which have appeared in an already existing festival custom. An example is the long story of the Ionic Bouphonia festival, which explains how it came about that a bloodless sacrifice gave place to one in which blood was shed. Instances of aetiological tales describing the occasion of the founding of a cult are common. In Corinth it was the custom for seven youths and seven maidens in mourning garments and with clipped hair to mourn—according to a practice not unusual in the hero-cult—for certain child-heroes who lay buried in the shrine of Hera Akraia. The story said that they were Medea's children, whom the Corinthians had slain ; to atone for the deed the cult had been founded. Euripides is the first to make Medea herself kill her children. This type of story had such an influence that several of Euripides' tragedies are aetiological. Reconciliation is achieved at the conclusion by the founding of a cult.

This prolific group is principally important for the history of the cult, and the tales often throw light upon the cult practices themselves. Thus, for instance, I have tried to reconstruct from the aetiological myth the customs at the Aiora festival.[2] It appears that virgins walked singing

---

[1] This explanation has been confirmed by discoveries at the spot where the annual fire was lit on Mount Oeta. See my article *Fire Festivals in Ancient Greece*, *JHS*, xlii, 1923, pp. 144 et seq., and especially *Der Flammentod des Herakles auf dem Oite*, *ARw*, xxi, 1922, pp. 310 et seq.

[2] M. P. Nilsson, *Die Anthesterien und die Aiora*, *Eranos*, xv, 1915, pp. 187 et seq.

around the vine-hills and sacrificed a dog to promote the harvest. Historically considered, the importance of the cult *aitia* is paradigmatic. They are often mechanically constructed according to a certain scheme and have frequently only a superficial connexion with the current myths.

Nearest to this group stands another which also has its origin in the cult. It consists of aetiological tales intended to explain peculiarities in the god's form of appearance, his attributes, even his images. To this group no doubt belong *inter alia* a number of animal-transformation tales, although the conquering anthropomorphism has obliterated most of the traces. The clearest example comes from backward Arcadia. At Thelpusa and Phigalia it was said that Poseidon in the form of a horse united himself with Demeter in the form of a mare ; she gave birth to a filly or to a daughter Despoina, and to the colt Areion. So far the story resembles an ordinary tale of animal-metamorphosis. The aetiological basis becomes evident when we know that at Phigalia Demeter was represented with a horse's head. At Lycosura Despoina was said to be the daughter of Demeter and Poseidon Hippios (' the Horse-Poseidon '). It is a reminiscence of the representation of gods in the form of animals that this aetiological tale seeks to explain. An epithet is often all that is left of this representation. Its traces have usually been obliterated, so that we have to draw more or less certain conclusions from the connexion of a god with the animal tale. The nymph Kallisto, who was transformed into a bear by the wrath of Artemis, is regarded with probability as a form of the epiphany of Artemis herself, who has certain associations with the bear. Little girls, who were her temple-servants in Athens, were called ' bears '.

I regard as belonging to this group an aetiological tale of another type, viz. the myth that Hera hurled the new-born Hephaistos to the earth, so that he injured himself and

became lame. Stunted limbs or severed tendons distinguish
the smiths of mythology, and even to-day smiths still tend
to acquire strong arms but weak legs by constantly standing
hammering at the anvil. Men choose the trade for which
they are fitted, and therefore under primitive conditions
blind men became minstrels and lame men smiths. Accordingly, their god too is lame, and it is this fact which the myth
seeks to explain.

The aetiological tales explaining attributes are of little
importance. Athene received the Gorgon's head from
Perseus ; Hermes threw his staff upon two snakes in combat,
which wreathed themselves around it ; hence he got the
caduceus. As a new-born child he made the first lyre out
of a tortoise-shell and gave it to Apollo. Nor of the images
of the gods is there much to say. Most of the tales relate
their origin, for instance, those of the palladium and the
image of Tauric Artemis, to which various places laid claim.
When Hermes had killed Argos, the gods were to judge him.
To avoid coming into contact with the blood-contaminated
deity they cast their voting-pebbles at him ; these collected
in a heap around his feet.[1] The myth seeks to explain why
the herme usually stands amid a pile of stones.

With the next group we come to explanatory tales of
a kind extremely common among other peoples also, both
primitive and modern, viz. the Nature *aitia*, which attempt
to explain peculiarities in surrounding Nature, both animate
and inanimate.

A tale which has spread to every corner of the world tells
how a human being, among us a giant, has been turned to
stone. It is a transparent aetiological tale which seeks to
explain a human resemblance in a block of stone. In the
excess of her grief Niobe is transformed into a constantly
weeping rock. It exists to this day on the top of the moun-

[1] Schol. to the *Odyssey*, xvi. 471 ; compare my *Griech. Feste*,
p. 338, n. 2.

tain Sipylos. A spring wells up and flows down over its head. When Poseidon in the *Odyssey* turns the ship of the Phaeacians into stone, this is probably an aetiological attempt to explain the ship-like formation of some rock in the sea.

Prominent trees are associated with the myths. Under a great plane-tree at Gortyn Zeus and Europa had celebrated their nuptials. But in such cases the tree had no doubt most usually been the object of a cult from the beginning. The place *aitia* are in Greece often cult *aitia* also. We know how among ourselves historical reminiscences are used to explain peculiarities of places, which become monuments to minor kings, the scenes of encounters with marauders, and so on, and how legends such as those of Robin Hood in England wander and become attached now to one place, now to another. In Greece, mythology was constantly ready for a similar service. Universally known stories became attached and gave their names to localities which occupied the popular imagination. Therefore, when the name of a famous legendary hero is associated with a shrine or a grave, we shall do wisely to reckon with the possibility of a later ascription of the name. Oedipus, for example, had four tombs, none of which is the original. For he was from the beginning not a hero of a cult but a legendary hero.[1] The attempts made by the help of these local traditions to show that the Trojan heroes originally belonged to the mother country must therefore be regarded with extreme suspicion.[2] They were so famous that a half-forgotten cult or a nameless grave might anywhere be christened by their names.

Pausanias tells of one obvious instance from Argolis.

[1] My arguments against Robert's view that Oedipus was originally a god and that the place of his cult (the grave) at Eteonos is the real one are developed in a review of his *Oidipus* in *Götting. gelehrter Anzeiger*, 1922, pp. 36 et seq.

[2] The chief defender of this view is E. Bethe; see his essay, *Homer und die Heldensage*, *NJb*, vii, 1901, pp. 657 et seq.

On the road between Mycenae and Argos lay the tomb of Thyestes. It was adorned with a stone image of a ram and the place was called Krioi (' The Rams '), so that there were no doubt several images of the kind. In older times more particularly the tombs were often ornamented with images of animals—they are found in great numbers on the burying-ground of Athens at Dipylon—and the association with the myth of the Golden Lamb stolen from Atreus by Thyestes caused this particular tomb to be assigned to Thyestes.

Aetiological tales explaining characteristics of animals are extremely common among all peoples who live in close contact with Nature. Kipling relates an Indian legend of how the tiger, after his first slaughter of a living creature, fled through the jungle ; the reeds struck his sides and therefore he became striped. The swallow has her round, red throat and cloven tail because she was a thieving servant-maid, who stole a red ball of wool and a pair of scissors from the Virgin Mary. The idea of animal-transformation also enters in here.

Greek mythology has a brilliant and oft-quoted example. No one could suspect an animal-tale in the bloody tragedy of Prokne and Philomela, but when the heroines are also called Aëdon and Chelidon (the Nightingale and the Swallow) the connexion begins to be clear. I take a later and less-known version of the story.[1] At Colophon lived Polytechnos (the skilful artist) with his wife Aëdon and their only son Itys. They had a contest in artistic skill, Aëdon weaving and Polytechnos making a chariot. From this contest a quarrel arose. Polytechnos enticed his wife's sister Chelidon to him and seduced her, and when the sisters recognized each other they revenged themselves by killing Itys. All the personages of the story, including their relatives, were transformed into birds, Polytechnos to a wood-pecker. In the Prokne story Tereus cuts out Philo-

---

[1] The so-called Boios in Antoninus Liberalis, ch. II.

mela's tongue so that she shall not be able to betray his misdoing. The explanatory nature of the tale is clear. The swallow twitters so unintelligibly because her tongue has been cut out; the nightingale is constantly crying ' Itys, Itys ', in grief for the child whom she has murdered. The wood-pecker, the carpenter of the animal world, hammers constantly. The different versions show how greatly details may vary while the main aetiological idea is constantly kept in view. In another of them, for instance, Prokne, jealous of her sister's flourishing tribe of children, wishes to kill one of them, but kills by mistake her own son Itys. These versions also show, as has been remarked above, how the aetiological character of the tale may entirely disappear and the animal-tale be raised to the level of the ordinary anthropomorphic mythology. The animal names are changed to others, and the motif of the severed tongue has already fallen out in Homer as being too crude.

Metamorphoses are very popular in the later mythological poetry, their occasion being usually some great grief or else the wrath of the gods. Arachne (the spider) was so proud of her skill in weaving that she gave herself out to be superior to Athena. The goddess therefore changed her into a spider, constantly weaving its web. The peasant boy Askalabos (the lizard) mocked at Demeter as she was thirstily drinking a broth. In her wrath she poured the mess over him; he was spotted by the solid pieces, and was thus transformed into a spotted lizard.

It is noticeable that mammalian animals hardly occur in this group; we find chiefly birds and also sometimes lower animals. The reason must be that the stories of metamorphosis into mammals are bound up with representations of the gods in animal form, and have accordingly found their place elsewhere. The other animals were, therefore, left for explanatory tales of the present type.

From the earth man raises his eyes to the sky, the

phenomena of which very soon lay hold of the primitive imagination. The nature peoples tell numerous stories intended to explain the creation of the heavenly bodies, the course of the sun, the markings and varying phases of the moon. All these stories are Nature *aitia* but belong to another domain. In regard to the starry world, primitive peoples already group the stars together into images, which may then represent anything within their world of ideas. This grouping of the stars is not in itself aetiological but readily suggests an aetiological tale. The constellations become objects and living creatures which have been carried up from earth to heaven.

In regard to the greater heavenly bodies the Greeks have only short explanations to give, which are by no means developed into the long myths found among the nature peoples. The sun rides in his chariot over the heavens and is carried back over the ocean from west to east in a golden bowl which Herakles once borrowed ; the moon rides or drives ; the morning-star rides. A vase-painting represents the stars as boys, who on the rising of the sun dive into the sea.

But there are very many star-myths, for these were extremely popular in Alexandrian times. It is not certain, however, that this branch of mythology is of native Greek origin. Homer knows a few of the larger constellations : Sirius or the Dog ; its master Orion, the huntsman ; the Pleiades ; the rainy stars, the Hyades ; the Bear or the Wain ; and the driver of the Oxen, Boötes. It is the common transference of terrestrial objects to the stars that may give rise to star-transformation myths, but the older Greek star-myths are few. The Orion myth, however, can hardly be separated from the constellation. Much later, in the sixth century, the zodiac and its signs were borrowed from Babylonia. It is possible that this gave rise to the development of star mythology ; there can be no doubt at least that the interest in astronomy in later times gave the star mythology its popularity.

There is still less to say about atmospheric phenomena. I shall only refer to Aristophanes' grotesque explanation of the rain,[1] and the common folk-tale which appears in the *Odyssey* about the winds being shut up in a sack. To the primitive mind man is a natural being like other creatures, and it is, therefore, obvious that he, his origin, idiosyncrasies, and institutions will be the object of the fantastic explanations of the aetiological tale. Whence comes the culture which, however insignificant it may be, distinguishes the world of man from that of the beasts ? The myth replies with the culture-bringer, among primitive peoples a powerful magician of ancient times or the totem animal, among more advanced races a god or a hero. Fire, the basis of all human culture, was stolen by Prometheus from the gods, just as by a certain Indian tribe a fish was said to have stolen it from the Creator Quawteatl. Agriculture, the next great step in civilization, is taught to man by mythical personages. Sent forth by Demeter, Triptolemus goes about the earth in his chariot and spreads the knowledge of it. Upon this myth is modelled that of the first vine-grower, Ikarios. The culture-heroes of the Greek myths are Prometheus, who in Aeschylus boasts that by his inventions he has drawn man out of his half-bestial sloth, and Palamedes, who invented writing, the calendar, and the game of draughts.

The aetiological tale explains the origin of man and animals. Poseidon created the horse by a blow of his trident on the rock. Prometheus made woman from clay and the gods equipped her with soul, beauty, and cunning. Similar tales are told everywhere. The Greek story reminds us of the biblical in that woman is created after man, as well as in other respects. Its self-conceit shows that it was the male sex that created the myths. It is related in many

---

[1] Aristophanes, *The Clouds*, v. 373.

tales that man proceeded from the earth, from trees, as in Norse mythology, or from the animal world—this last especially among totemistic peoples. But when a Greek myth tells how Zeus, at the prayer of Aiakos that his country might be peopled, turned ants (μύρμηκες) into men, Myrmidons, this is an aetiological tale which has been brought into existence through a play on words. Such etymological myths are not rare. It has been thought that a reference to the above-mentioned idea that man proceeded from trees or stones is to be seen in Homer's stock question : ' Thou wast not born of an oak or a stone ? ' It is found in the story of Deucalion and Pyrrha. When the world was destroyed by the Deluge, they threw stones behind them and from these arose new men and women ; but this myth too has an etymological background, the resemblance of sound between λᾶας, ' stone ', and λαός, ' people '.

When the aetiological tale tries to explain the origin of the human race and of culture, it has reached the highest and most comprehensive questions, and it is no long step to the attempt at explaining the origin of the whole world in which men live and move. The answer is very simple and easy. Just as man arranges matters as conveniently as he can to suit his simple needs, building a hut and making his few tools, and just as the advance of culture is brought about by culture-heroes, so, it is said, there was at the beginning of time some one, though much more powerful than man, who arranged the world as conveniently as possible to supply man with all that he needed. This creator, who is found among many primitive peoples, is called by the Australians characteristically enough ' the Maker' (Baiame). He has also fixed the customs and institutions of the tribe. At first sight it would seem as though we had here a highly developed monotheistic type of divinity, but the idea is in reality due to the indolence of primitive habits of thought. The creator is a mythological, not a religious divinity ; and, therefore, he has no cult and no one troubles about him.

It is natural that among less primitive peoples, who have developed a system of divinities, the Creation should be ascribed to the gods, as it is in Babylonia and Scandinavia. Greek mythology has neither of the two theories. ' The Maker ' is found only among primitive peoples, and the Greek gods were not great and mighty enough to create the world; they were too strongly anthropomorphic. Rationalism had early deprived them of the magic power which gods require for such a work.

In Greece we consequently find only the other kind of creation myth, in which the creation proceeds automatically. This too is very common among other peoples at a somewhat higher stage of development than the lowest. A widespread idea is that the world arose out of the water or came from an egg. When Homer speaks of Okeanos as the origin of the gods and of Tethys as their mother, the idea of primeval water probably underlies the statement. It recurs in the Orphic cosmogony, which rests upon a primitive foundation. In the beginning was the primeval water, from it arose an egg, and out of this proceeded the first creature, the god Phanes. Still more crude is the cosmogonic myth in Hesiod. Ouranos (the sky) settled down upon Gaia (the earth), completely covering her, and hid their children in her entrails. Gaia persuaded her son Kronos to part them by cutting off the genitalia of Ouranos. There are curious parallels in the Egyptian myth of Keb and Nut, the earth-god and the goddess of heaven, and in the Maori myth of Rangi and Papa. The sky lay in a close embrace upon the earth, and in the darkness between them the gods had to dwell. Tane Mahute separated them and raised up the sky. The gods then departed each to his separate place in air, earth, and sea, and thus the world was established.

In the last-mentioned tales the parts of the world, heaven and earth, have been anthropomorphized. The cosmogony has become a divine myth, but the personal names are only a transparent disguise. These gods, like the ' Maker ', are of mythological, not of religious origin and are without any importance for the cult. Examples of such mythological deities in Greece are Ouranos, Okeanos, and in most respects Gaia also. Helios and Selene resemble them. They play an insignificant part in the cult, with the exception of Helios at Rhodes, this exception being probably due to foreign influence. Hades had practically no cult. The name seems to be a collective term used to describe the kingdom of the dead and then personified. Several similar and still paler cosmic deities were added when meditation, seeking to explain the origin of the universe, carried the cosmogony still farther back into its formless beginning. Chaos, Erebos, Nyx, and other names in Hesiod stand for nothing but cosmic principles, although the words are spelt with an initial capital like personal names.

The Greek form of imagination is anthropomorphic and the creation of the world takes place as a series of procreations ; it is brought into the customary genealogical form. Through this thin veil the real nature of the process is clearly seen. The creation is a development of the cosmic material existing from the beginning and proceeds of itself, a development in the only form in which it could yet be imagined—that of procreation and conception. We have only to strip off the mythological disguise to have natural philosophy, and indeed natural philosophy for a long time called its principles by mythological names. The fundamental distinction between matter and force is already dimly perceived by Hesiod, when he gives to Eros, Love, the driving-force of generation, a place as one of the cosmic powers. Thus the aetiological tale in its highest form gives rise to the beginnings of science. The first elements of a scientific explanation of the universe were among other peoples just as inseparably united with the mythical as Ouranos with Gaia in the myth of Hesiod. But the Greeks separated them with the keen edge of thought. Their marvellous qualities of mind, their rationalism, and clarity of thinking could brook no ambiguity or confusion. Hence was born among them that independent searching after truth which is Science, the greatest offspring of the spirit of Greece.

We have seen that the same quality in a lower form, for which I should perhaps use the term rationalism, gave to the Greek myths their peculiar character, in contra-distinction to the primitive tale and folk-tale out of which they sprang. An outgrowth of the same kind is the humanizing of the myths, the anthropomorphism characteristic of Greek mythology. It is due not only to the plastic imagination of the Greeks, with its power of intuition, but also to their antipathy to the primitive and fantastic ideas and characteristics of the folk-tale, which led them to clear away all that too sharply contradicted the experiences of human life. The Greek myth has thus become something other than the ordinary folk-tale, and rightly bears a separate name. What, through this rationalizing and humanizing process, it lost in religious importance, it made up in independent worth. It became a power which defied changes of religion and the lapse of centuries, and which even to-day is not dead.

The correctness of the conception here generally outlined must be proved by a detailed analysis of the myths. I have carried out this analysis for certain important cycles, but I am unable, from lack of space, to reproduce it here. We shall return below to the later development of the Greek mythology. But the basis on which it was to develop throughout all future ages was laid down in prehistoric times.

III

PRIMITIVE BELIEF AND RITUAL

In the preceding pages I have made an attempt to enter into the religion of the Minoan-Mycenaean Age and to demonstrate its influence upon later Greek religion and myth. The Minoan-Mycenaean Age was highly developed artistically, and we may conclude from certain signs that it had also attained a high level of social and religious development. It must have already left behind it the more primitive forms of religion. But it is just the relics of these primitive forms that modern research in the history of religion seeks to unearth and bring to light, and they must of necessity find a place here, even though it be chiefly well-known facts that I have to point out.

A word or two first as to the method which has necessarily to be adopted, for it is important that the nature and limitations of this should be made clear in order that the extent of its applicability may be rightly understood. It is not historical in the strictest sense of the term. The material is collected principally from later times, from the written tradition of the post-Homeric period. Historically regarded it is therefore far later than the material dealt with in the first chapter, and later than the extensive remodelling of the religion in Homer, of which I shall speak presently. Yet our justification for seeing in this material survivals from a religious stage which was far earlier than the Homeric or even the Minoan-Mycenaean period lies in its primitive character, and in the fact that it recurs among all peoples of the world, among the primitive races as well as among the rustic populations of the countries of Europe.

To use an old illustration, a highly developed religion is

like the total vegetation of a forest. The great gods are the tall trees, which raise their mighty heads the highest, are most conspicuous to the eye, and determine the character of the forest. But it is also easiest to fell them and plant new ones instead. It is more difficult to eradicate the brushwood, which their crowns conceal and deprive of air but cannot stifle—what we are accustomed to call the lower figures of popular belief. And the grass upon the ground is still more stubborn, ever the same blades springing up and the same simple flowers blooming. It is this under-vegetation of belief and custom which we shall now try to examine.

By an analysis of the whole complicated scheme, but chiefly by an investigation of the state of primitive peoples among whom the more rudimentary beliefs are still preserved unimpaired, ethnological research tries to construct the rising curve in religious and social development, for the two are intimately connected. There are revealed in the process certain important and widespread groups of ideas and rites associated with certain primitive forms of society, and the question arises whether these are necessary transitional stages in the general development which we must look for everywhere. The point most discussed is whether the curious association between a consanguineous group of men and a certain species of animal, together with the remarkable social system called totemism which is built upon it, must also be presumed to have once existed in the case of the early ancestors of the Greeks. Although earnest attempts have been made to discover traces of it,[1] there is nothing in the Greek religion which necessarily demands a totemistic explanation ; totemism has no monopoly of animal worship and animal tales, they may also have another origin. It will probably be wisest to formulate

[1] More particularly S. Reinach in several essays reprinted in *Cultes, Mythes et Religions*, 5 vols.

our answer thus : It is unproved and doubtful whether totemism ever existed among the forefathers of the Greeks, and, if it did exist, the totemistic ideas and rites were transformed under the influence of a new world of ideas, in particular agrarian ideas, so that they can no longer with certainty be pointed to as totemistic.

Still less do I believe in the attempt recently made [1] to discover traces of that curious social and religious state in which society is grouped according to age, the initiation of the young into the confederacy of full-grown men is the principal ceremony, and general conceptions prevail from which deities are ultimately developed. This is a form of religion which more than any other is indissolubly associated with a definite social stage of development and which, with any change in the latter, must itself also change and disappear ; it belongs to that primitive democracy which we find only among races at a low stage of civilization. In Greece the Minoan-Mycenaean culture prevailed for a millennium before the beginning of the historical period, and this culture was highly developed socially and belonged to a totally different type, one in which a king or priest-king ruled, more or less absolutely, a state with a population clearly marked by differences of rank and class. A social order of this nature must have discarded the system of age-groups and everything connected therewith. If we turn to the invading Greeks, the chances of the survival of such a system are no greater. For one thing is clear : the Greeks, like all other Aryan peoples, built up their social order upon the patriarchal family. The latter is in opposition to the group-system, which must disappear where it prevails. The theory of the survival of the group-system involves an inadmissible ' foreshortening ' of the historical perspective.

The indisputable remains of primitive ideas and rites are

[1] Jane Harrison, *Themis, A Study of the Social Origins of Greek Religion.*

of a more general nature than the ideas and customs just mentioned, which represent a system built up under special conditions. Whether they derive from the original population of the country or from the invading Greeks it is impossible to decide, and the question is of no importance since the ideas are universal and in their main features must have existed among both peoples. As has already been said, we must look for our knowledge of them to the historical period, when they had become interwoven with Greek polytheism, and it is by inference as to their character that we trace them back to the primitive foundation of religion. The most accurate method should therefore be to begin with a portion of the fabric which shows the threads woven together, and then gradually to disentangle them and trace them to their separate origins.

From the standpoint of a more advanced religion it is obvious that all that belongs to the gods is withdrawn from profane use and must be treated with due reverence and respect. But this respect manifests itself as a scrupulous awe which performs works of unnecessary devotion. We cast away our useless rubbish upon the rubbish-heap, but the property of the gods must not be treated so, even if it be entirely worthless. In the temples the poor votive offerings accumulated, were damaged by time, and became no more than rubbish. Sometimes a great clearance had to be made, but even then the rubbish was not simply thrown away but was hidden in crevices or pits dug in holy ground, and was covered with earth. It is these deposits that the spade of the archaeologist has turned up in later times. The same obligation applied to the common animal-sacrifice. Very often, although far from universally, it was the rule that the flesh of the animal sacrificed must not be taken home but must be eaten on the spot within the domain of the god. Curiously enough, the rule seems to have applied still more strictly to the offal from the sacrifices.

Around an altar belonging to the archaic period we usually find layers of ashes, charred animal bones, and votive offerings. They were the property of the god and must not be removed from the spot, although according to our ideas they must have formed an objectionable rubbish-heap. Even in later times the ashes were left upon the place of sacrifice and piled up into ash-altars, a famous example being the ash-altar of Zeus at Olympia. The skulls of the sacrificial victims were nailed up on a tree in the sacred grove or on the temple wall. The boucranion therefore became a common motif in the ornamentation of temples and altars.

The temple was holy, but there were varying degrees of holiness. Some temples could only be entered at a certain time—that of Dionysos Limnaios at Athens, for instance, only on the feast day, the 12th of the month Anthesterion—others might be entered by the priests alone ; the inner *cella* in the temple of Sosipolis in Elis could only be entered by the priestess and even she must veil her face. Other temples had at least an adytum from which the public was debarred. There were sacred areas which must not be trodden at all by human foot, for example, the grove of Demeter and Kore at Megalopolis, and the ground sacred to Zeus on the top of Mt. Lykaion. Any one who trespassed upon this would lose his shadow and die within the year. The gods themselves might mark out a place as holy. A spot which had been struck by lightning must be fenced in and be trodden on no more, and therefore a person who had been killed by lightning must not be removed but must be buried on the spot.

That which is sacred is inviolable, and this quality has in the last-quoted examples been so far developed as almost to resemble a curse. So it is also with the land which belongs to the gods. It might happen that it was rented for use, but trees must not be felled or taken away from the sacred grove. Sometimes the prohibition against profaning the land belonging to the god was understood so strictly that the land was not cultivated but had to lie waste. This was so, for instance, with the Crisaean plain, which was dedicated to Apollo. It is well known what a part the complaints against the cultivation of this land played in the political struggles of the middle of the fourth century. No less a part was played in the Peloponnesian War by the district at the foot of the Acropolis of Athens known as the Pelargikon. An oracle commanded that it was to lie unused, but when the population of Attica was crowded within the walls of Athens, dwelling-places were sought upon the Pelargikon as well; many saw in the transgression of the command a reason for the disasters of the war.

Here we have a clear example of that twofold significance of sanctity to which reference has already been made. The Pelargikon was according to our conception under a curse. In Latin the word *sacer* had both senses; it means both ' sacred ' and ' accursed '. The Greek language has the corresponding idea but not the word. The verb ἀρᾶσθαι, however, means both ' to pray ' and ' to curse '; and the priest is called ἀρητήρ by Homer. The connecting link is the fact that both the sacred and the accursed are withheld from common use; they are handed over to the gods, whether to their care or to their wrath. But the origin goes much farther back, before the emerging of the gods. The might of the gods is not necessary to remove a thing from the sphere of ordinary use. Among most peoples there is a belief in ' power ' (*mana*, &c.), which penetrates everything; in Greece alone it was pushed aside—we shall presently try to find its traces—until with the recrudescence of religion in a later age it came back again as δύναμις, ' magic power ', in a higher sense as φῶς, ' light, knowledge ', and in Christianity also as χάρις, ' grace '. In the last two words ' power ' is regarded under its good and noble aspect. ' Grace ' is

granted by a personal God, and so also often is light, but this
is also a force in itself. Among primitive peoples ' power '
is its own cause ; it exists before and independently of gods
and spirits. It is merely ' power ', and whether it is good or
evil depends upon how it comes into contact with man.
Man must beware of it and proceed cautiously in regard to
it, for if it can help, it can also harm. Anything which is
filled with ' power ' must therefore be treated with certain
measures of precaution; only certain specially qualified
persons can come near it, others must avoid it. It is *tapu*.
The idea of taboo is the root and origin both of that
which is sacred and of that which is accursed. There has
only been a displacement of the causal motive : the essential
of sanctity is possession by a god. That which is under
a curse is also dedicated to a god, but to his anger and
vengeance.

Taboo ideas permeate the whole life of primitive man.
They accumulate more than elsewhere about the critical
points of human life, about birth, death, and marriage,
when man is more exposed than at other times to the
attacks of ' power ' or ' the powers '. At these points we
find them also in the Greek religion. Certain herbs were
laid beside a woman in childbed to ward off evil from her,
and in Athens her clothing was disposed of by being dedicated
to Artemis Brauronia. On the fifth day the child was
carried round the hearth and was thereby received into the
protecting bosom of the family. The neighbourhood of
death involves the presence of dangerous forces, against
which protection is sought in many ways. The means of
protection are most often called purifications, for they are
intended to ward off the evil force which, like a plague, is
communicated to every one who comes into contact with it.
Hence the woman in childbed and the dead man came to
be regarded as infectious and unclean, and many ordinances
of purification were instituted. Any one who visited their

house became unclean and had to purify himself. Outside the house of mourning was placed a bowl of water, so that those who went out might be able to cleanse themselves. The water, and even the fire and the food, in the house became unclean, and these had to be fetched from outside. After the burial the house was purified, just as Odysseus purified his palace with fire and sulphur after the slaughter of the suitors.

The ideas of taboo became transformed into ideas of purity and impurity [1] when they were associated with a belief in the gods. Above all else the gods demand purity in those who approach them. Hence the bowl of water is placed at the temple door, so that those who enter may cleanse themselves. In Homer, Hector, when he returns from battle, will not pour out a libation to Zeus with unwashed hands. Hesiod demands that the bringer of a sacrifice shall be pure and clean (ἁγνῶς καὶ καθαρῶς) ; it is a rule of general application that the worshipper must be clean at sacrifice and prayer and when entering a shrine. The sacral laws exhibit a varied and comprehensive casuistry. The forbidden periods are determined so to speak according to the strength of the infection. Here are a few examples : Women in childbed are excluded from the temple for forty days, those who have come into contact with them only for two, those who have had a death in the family during twenty to forty days, those who have visited a house of mourning for three days, and even those who have merely seen a corpse or taken part in the general ceremonies in connexion with a funeral are forbidden for the time being to visit the gods. Sexual intercourse between man and woman also renders both unclean for a shorter period. Hence none must be begotten, born, or die within the sacred precincts. The Athenians even went so far as upon two

---

[1] Th. Wächter, *Reinheitsvorschriften im griechischen Kult, RGVV*, ix. 1 ; compare also certain portions of Rohde, *Psyche.*

occasions to dig up all the old graves on Apollo's sacred island of Delos, and take away their contents.

At the great festivals the severity of the purifying ordinances was increased and they were blended with others of magical import, such as the forbidding of the tying of the hair into a knot or the wearing of rings, or with ordinances which sought to maintain an old-fashioned simplicity of worship, such as the prohibiting of valuable jewels, or purple-coloured or embroidered garments. The mysteries often began with a purification rite. The opening day of the Eleusinian mysteries takes its name from the bath of purification in the sea, and those who were to be initiated were specially purified by the sacrifice of a pig. Priests and other officials of the cult were subjected to even stricter regulations. A priest was forbidden, for instance, to enter a house where there was a woman in childbed or a house of mourning, to visit a grave or to take part in a funeral-banquet. At Messene a priest or a priestess had to resign office if his or her child died. For the same reason the boys who assisted in the cult must have both father and mother alive (παῖς ἀμφιθαλής). But the Greeks were not prone to the exaggerated scruples of which so many examples are found among the nature peoples. The regulations applying to the priest and priestess of Artemis Hymnia at Orchomenos in Arcadia are unique in Greece. They must have no intercourse with one another, must not bathe or take their food in the same manner as other people, and must not enter a private house. They remind us more of the Mikado or of some New Zealand chieftain than of a servant of the Greek gods.

The demands for cleanliness and purification extend throughout the whole of life but are modified for practical reasons. In their strict and literal meaning they are observed only by the few whom the Greeks disapprovingly called δεισιδαίμονες, a word for which we have no exact translation ;

' superstitious ' is not a precise equivalent, for the Greek word is used of those who are too much afraid of ' the powers '. It is psychologically easy to understand that the strength of the claim depended upon the strength of the impression made by the cause of the uncleanness. Therefore the homicide was intensely unclean. He had to be purified with an elaborate sacrifice before he was once more allowed to enter the temple in common with other men. Accidental death or suicide produced the same effect. On Cos it was a rule that if any one hanged himself, not only the corpse but also the rope and the tree to which it was fastened were to be sent beyond the borders of the country. In Athens the object that had caused a person's death was treated in the same way. In later times it happened that heated political passions led to the wholesale murder of opponents. The terror that this caused is revealed by a couple of anecdotes. When envoys from Cynaetha, where a wholesale slaughter of the kind had taken place, visited Mantinea, the inhabitants caused purificatory sacrifices to be borne round the town and its whole neighbourhood. The Athenians again, having merely heard how the democrats of Argos had beaten their opponents to death with cudgels, at once had the popular assembly purified in the same manner. Here the natural feeling manifests itself in the form of the rite. The demand for purification contained a seed which was to bear fruit in the future and we shall later see what grew out of it.

Uncleanness was conceived of as an infection, as a material substance which could be washed away with water or the blood of sacrificial victims, rubbed off or else burned away with fire, or smoked out with sulphur. This simple primitive conception appears clearly in the case of sickness, which was also regarded as the work of an evil power and was removed by the same means, as is done among the nature peoples. The classical example is contained in the first book of the *Iliad*. After the plague a great cleansing was carried out in the Greek camp and the off-scourings (λύματα) were thrown into the sea. Thus both they and the evil power residing in them were got rid of. And this was a common practice. It is said of Aesculapius that he wiped away (ἀποψάω) disease, and inversely he pours all his healing power into man by touching him with his ' gentle hand ' (ἤπιος χείρ).[1] Any who sought to be cured of leprosy by the nymphs of Samicon first wiped his diseased limbs and then swam over the stream. The Greek word for pollution, ' miasma ', still keeps this material sense to-day.

The same custom and the same idea recur in the established rite. The pig was the usual sacrificial animal in purifications and expiations. By the sacrifice of a pig the homicide was cleansed and so also was the candidate for initiation into the Eleusinian mysteries. Before every popular assembly in Athens the place of meeting was purified by the sacrifice of a pig, which was carried round it. Other animals were also used. When the Macedonian army was purified in the month Xandikos, the method adopted was to cause the soldiers to march between the bleeding parts of a dismembered dog. The people of Boeotia were purified in the same way, and the myth relates that a human being was cut up instead of a dog in these purifications. This is not incredible, for it is precisely in purificatory rites that human sacrifices occur far down into historical times. Over all the Ionian district the Thargelia festival [2] was widespread. It was held shortly before the ripening of the corn and was intended to ward off all injurious influences from the crops, and the rites were naturally celebrated with reference to both country and town. It passes for an Apollo festival, but the rites are much older than Apollo ; their inner meaning is a purification, working of itself without the intervention of the god. At this festival a human being, in historical

---

[1] O. Weinreich, *Antike Heilungswunder*, *RGVV*, viii. I.

[2] See my *Griech. Feste*, pp. 105 et seq.

times a criminal, was carried about the town, after which
he was killed, his body burned upon branches of unfruitful
trees, and the ashes thrown into the sea.

These rites are usually called sacrifices, but the term is
misleading. They are not sacrifices in the ordinary sense
in which the victim is handed over to the gods or serves as
a medium of communication with them. These so-called
sacrifices are nothing but a means of purification, designed
to take away the impurity attaching to town and country.
And therefore they are carried round the town, or men have
to march between the parts of them. When, like a sponge
with which one dries a table, they have absorbed all the
impurity, they are entirely destroyed so that this impurity
shall be altogether removed with them; they are thrown
away, burned up, cast into the sea. And that is why this
' sacrifice ', so-called, need not, like others, be without
blemish or defect. A dog may be used, which was otherwise
never sacrificed, or a condemned criminal. He was called
φάρμακος, ' remedy ', κάθαρμα, ' off-scouring ', περίψημα,
' that which is wiped off '; this last word in particular
clearly shows the meaning of the rite. We can understand
how these words came to mean ' scum ' and became the
worst terms of abuse in the Greek language. A victim of
this nature is a scapegoat upon which all evil is loaded, but
which, instead of being let loose and driven into the desert,
is completely destroyed, together with its evil burden.

A prominent feature of these rites is the marching about
in the city or other place.[1] A rite which seems very similar
was observed at Methana when the south-west wind threatened to damage the vineyards. A cock was cut in two and
two men bore the pieces one in either direction around the
vineyards ; where they met, the two parts were buried.
And yet a new idea enters in here : a magic circle is drawn,

[1] See my article *Die Prozessionstypen im griechischen Kult*, *AJ*,
xxxi. 1916, pp. 319 et seq.

which nothing evil can pass. The farmers had many customs
of the kind. A maiden must walk around the farm with
a cock in her hand to ward off weeds and injurious insects,
but these were still more certainly destroyed by a men-
struating woman, walking about in the garden. This is
evidently a destruction by magical means ; in the menstrual
blood a dangerous power resided, just as in the evil eye,
and the power was used with intent to destroy, although it
was only directed against noxious plants and insects.

I cannot see that this magic differs in principle from that
which is employed to injure other people, in other words
I cannot make the difference between magic and religion
correspond to a distinction between an antisocial and a
social purpose. The essential difference still seems to me
to be whether an action takes place as an *opus operatum*
of itself or whether it addresses itself to a higher will, through
which it strives to see its intention fulfilled. It is true that
the most transparently magical practices are preserved in
antisocial sorcery and witchcraft. A wax figure is melted
or stuck full of pins in order that the person whom it
represents may suffer in the same way. Leaden figures
are laid down fettered in a grave to bind the enemy whom
they represent. Popular superstition believed that it would
hinder a sick man's recovery if one crossed one's hands or
laid one foot upon the other. And therefore all knots had
to be untied at child-birth, and at the mysteries at Lycosura
it was forbidden to wear rings or braided hair.

These are practices which are not recognized and which
are condemned because their purpose is evil ; but a search
will reveal entirely analogous rites in the official religion,
whose observance is enjoined by tradition and respect for the
gods ; their magical character was forgotten when they were
adopted by the religion and associated with divine worship.
In the so-called ' sacrifice of the oath ' the real nature of
the ceremony is clearly seen. Its usual form was for the

taker of the oath to touch the sacrificial victim and call down the curse upon himself in case he should break the oath. A passage in the *Iliad* makes the matter still more clear. An animal is sacrificed and a libation of wine is poured out and accompanied by the words :

Which nation soever shall first transgress this covenant-
 plight.
Be the brains of them spilt on the earth as yonder wine this
 day.

The words would be still more appropriate if they were spoken just as the sacrificial victim was killed. This is conditional magic. The perjurer calls down upon himself the fate of the sacrificial victim. And the latter is not really a sacrifice but, like the purificatory sacrifice, a magical instrument which is got rid of when the ceremony is completed.

Before man learns to address prayers to the gods for the success of his undertakings, he uses magic to effect his object ; and when he has learned to believe in the gods, he does not forget his ancient rites. They survive within or alongside of the cult, that is, if it be a cult with old traditions.[1] The younger cults of Greece repeat with wearisome monotony the so-called Olympic ritual—the ordinary sacrifice with procession, hymns, choric dances, and sacrificial banquets. Peasants are always conservative ; and just as in modern Europe, so also in ancient Greece, the rustic customs have preserved many relics of an outgrown religious stage.

In Greece rain is a much-desired gift and is often all too rare. Consequently the art of rain-making was important. The town of Crannon depicted on its coins a cart with an amphora which was used for this purpose. Probably the

[1] Most of the material for the following paragraphs will be found in my *Griech. Feste.*

vessel was filled with water and the cart was pushed hither and thither so that the water splashed in all directions. On Lykaion, the mountain of Zeus in Arcadia, there was a well called Hagno. When there was a drought the priest of Zeus went to the well, dipped a twig into its waters, and stirred them up. At once a mist was seen to rise from the well; it thickened into a cloud, and there was rain all over Arcadia. The rite is the simplest possible example of ordinary rain-magic, but it is performed by the priest of Zeus and is accompanied by a sacrifice; religion has taken it in hand. To Zeus, the god of rain, men turn when rain is wanted; he lives on the mountain-tops and there they go to pray for rain, for example, on Mt. Pelion, or on Kos and Keos. Those who climbed up to the shrine of Zeus Akraios on Pelion were clad in newly flayed sheepskins. In this costume an old piece of weather-magic lies hidden. In popular custom the fells of various animals were used as a protection against lightning and hail. When Empedokles the philosopher hung up asses' hides on the mountains round Akragas as a protection against the wind he was following an old popular belief. Zeus' fleece, the much-discussed $\Delta\iota\grave{o}s$ $\kappa\acute{\omega}\delta\iota o\nu$, belongs to 'the boisterous Zeus' ($M\alpha\iota\mu\acute{\alpha}\kappa\tau\eta s$). I am inclined to think that in these rites lies the key to the explanation of the myth of the Golden Fleece; it is associated with the Zeus of Mount Laphystion.

In our climate fire-magic is more common than rain-magic. It is a matter of dispute whether it is to be regarded as sun-magic or as a purificatory rite. I need not enter into this undecided question but will only point out that the annual fire is quite common in ancient Greece. In it were burned, as is also the modern custom, male and female puppets, living animals, and votive offerings. This was done, for instance, at the Elaphebolia held at Hyampolis in Phocis, and at the Laphria at Patrai, transferred thither from Calydon. Sometimes, as is done to-day, the fire was lit on the top of a mountain, for instance, on Oeta and on Cithaeron at the Daidala festival.[1]

Everywhere in the rites specially associated with agriculture we find examples of the same magical circle of ideas. The most widespread festival in Greece was the Thesmophoria, celebrated in autumn in order to ensure that the fertilizing power might cause the seed, soon to be committed to the ground, to grow and thrive. The festival was held in honour of Demeter, but the rites proceeded independently of the goddess. A repulsive but instructive example of a charm to induce fertility is the rite known as μεγαρίζειν. Living pigs were thrown into a subterranean chamber. After a while their corrupting remains were brought up, laid upon the altar, and mixed with the seed. The myth relates that when Hades carried off Persephone and the earth opened to receive him, the swineherd Eubouleus vanished with his herd into the abyss. This is an aetiological tale intended to explain the practice. Subterranean chambers (μέγαρα) were a distinguishing feature of Demeter's cult. At Cnidos, from which came the famous statue of Demeter in the British Museum, a crypt of this kind has been found and in it a number of marble pigs and other animals.

Other things having an association with fertility were placed in the subterranean chambers as well as pigs, for instance, pine cones and phalli. A phallus is the evident symbol of the procreative power in Nature. With the parallelism between human and vegetative fertility which is obvious to all agricultural peoples at a more primitive stage, it has its natural place in the rites of fertility. It occurs in the cult of another vegetation god, Dionysos, still more often than in that of Demeter. It was borne at the head of the procession at his festivals. Even the great

[1] See my paper, *Five Festivals in Ancient Greece*, *J.H.S.*, xlii, 1923, pp. 144 et seq.

Dionysia, which were celebrated with that noblest creation of the Greek spirit, tragedy, were introduced by a similar phallic procession, to which the Athenian colonies were required to send phalli.

So long as the crop stands on the soil it is committed to the care of the powers and must not be touched by man. When it is reaped, special rites must make it accessible to human use. This is the meaning of the sacrifice of the first-fruits. With these rites, which imply the raising of a taboo, are mingled others signifying the transference of the force of vegetation to man and to the new harvest which will spring up from the garnered corn. First-fruits of all kinds were boiled in a pot or were ground and then baked into a cake. The Greek name of this is *thargelos* or *thalysion*, and the mixture of all the fruits was called *panspermia*. This is found at a great many festivals, at the above-mentioned Thargelia which preceded the harvest, and at the real festival of harvest, the Thalysia. At the Pyanopsia, which were held in the autumn and took their name from the pulse which was boiled into a *panspermia*, the latter was eaten by all the members of the household, and so also at the Oschophoria, an Athenian festival at the vine- and fruit-harvest. The *panspermia* has its counterpart in European harvest customs : in Sweden it is known as the ' sowing-cake ', which is baked from the corn of the last sheaf, lies on the Christmas table, and before the beginning of farm-work in spring is eaten by the people of the house, sometimes also by the teams. The ' power ' which dwells within the crop of the year is embodied in the *panspermia* and the ' sowing-cake ', and through this it is transferred to the people of the house and to the new harvest which will grow up from the seed of the old. In later times the *panspermia* was certainly regarded as an offering to the gods, to Zeus Georgos (' the Farmer '), for instance, but in the popular custom the original meaning is clear. In Sicily there was a practice which suggests our modern May customs, the rite known as the Boucoliastai. A band of people went about with a bag of lentils and a skin of wine. When they came to a house, they sang a simple song, strewed the threshold with the lentils, and offered the inhabitants a draught of wine, with the words : ' Take the good fortune, take the blessing which we bring from the goddess who commanded this ' (viz. the custom). Artemis is represented as the origin, but there can be no doubt that the blessing is supposed to reside in the lentils and the wine and to be communicated by them, just as it dwells in the bough with fresh foliage planted according to modern custom before the houses on the first of May. In Sweden the lads who do this sing a song of blessing. Similar processions, in which a number of people, often boys, carried round from door to door something which brought blessing, sang a song with reference to this, and then received gifts, were just as common in ancient Greece as they are in modern Europe. On the island of Samos the *eiresione* was carried about ; at Rhodes an image of the swallow, messenger of Spring, was borne around as is done to-day in Macedonia ; at Colophon the crow.

I have mentioned the sacred bough, which confers life and fertility and plays so prominent a part in the agricultural customs of modern Europe. It played the same part in ancient Greece, where it was called *eiresione* or *korythale*. It is found at the Thargelia before the harvest and at the harvest festival proper, the Pyanopsia. The *eiresione* of the Pyanopsia closely resembles the bough which is carried about in modern harvest-customs. It consisted of an olive-branch hung about with all kinds of fruits and small bottles of wine and oil, which was carried in procession and set up before the house, where it was allowed to remain for a year, its place being then taken by a new one. But Apollo appropriated the festival, so that a bough was set up before his temple also. At the Oschophoria, the festival of the vintage, a branch with a cluster of grapes was employed for the purpose.

In our popular customs the beneficent power residing in the sacred bough has been made to apply to all the important occasions in life. It is raised when a wedding is celebrated or a new house is built. It was the same in Greece. The sacred bough was set up at a wedding and on the important occasion when the ephebe was received into full-grown manhood. It became an inseparable accompaniment of all rites and festivals. Any one who sought the protection of the gods bore the suppliant's bough (ἱκετηρία), a branch bound with woollen bands ; and the wreath encircling the heads of the participants at all sacrifices and festivals certainly has its origin in the belief in the beneficence of the flourishing bough.

The power residing in the sacred bough was transferred by its mere presence or through contact with it, just as power is transferred from the ' sowing-cake ' to those who eat it. At the festival of Artemis Orthia at Sparta the young boys were scourged at the altar of the goddess. This was regarded as a test of endurance of pain, and formed an element in the rigorous Spartan training. But such was not the origin of the practice. In this custom there has been recognized with great probability the blow with the sacred bough, whereby its power is communicated to man, a popular custom which is very common even in modern times. In all these customs the fundamental idea is clearly magical. The power residing in the cake or the bough passes over from these to anything with which they come into contact. Man enters into communication with the supernatural power. It might even be called a communion, if the use of the word were not restricted to the cases in which man is filled with power proceeding from a god. Yet even here the conception is fundamentally the same.

The communion, the union with the divinity, plays a very great part under various forms in the later, mystically inclined religions of antiquity. In the older Greek religion it occurs in one typical and important case, the worship of Dionysos. The central rite in the orgies of Dionysos was the omophagy. In the intoxication of their ecstasy his worshippers tore an animal to pieces and swallowed the flesh raw. The god himself was incarnated in the animal, man by virtue of the omophagy received him into his own being, was filled with his power, and was caught up from the human sphere into the divine. Here the primitive rite is transformed into a means to mystical ends, and it is because the rite provided an outlet for this tendency that the cult of Dionysos was of such great importance in the history of the Greek religion. We shall return to this cult later; here I would only point out its origin in primitive rites and ideas.

The ordinary Greek animal-sacrifice shows certain peculiarities which prove the insufficiency of the old explanation that it is a gift to the gods. The sacrificial animal is transferred into the sphere of the sacred by means of a special consecration—even the offal is sacred—but does not fall to the portion of the gods. On the contrary they obtain only a small part, the bones and a few scanty pieces of flesh wrapped in the adipose membrane. These are burned upon the altar, but the human worshippers appropriate the best morsels and celebrate a sacrificial banquet, although in many instances the flesh of the sacrifice must not be taken away from the holy place and must sometimes be devoured on the spot before nightfall. Attempts have been made to explain these peculiarities by the idea of a totemistic communion.[1] The god was incarnated in the sacrificial victim and his worshippers received his power into themselves, strengthening the bond of connexion with him by eating the flesh of the animal sacrificed, that is, of the god himself. The applicability of a totemistic explanation in Greece is doubtful, but under primitive conditions every

[1] W. Robertson Smith, *The Religion of the Semites*.

banquet has a sacral significance. Any one who eats and drinks in the company of a group of men is united with them by a sacred bond ; the admission to a meal means the admission into peace and protection. Odysseus takes a solemn oath at the table of hospitality. In the most holy form of marriage in ancient Rome, the *confarreatio*, the contracting parties ate bread together. That the gods were included in the community of the banquet appears clearly in the sacrifice of Eumaeus in the *Odyssey*. Of the seven parts of the animal slaughtered those present receive six, Hermes and the nymphs one. Thus the common banquet already becomes in itself a communion, uniting the participants in one fellowship ; the gods also take part in the banquet. In this sense the explanation of the animal sacrifice as a communion is undoubtedly correct. Into it enter not only the flesh of the sacrificial victim but also bread and wine, and the animal is consecrated by being sprinkled with crushed grains of corn ; this is the form in which cereals were eaten in ancient times.

The idea of communion also lies at the root of certain votive offerings. Usually the objects dedicated to the gods and placed in temples are regarded as gifts through which it is desired to win the favour of the god or show gratitude to him. This is correct in many cases, especially in later times, but other instances have peculiarities which cannot be explained in this way. The habitual gift to a god of healing is a representation of the diseased limb. Regarded as a gift this is curious. The explanation probably is that the image, as is so often the case, is meant to take the place of that which it represents. The diseased limb is consecrated to the healing god in order that it may partake of his healing power. The hair-offering is probably to be explained in a similar way. At the entrance upon adult age, when the girl is married, when the ephebe becomes a man, a lock of hair is cut off and dedicated as a reward for the child's upbringing, a ' foster-wage ' as it is usually called (θρεπτήρια), to some god, generally the river-god or fountain-nymph of the locality. The hair represents the man ; a lock in the possession of the gods places the whole man under their protection and care.

The primitive world of ideas into which we have been looking has two sides, one positive, magic, which by certain actions seeks to bring about certain results, and the other negative, the taboo, which forbids certain actions for fear that evil may ensue. Both are aspects of the same belief in ' power ', whose injurious influence it is desired to avoid, and by whose beneficial influence it is desired to profit. The taboo is a general conception which has its application to every religious action and state. In its nature it is but a prohibition. It is therefore capable of elevation and refinement through the transforming and elevation of its contents. The taboo prohibitions are easily adaptable to a higher religion. They are regarded as the will of the gods and are exalted into decrees of purity and respect for all that concerns the divine. These decrees preserve their ritualistic character, but in principle they pave the way for an all-important change of motive whose starting-point is the fear of harm but whose concluding stage is the dawn of moral conscience. The taboo gives rise to sacral rites only with a view to removing some pollution or atoning, for an offence, and only few of these rites have any special character. The reverse is the case with the positive magical rites, which are both specialized and varied. A definitely specialized rite is much more difficult to change and transform, and therefore the magical rites are preserved in their original shape in the higher religion ; it is only that the magical motive is forgotten, and tradition and the commands of the gods take its place. Then aetiological tales are invented to explain customs which are no longer understood.

Thus the belief in magic vanishes from the Greek religion,

although the rites upon which it was created remain. With it, its servants also vanish. Men gifted with magic powers are conspicuously absent in Greece, whereas among most other peoples they abound. There are no magicians and it is with difficulty that we can discover in a Homeric passage [1] a trace of the primitive god-king, in virtue of whose justice the earth yields her crops, the trees are loaded with fruit, the ewes give birth, the sea produces fish, and men prosper. The myth of Salmoneus, who imitated the lightning and thunder, has been thought to contain a reminiscence of the old rain-maker, magician, and king in one. The absence of magicians is no doubt partly due to a special characteristic of the Greek mind, which refused to allow itself to be fettered by superstition, sorcery, and a sacerdotal rule, but the reason is also in great measure to be sought in the patriarchal institutions of the immigrating Greeks, as a result of which every head of a family was his own priest and magician. This prevented the specializing of the profession and the accumulation of power and authority in the hands of its special representatives.

The magical rites were adopted into the worship of the gods and became sacral rites. Hence it comes about—and the fact can hardly be too strongly emphasized—that a great many of the sacral rites, apart from the commonest of them, the animal sacrifice, are older than the gods. As a matter of fact neither the scapegoat of the Thargelia, nor the rain-magic on Mt. Lykaion, nor the sacred bough, nor the *panspermia* and similar rites, presuppose any god. A rite of this kind is pre-deistic; it is an *opus operatum* which works in and by itself, without the intervention of any anthropomorphic deity.

If we examine the Greek sacral customs, and especially those that recur annually at definite seasons of the year, the festival-rites, we accordingly find a great number of

[1] *Odyssey*, xix, vv. 111 et seq.

these pre-deistic, magical practices. They are particularly associated with agriculture, which far back in prehistoric times must have been the most important, in any case a necessary, source of livelihood. Agriculture follows the changes of the year and all its phases need the protection of some power : when the seed is put into the ground, when the crops are standing and ripening towards harvest, when they are reaped, threshed, and gathered into the barns—not to speak of the fruit crops. Hence Aristotle has already traced the festivals back to agriculture, and in all essentials correctly. Peasants are even more conservative in their religion than in their methods of cultivation ; and therefore the pre-deistic, magical rites are found in great numbers precisely in the agrarian festivals—Thesmophoria, Thargelia, Oschophoria, Pyanopsia, and many others unmentioned here but not forgotten. These rites are associated with the changes of the seasons and a cycle of festivals arises. In later times this brings in its train the regulation of the calendar.

The second great domain of primitive religion is the relationship with the world of the dead. Here, shortly before the historical period began, a great change came about which we can document archaeologically : cremation took the place of burial. During the Minoan-Mycenaean period the dead were buried. The first immigrants adopted the burial customs of the country, but with the last and most powerful wave of immigration, the Dorian, cremation gained ground. It is probable, therefore, that we must see in it the method by which the immigrating Greeks disposed of their dead. It is suitable, too, for a semi-nomadic people, such as we have reason to suppose them to have been. In the change of funeral practices it has often been the custom to see an expression of a profound change in the views regarding the dead. Certainly this had some influence—we shall return to the point in dealing with the Homeric religion—but on the whole the theory is not corroborated in Greece, so far as we can test its accuracy from known customs and beliefs. We shall here follow the line of continuity.

The most primitive and substantial feature is the rude belief in the continued life of the dead in the grave, from which they sometimes rise up in complete bodily form to help their friends and injure their foes, as the city-heroes do. We have from later times a number of typical stories of ghosts.[1] The best known is that treated by Goethe in his *Bride of Corinth*. Pliny the younger tells of a house in Athens where the ghost of an emaciated and dishevelled old man in fetters appeared and drove away the inhabitants. When they dug in the garden where the ghost had disappeared, they found a skeleton in chains. Such stories are by no means those which growing superstition brings with it ; they represent original popular belief, arising from the obscure depths. I will not appeal to the apparitions of tragedy, where it is usual for spirits to appear in the form of men ; but Aristophanes speaks in one place of an old woman who had risen from the dead, and earlier folk-lore knows of similar figures, though it calls them heroes. The inhabitants of Temesa had stoned an athlete who had outraged a maiden. To avert his wrath they had to sacrifice a maiden to him every year, until the boxer Euthymus conquered him in open fight and drove him into the sea. According to Athenian popular belief the ghost of Orestes used to walk at night, plundering and beating any whom he met. A similar motif lies behind the old myth of Protesilaos and Laodamia. There was a brutal primitive custom known as μασχαλισμός, in which the murderer cut off the hands and feet of his victim, threaded them on a string, and hung

---

[1] Collected by Collison Morley, *Greek and Roman Ghost Stories*, and P. Wendland, *Antike Geister- und Gespenstergeschichten* (*Festschrift der schlesischen Gesellschaft für Volkskunde zur Jahrhundertsfeier der Universität Breslau* (1911), pp. 33 et seq.).

them round the neck of the corpse. His idea was to prevent the dead man from taking vengeance, just as the Australian aboriginal cuts off the thumb of the murdered man so that his spirit shall not be able to fling his spear at his murderer.

A more important feature is that burial customs and the cult of the dead reveal the same idea.[1] In Mycenaean times weapons and jewels, food and fire-pan were placed in the grave of the dead man, so that he might continue life in the same way as in the past. It is often said that in the mound over the shaft-graves at Mycenae there have been found bones of sacrificed slaves, who have had to accompany their masters in death. This is not correct. When the place was planned, in late Mycenaean times, bones from other graves were brought there in the earth which was spread over it to fill it up. But the images of animals and human beings found in great numbers in Mycenaean graves are meant to answer the same purpose as the Egyptian *ushebtis*—to serve the dead man in the other world. In Homer there is one celebrated reminiscence of these older burial customs when Achilles sacrifices on the pyre of Patroklos twelve Trojan prisoners, as well as horses and dogs, oxen and sheep. The great vases which adorned the tombs of the Dipylon age have no bottoms ; the offerings poured into them ran down into the tomb. If an animal was sacrificed, the blood was poured into a hole in the ground and the body was burnt. Meals were set out upon the tomb ; they are called ' banquets offered by law and custom ' (δαῖτες ἔννομοι) and the dead are εὔδειπνοι (' well feasted '). Sometimes the tombstones have the shape of a table. Later on we find pipes leading from the surface of the tomb to the cinerary urn. Cremation could not overcome the idea that the dead man

---

[1] Separate chapters *Die Heroen* and *Der Seelenkultus* in Rohde's *Psyche* ; P. Foucart, *Le culte des héros chez les Grecs* (*Mémoires de l'Académie des Inscriptions*, xlii, 1918) ; L. R. Farnell, *Greek Hero Cults and Ideas of Immortality*.

in his tomb needed to be supplied with material food and drink, and even the nameless dead, whom no one any longer remembered, must receive their portion. Once a year a general festival of souls was celebrated. The dead visited the houses and were welcomed with a *panspermia*, and at the end of the feast they were requested to vanish once more. The same festival is found, and in some cases under the same form, among most Aryan peoples from the Indians to ourselves. It would be strange if there were no connexion here. According to these practices the life of the dead is a continuation of their life upon the earth. Every night the clang of weapons and the neighing of horses could be heard around the burial mound at Marathon. The Nekyia of the *Odyssey* preserves the idea but has transferred it from the grave to the lower world. Minos there is still a king dispensing justice to his subjects, and Agamemnon appears with his kingly train, who had suffered death at the same time as he.

This essential unity of the living person with the form in which he continues after death was very early dissolved. No doubt there exists among all peoples a conception of the soul in one form or another, but alongside of it the idea of the ghost stubbornly persists. In Greece there are a number of conceptions of the soul, oscillating, as is always the case, between a life-force and a double. Nearest to the life-force comes the *psyche*, which must once have meant ' breath ' but came to denote ' spirit '. The soul as a double of man is represented in a grossly material form, often as an animal. The snake is the usual soul-animal, but the bird is almost equally common. The soul of Aristeas flew out of his mouth as a raven ; in allegorical representations the soul-bird is extremely common. Sometimes it takes a semi-human form. This is the type which, through the tale of the Sirens in the *Odyssey*, is familiar in quite another aspect. The figure which the Greeks themselves called *eidolon* ('image') and which is the classical representation of the soul is a compromise between all three types. It is a shadowy image of the dead man, represented in art as a diminutive and often winged figure. It has borrowed the physical resemblance from the ghost, its lightness from the air-soul, and its wings from the bird-soul. The introduction of cremation may have promoted a more spiritualized conception of the soul, but on the cult of the dead it had astonishingly little influence. This continued in the same forms, based on the belief in the survival of the dead man in complete bodily shape.

Equality in death is a chimaera. Even more than now it was so at a time when men believed in the continuance of the power of the dead. The man of the people was equally insignificant in life and in the grave. He was soon forgotten even by those nearest to him. But the prince was a prince even in the tomb ; his power was not diminished by death, it was only transferred to a sphere in which it was regarded with greater veneration. The archaeological finds bear witness to the continuation of the cult of the grave as the material expression of this power and this belief. We may presume that whereas an ordinary man was remembered after death only by those nearest and dearest to him, the prince was revered by the whole people in life and death alike. His grave-cult was the business not only of his family but of the whole people.

Herein lies the key to the Greek hero-cult. It arose from the cult of the dead and may have been strengthened by the patriarchal institutions of the immigrating Greeks and extended to a wider circle by the self-esteem of the powerful families. For the social conditions based upon the idea of kin and family find their religious expression in the cult of ancestors. The hero-cult is originally nothing but the cult of a dead man who belongs not only to a single family but to the people in general. If we go back to the Greek age of chivalry we can understand that the word ' heros ' originally (and also in Homer) means a prince or nobleman ; ' lord ' is the best translation, if we mean by the word a person belonging to the class of gentlefolk ; we can see, too, how the horse, the symbol and pride of the gentry, became the symbol of the hero,[1] and is placed upon the tombstone as regularly as the coat of arms in modern times. The hero-cult sprang from the belief in the continued corporeal existence after death of a powerful man. The hero works from his grave and only in the place where his bones rest. His power is bound up with his physical remains. The cult of heroes has absorbed foreign elements, but it is at bottom a cult of powerful dead men, whose power is extended to apply to the whole of their country and all its people. Setting aside the Greeks' own general conception of the heroes and their cult, we may find the proof of the above statements in the nature of the cult itself, which is a continuation and expansion of the old cult of the dead.

The background of the Greek religion is therefore formed out of the universal ideas concerning the dead, who are to be nourished and honoured by the living and who rise up from their graves to help and to avenge their kinsfolk ; and concerning the power which pervades everything, threatening men with dangers which they seek to avoid, but able also to confer blessings which they desire to obtain. We have already taken note of the changes which these ideas underwent as a result of the belief in the gods. To this belief, the religious stratum which overlay and blended with the lower, we shall now turn our attention.

[1] I cannot therefore share in the usual chthonic conception of the horse most recently developed by L. Malten, *Das Pferd im Totenglauben, A J*, xxix, 1914, pp. 179 et seq.

IV

GODS OF NATURE AND OF HUMAN LIFE

THE gap between ' power ' and ' the powers ' is not great
no greater than the difference between the singular and
plural of the word. Yet we at once feel the change of sense
when the word is put into the plural. The undivided, homogeneous stream of power, which is ever breaking forth and
expressing itself in individual manifestations, is split up into
centres of power. Man projects his own conscious and
volitional ego into the world about him ; he must do so,
for it is only by way of analogy that he can attain to any
knowledge of that which lies behind phenomena, whether
real or imagined, and the first analogy is his own being.
Hence he ascribes to the powers feeling, will, and purpose.
So far the powers can hardly be called personal, still less
anthropomorphic, but when they are possessed of the same
psychical properties as man they are on the way to becoming
so. The Keres, as the Greeks often call the powers who
exercise a pernicious influence on human life, have been
compared with bacilli.[1] The comparison is illuminating,
although its correctness is doubtful. The question no
doubt belongs rather to the domain of semasiology than to
the history of religion.

In the sequel I shall endeavour to indicate traces of the
idea of ' power '. It was ousted by the strongly developed
anthropomorphism which also transformed ' the powers '.
The latter were called *daimones* by the Greeks, but the
daimones became in great measure personal, anthropomorphic, and the word *daimon* may also denote one of the great

[1] Jane Harrison, *Prolegomena to the Study of Greek Religion*,
especially ch. 5.

gods. Daemonistic traces in the rites are extremely rare, but the exchange of clothes by bridegroom and bride at the wedding may possibly be so interpreted. The idea may be to mislead the spirits on this critical occasion, just as primitive peoples change the clothes of a sick person so that the spirits of disease may not be able to recognize him but may pass him by.

The belief in *daimones* peoples the world with spirits. They live in the deserts, among the mountains, in the forest, in stones, in trees, in water, in rivers and springs; they are the occasion of everything that concerns man, they send fruitfulness and dearth, good fortune and disease. It is they that have given rise to the old saying that 'fear created the gods'. For man is much more strongly roused to a consciousness of the interference of higher powers in his life when misfortunes come upon him than when things are taking their normal course. As a necessary consequence of this conception, the object of the earliest cult is by one means or another to keep the powers at a distance from life; it is apotropaeic, a warding-off of evil. This view of religion and cult either ignores magic or represents it as harmful, but magic, in its primitive stage, has quite another function. By magical rites men try to secure for themselves and for others fertility and prosperity; magic serves the individual and the social good. And thus appears the higher purpose of religion: it is directed, in the form of magic, towards the general good, a development of which the previous chapter has given many examples.

A magical rite has reference to 'power' in general, but 'power' may give place to 'the powers' or to a certain power, and we have here the first step towards the gods. When the totemist, undertaking certain rites, for instance, for the multiplication of the totem animal, believes that their success depends upon the favour of the totemistic primordial being, a god in the form of an animal may arise.

This appears in some instances to have happened, but as regards Greece it is unnecessary to discuss the possibility. There are surer and more evident examples among the agrarian rites.

The vegetation spirits belong to one of the best-known chapters in European folk-lore and non-European religion. The ' power ' which expresses itself in the green foliage of the trees and the corn of the field is split up into ' powers ' and these take the shape of an animal or a man. In addition to the purely magical rites, above referred to, in which ' power ' is concerned, others develop which involve ' the powers '; man does not at first approach the latter by prayer and sacrifice, for he is so possessed by the magical reasoning that like produces like that, in order to promote the growth and increase of vegetation, he performs certain actions with the representations and images of the vegetation spirits. An idea of frequent occurrence is that the vegetation spirit in animal or human form shall be captured at the harvest and killed. The Lityerses myth is explained in this way, though it is hardly Grecian but rather Phrygian. At the Carnea, a harvest feast in Sparta, boys carrying bunches of grapes ran a race, the leader was adorned with fillets, and it was regarded as a good omen if he was caught. Wide has concluded upon certain grounds that this boy had been substituted for a ram.[1] A similar custom was followed at the Oschophoria at Athens. Here the interpretation depends entirely upon the extent to which we are willing to apply the parallels which we find in modern European harvest-customs. A custom from Magnesia on the Maeander speaks with greater certainty.[2] At the beginning of the sowing a bull was bought, which was dedicated to Zeus Sosipolis. He was fed at the public cost and those who traded in the market were told that they were

[1] S. Wide, *Lakonische Kulte*, pp. 78 et seq.
[2] M. P. Nilsson, *Griech. Feste*, pp. 23 et seq.

doing a good action in giving him food. He was sacrificed at a time coinciding with the harvest, and the flesh was shared out among all who took part in the festival. There can be no doubt that this bull personifies the standing crop between seed-time and harvest and that the sacrifice is a communion with the vegetation spirit. This custom makes it certain that the curious rite at the Bouphonia at Athens and other Ionian cities is to be similarly explained, as has long since been proposed. A labouring-ox was slaughtered amid ceremonies which testify that the slaughter was felt to be something unlawful. Then the skin was stuffed and set before the plough, while the flesh was eaten by those present at the feast.

In these cases the vegetation spirit appears in the form of an animal. It might also appear in human shape and did so in a harvest-rite which is of far greater importance, because in it originated one of the great divinities of Greece. It is well known that the spirit of the crops is represented by the last ears that are reaped, and is often imagined under human form as the Corn-mother. The Greek Corn-mother is Demeter [1]—the name itself has very probably this meaning—and at the harvest festival her image was erected beside the heaps of grain with a sheaf and the poppies of the cornfield in her hand. This interpretation is disputed but it is supported by the fact that in the mysteries of Demeter at Eleusis the reaping of a few ears in silence was regarded as the most sacred rite. Our information is of late date, but it is corroborated by a vase-painting which shows some ears of corn in a temple. The ears of corn had their place in the cult ; it is therefore an authorized conclusion that the goddess of the corn originated in them. There is a long series of epithets of Demeter referring to cereals, the sheaf, the harvest, the threshing, and the piles

[1] W. Mannhardt, *Mythologische Forschungen*, pp. 202 et seq. ; compare my *Griech. Feste*, pp. 311 et seq.

of grain. The corn is called Demeter's fruit and it is she who parts the grain from the husk. The genius of the sheaf has had the way left free for it to grow into a goddess and has not been handicapped in its development by religious conceptions of a higher order. She extends her protection to agriculture in general and its rites become associated with her. The oldest of the fables on this subject, her nuptials with Jasion upon the thrice-ploughed fallow, is mentioned by Homer and is a mythical disguising of a well-known rite which by human procreation seeks to arouse the fertility of the fields. The vegetation-magic of the Thesmophoria (cf. p. 91) was associated with Demeter, and in the Eleusinian mysteries, which originated in an agrarian festival, the germination and decaying of the crops were by an easy analogy transferred to human life and occasioned the deepest expression of Greek religious feeling. Her daughter is Kore, ' the maiden, the daughter '. The daughter of the Corn-mother, the Corn-girl as she is sometimes called in modern Europe, has her natural place in this circle of rites and ideas ; she is the new harvest that is to be, but she has become involved in another cycle to which we shall presently return.

Hermes has behind him a similar development.[1] The name is one of the few that are etymologically transparent and means ' he from the stone-heap '. There are various examples of stone-cults in Greece. In the stone a power resided, and it was therefore anointed and wrapped round with sacred *taeniae* and received a cult. The famous omphalos at Delphi is a stone of this nature : so too is the stone pillar which stood before the house and protected it. Apollo took over both of these and the latter bore his name, Apollo Agyieus. On the top of the grave-mound a tall stone was erected, and the mound was often composed of lesser stones. It is a widespread custom for every one who passes

[1] M. P. Nilsson, *Griech. Feste*, pp. 388 et seq.

any such heap of stones to add his stone to it ; in a country without roads these cairns would be the landmarks, and perhaps not all were originally barrows. In the cairn and its monumental stone lived a *daimon*. Since the cairn was a landmark, this *daimon* became a guide and the protector of the traveller ; since it was also a grave-mound, he became the guide of souls, showing them the way to their kingdom, and since he appeared in Arcadia, the land of shepherds, he promoted the increase of the flocks and was the shepherds'. patron. Thus his functions centre round the cairn with its monumental stone. His image, the herme, was nothing but a monumental stone standing on a stone-heap ; from the beginning this stone was the abode of the *daimon*, and afterwards it was regarded as his image and was given a human head. It did not become fully anthropomorphic, and it continued to protect roads and streets and was set up on graves.

In these two examples we can tráce how a god has originated from the belief in the daemonistic power and from the daemonistic rite. But a question of fundamental importance remains. Every field has its last sheaf and its corn-mother, every stone-heap has its *daimon* living and working in it. How from this multiplicity did unity arise, the one corn-mother, protecting all the fields, and the one god from the stone-heaps, living in them all ? The process was somewhat different in the two cases. Every year the harvest-rite returned, and with it the corn-mother : the fruitfulness of one year proceeds from that of the last, and the same corn-mother returns every year just as the same sun reappears every day. Similarly the corn-mothers of the different fields were bound to coincide, just as the name was the same. There was nothing which could keep them separate : the cultivation changed ground every year in virtue of the two-field system. On the other hand the spirit of the cairn was localized to the particular heap in which he lived. Here, too, the common name led to the finding of the same spirit in all heaps, but another development would also have been possible, namely, for every spirit, localized to his heap, to have become a god on a small scale. Local minor deities of the kind are common enough in Greece.

The Nature *daimones* form the most numerous group. They are found everywhere, nymphs live among the mountains as well as in trees, springs, rivers, and seas. The Sileni are fountain-*daimones*, and both they and the satyrs are *daimones* of fertility. The Panes are of the same nature and owe their peculiar character to the fact that they arose among a pastoral people. The Centaurs also belong to this category, although they appear principally in mythology. Nature is full of these *daimones*; they are innumerable, for every spring, every tree, every natural object has or at least may have its *daimon*. Hence crowds of Nature *daimones* of various kinds arise. Within each homogeneous group the individual disappears in the aggregate; the *daimon* residing in a particular natural object has an extremely limited circle of worshippers; most have no cult but exist only in belief and imagination. In other domains also similar collective groups of spirits or gods appear, such as ' the gentle gods ' (θεοὶ μειλίχιοι), ' the boisterous ones ' (Μαιμακτῆρες), the goddesses of childbirth (the Ilithyiae), ' the holy goddesses ', the Erinyes (σεμναὶ θεαί), and the ' Rulers ' (Ἄνακες), the two sons of Zeus, the Dioskouroi.

And these spirits intervene in human life and fortune. Men turn to them for peace, happiness, and prosperity. Just as the harvest-rite could not embrace the entire crop standing upon the field, but a single sheaf was selected as representing the whole, so the cult cannot address itself to the collective group. The attention is fixed upon some particular one from among the host of similar spirits. If they are localized, the nearest is chosen ; then a local god arises. If the localization is not made prominent, the singular is simply put for the plural : Pan is invoked instead of the Panes. It is significant that in so late a document as the record of the secular festival of the Emperor Augustus the Ilithyiae are everywhere named in the plural except in the prayer, where we read ' O thou, Ilithyia ! ' In a cave dedicated to the cult of the nymphs in Attica, in which various inscriptions were carved in the fifth century B. C., the nymphs are as a rule spoken of in the plural, but one dedication reads : ' Archedemos built to the nymph.' [1]

The needs of man created the gods, and the cult is an expression of his need. A god is a *daimon* which has acquired importance and a fixed form through the cult. From among the crowd of similar beings the cult chooses one as its object, and this becomes a single god. But the belief in the numerous *daimones* lives on, and if both the single divinity and the group of *daimones* are present to the mind together, the latter acquire a leader. Thus we have Pan and the Panes, Silenus and the Sileni, but Silenus was reduced to a semi-comic figure when his retinue was absorbed in that of Dionysos. A great goddess who seems to have arisen in this way is Artemis. She is essentially nothing but the most prominent of the wood- and mountain-nymphs. With these she hunts and dances in mountains and forests and amid green meadows. Like them she rules the animals in wild Nature and fosters their young. Like them she extends her sway to men, helps the mother in her hour of need, and protects the rising generation, but she may also deal sudden death with her arrows. This tendency to exalt one among a number of similar beings to a position of supremacy was so ingrained that it has left an example dating from the time of transition to the Christian faith. The Lycian ' wild gods ' are represented as twelve similar

[1] *AJA*, vii, 1903, p. 297.

figures ; to them a thirteenth was added as their ruler, and he was placed in the middle and was somewhat larger in size, but was in other respects just like the rest.[1]

The above explains much but not the whole of the complicated and diversified process which led to the creation of the major gods of Greek polytheism. There is a distinction between the localized deities and the gods which rule over and express themselves in a certain phenomenon. A god of the latter kind is a universal deity who is everywhere the same. We have seen how the cult selects and creates such a god from the collective group of nature spirits ; but others must have been, or at least tended to be, universal gods from their very origin. The clearest example is the case of the sun-god and moon-goddess, for no one doubts that the same sun and the same moon shine over every place, but both these play a very unimportant part in the older Greek religion. Of far greater importance, on the other hand, is the god who rules over the atmospheric phenomena—storm, rain, and thunder. The rain is of more consequence than even rivers and springs ; upon it depends the fruitfulness of the fields, and it is in Greece sparsely meted out, so that the inhabitants had a lively sense of its importance. Every traveller in Greece will have noticed how the clouds swiftly gather round the highest mountain-top in the neighbourhood. In a short time the sky is covered with clouds, the roar of the thunder is heard, and the rain pours down. Up there upon the mountain-top dwells the cloud-gatherer and the flinger of the thunderbolt, who sends rain and therefore also grants fertility. Every such hill-top and every town has its Zeus, but notwithstanding this fact it is felt that it is the same Zeus who everywhere gathers the clouds, hurls the lightning, and sends the rain. The atmospheric phenomena cannot be localized.

[1] O. Weinreich, *Lykische Zwölfgötterreliefs* (*Sitzungsberichte der Akademie zu Heidelberg*, 1913, no. 5).

Thus the universal character of certain gods was inherent in them from the beginning, while others emerged from the crowd of nature spirits. On the other hand there were the gods who were bound to a certain natural object, a certain place. They had their limited circle of worshippers, but they too developed if the circle was extended. The population of a district and its importance might increase, and with this the importance of the god increased also. The god might also grow independently of the place. The circumstances which in modern times and even in ancient Greece enhanced the belief in a certain deity and created centres of pilgrimage must be presumed to have been present, although to a less extent, in the earlier period also. The position to which the local gods attained would depend on circumstances insufficiently known to us ; we can only surmise that the character of the people and even accident played a part in them. The Semitic religion affords an example of a development in which the local gods predominate. The local Baalim, alike in nature, different in locality, took over general functions and even became sun-gods. Every town had its deity which provided for all its simple needs. Within the tribe monotheism prevailed : the gods of the different tribes were friends or foes according as the tribes themselves were friendly or hostile. In a higher culture such as the Babylonian we further find the phenomena of Nature distributed among the gods, while the latter, in consequence, tend to acquire a universal character. But so strong was the localization of the Semitic divinities that the general functions were distributed among the city-gods, the sea-god Ea belonged to Eridu, the sun-god Shamash to Sippar, the moon-god Sin to Ur, and so on. The ruler of the pantheon was the local god whose city had gained a predominating position over the others—Marduk of Babylon.

These facts are useful in helping us to understand the development in Greece. There the tendency to universality, the distribution of elements and functions among gods who were everywhere worshipped, proved victorious and forced the local gods into a subordinate position. Local fountain-nymphs and river-gods were certainly worshipped but the god of water was one, Poseidon, who dominated and over-shadowed them all. The universal gods even became the individual protectors of the towns, and indeed from this function a universal city-goddess was developed—Athena. It is certainly true in some ways that Zeus or Athena in Athens is one divinity, in Thebes another, in Sparta still another, and so on, just as the Madonna of different cities varies, but on the other hand it cannot be too emphatically maintained that even in the general consciousness the same Zeus and the same Athena ruled (even though they bore different epithets) in Athens as in Thebes and Sparta and the other cities. A name is a power, and this is also true of names of deities, in regard to their unity and universality no less than in other ways.

In Greece the great deities grew at the expense of the Nature spirits and local gods. They even made the former their followers and retainers. Artemis was surrounded by mountain- and forest-nymphs, Poseidon by sea-nymphs, Dionysos by Sileni and satyrs. Or they might absorb the collective divinities. Instead of the ' gentle ' or the ' bois-terous ' gods (θεοὶ μειλίχιοι, Μαιμακτῆρες) there generally appears the ' gentle ' or the ' boisterous ' Zeus (Zeus Meili-chios, Maimaktes). The greater gods usurped the functions of the lesser, appropriated their names as epithets, or made them their servants and subordinates. Thus, for instance, Apollo appropriated the cult of the pre-Grecian god Hyakin-thos at Amyclae. Hyakinthos was reduced to the position of a hero who obtained a preliminary sacrifice at the festival of Apollo which had once belonged to him and which still bore his name, the Hyakinthia. In the myth Hyakinthos became Apollo's favourite, whom the god slew by accident.

Apollo sometimes received the addition of his name and was called Apollo Hyakinthos. The local gods who escaped this fate lived on in quiet and obscurity, their worship being limited to a small circle of devotees. Few of them adopted a more modest career like Acheloös.

It has been maintained that it was an essential feature of the gods that each should represent some speciality, some particular function. This involves the question : How far does the specializing extend ? Theoretically it may be carried on wellnigh indefinitely. Certain religions have created gods for special functions in the smallest detail.[1] The Roman gods of the *indigitamenta* are the best-known example. But these extremely specialized functional gods are not original but are the product of priestly speculation and scrupulous formalism. The natural man does not specialize his needs in this formal way, and it is the needs of man that create the gods. He picks out one of the powers or *daimones* that dwell in his imagination and turns to it to induce it to supply his needs. In the naturally developed Greek religion, therefore, there are few gods which can be regarded as special functional deities of this kind. Most of them are local deities or else transparent epithets, expressing a particular function of the god. I cannot see that such an epithet as κουροτρόφος (' foster-mother of the young ') as applied to Artemis or Demeter is very different from ἀστεροπητής (' lightener ') as an epithet of Zeus, even though the former appears as an epithet in the cult, and the latter only in poetry. ' The Lightener ' was never used as a name for an original functional god of the lightning, a god who otherwise might quite well have been suggested on general grounds. The needs of primitive man were little specialized, and therefore only a limited number of gods with special functions came into being. Out of them and amid mutual rivalry the great gods emerged. As they

[1] H. Usener, *Götternamen*.

developed they took up new functions answering to the more highly specialized needs which increasing culture brought to their worshippers. They may also have taken over functions belonging to other gods. Nor does anything hinder them from trespassing upon one another's domain.

There are, however, several other elements besides local gods and Nature spirits that went to produce the Greek gods. They received an extremely important addition from the rites. It was pointed out in the preceding chapter that when belief in the gods had arisen, the magical rites, which worked in and for themselves as an *opus operatum*, became attached to the gods and passed over to their cult. Thus the weather-magic passed into the cult of Zeus, purifications and the curing of diseases into that of Apollo, rites of fertility into those of Demeter and Dionysos, and the annual bonfires into that of Artemis. This is how the gods acquired the greater part of their rites and festivals, which were originally pre-deistic, at least as regards those which have the most interest for the history of religion. It goes without saying that this process, which followed a god in constant evolution from his first beginnings, powerfully contributed to develop his influence and authority. The gods repaid this by forcing the magical character of the rites into the background, which meant a gain in religious elevation.

In this attempt to explain the origins of Greek polytheism our conception of the fundamental significance of the various gods plays an important part. This is a difficult but not always an insoluble problem, if it be attacked from right premises. To illustrate the method, I should like to quote the words of an eminent philologist in regard to the fundamental significance of the linguistic forms.[1]

We should carefully distinguish between the general significance of a form and its original significance. The

[1] K. Brugmann, *Griech. Grammatik* (Müller's *Handbuch der klassischen Altertumswissenschaft*, ii²), p. 13.

first results from the fusion of the various uses of the form
into a higher, common conception ; it is a general formula,
to which we seek to refer separate functions, and as a product
of logical abstraction it is only of value in a survey of the
actual use of the form. The fundamental significance is the
original function from which in course of time the separate
significations have been developed, and is, therefore, strictly
speaking, that function alone which the form had when it
arose.

Mutatis mutandis the same thing precisely is true of the gods.
But the problem is perhaps even more difficult. A god
comes into being not only from an inward development
proceeding from the original function but also by the addition
of elements from outside. It may be that the original
crystallizing-point in the general conception of the god's
functions lay quite on the periphery. It is no doubt owing
to an exaggeration of the difficulties and an under-estima-
tion of its importance for the history of religion that no
great attention has been paid to the question of late years.
I venture to hope that my account has at least shown that
the solution of this problem is indispensable to any understanding of the development of the Greek religion.

A general view of the Greek pantheon as the outcome
of the development here sketched must break with the
traditional ideas. It must be based upon the proposition
that man's needs create the gods, and that beginning with
the gods of Nature he rises to those which are an expression
of the higher functions of his life. This implies that divine
personalities cannot be taken as unities, as is generally done,
but must be split up into their different component parts.

Any one who really wishes to understand the religion of
antiquity should have before him a clear and living picture
of the antique landscape, as it is represented, for instance,
in certain Hellenistic reliefs and Pompeian frescoes.[1] It is

[1] M. Rostowzew, *Die hellenistisch-römische Architekturlandschaft*
(*Mitteilungen des deutschen archäologischen Instituts zu Rom*, xxvi,
1911, pp. 1 et seq.).

saturated with religion in a manner quite foreign to us. One could hardly have taken a step out of doors without meeting a little temple, a sacred enclosure, an image, a cult-pillar, a sacred tree. Nymphs lived in every cave and fountain. These pictures completely answer to the description which the geographer Strabo gives of the lowlands at the mouth of the river Alpheus. ' The whole tract is full of shrines of Artemis, Aphrodite, and nymphs, in flowery groves due mainly to the abundance of water ; there are numerous hermae on the roads and shrines of Poseidon on the head-lands by the sea.' This was the most persistent, though not the highest, form of antique religion ; it was the form which gave way last of all to Christianity. And as it was in later times, so it was in earlier. The belief in Nature spirits was just as vigorous.

That which interests man is not Nature in herself, but the life of Nature in the measure in which it intervenes in human life and forms a necessary and obvious basis for it. The dangerous and terrifying powers of Nature are less prominent, at least in Greece, than a widely accepted theory of the origin of religion would lead us to expect. In the fore-ground appear the needs of man, Nature as a means for man's existence, her generosity, for upon that depends whether man shall starve or live amid abundance. In a scantily watered land such as Greece, groves and green fields where the water produces a rich vegetation are therefore the dwellings of the Nature spirits, and so are the forests and hills among which the wild beasts live. In earlier times hunting was an important means of livelihood. In the forests the nymphs dance and hunt, satyrs, Sileni, and centaurs roam about, the Panes protect the herds but may also drive them away in a panic. The life of Nature has become centred in Artemis, who was in early times the mistress of the wild beasts, and herself was once perhaps represented under the form of an animal ; she loves hills and groves and well-watered places, and promotes the natural fertility that does not depend upon the efforts of man. Aphrodite, less frequently, appears as the goddess of rich vegetation ; she is sometimes known as ' the one from the gardens ', and she, as well as Artemis and the nymphs, had shrines at the mouth of the Alpheus.

There is an Arcadian type of goddess [1] which resembles Artemis but often appears in the plural ; it extended its protection to cultivated Nature also, to the fruitfulness of the field, being therefore chiefly identified with Demeter and Kore. These goddesses are often nameless and are known as ' the Great Goddesses ' ; one of them is called Despoina ' the Mistress '. It has already been mentioned that they afford the best example of deities in the form of animals. Animal figures in the clothes of men adorn Despoina's mantle on her statue at Lycosura—they may possibly have reference to an animal masquerade in the cult—and she, like Artemis, has a sacred hind. These deities have sprung from the same root as Artemis but are more primitive, were originally not so strongly specialized, and in their plurality still preserve something of their original collective nature.

Such goddesses appear in connexion with Poseidon, whose sphere of activity is far wider than the sea to which he is limited by the orthodox mythology, created among the seafaring Ionians. He was also ardently worshipped in the interior, in Arcadia, Boeotia, Thessaly. On the Acropolis of Athens he had caused a spring to break out at a blow of his trident, in Thessaly he opened the Vale of Tempe to the river Peneus. In the Peloponnese, where the rivers often follow their course in subterranean channels, he is ' the one who drives underground ' (γαιάοχος). For coast-dwellers like the Ionians he is naturally the sea-god. The currents of rivers and the waves of the sea to many people's imagination take the forms of bulls or horses.

[1] M. P. Nilsson, *Griech. Feste*, pp. 342 et seq.

A belief in a water-spirit with the form of a horse still persists in Scotland, and we speak metaphorically of ' white horses ' and the sea-queen's cows. Poseidon is therefore the god of horses and bulls (ἵππιος, ταύρειος), he has created the horse and in Arcadia transforms himself into one. ' Horse ' enters into the names of many wells—Hippe, Hippocrene, Aganippe. Acheloös is a river in west Central Greece. This divinity was on the way to becoming a general river-god and was worshipped in many places in Greece. He is represented as a bull with a human head. Poseidon is principally the god of the element—few gods are so strictly bound to their element as he—and the fertilizing power of water is seldom prominent in his cult. Occasionally he is worshipped as the one who makes the plants germinate (φυτάλμιος), and he has a place in the Haloa, the Attic festival of the vegetation.

The corn from which bread is made is the most important means of subsistence, and therefore the water that falls as rain is more important than any other. It comes from Zeus the weather-god, and Zeus accordingly becomes the giver and god of fruitfulness. Sometimes he is called by such names as ' the Farmer ' (γεωργός). This aspect of his nature appears still more clearly in the above-mentioned agrarian rites which were included in his cult. The family of the Bouzygai, who performed the sacred ploughing at the foot of the Acropolis—that native agrarian rite of Athens— was at least closely associated with his cult. The analogy between the human child, coming from the seed laid in its mother's womb, and the grain germinating from the seed laid in the ground was present to the mind of the Greeks as to that of many other peoples, and took expression in customs which by human procreation sought to promote the fertility of the fields. Certain of these have already been mentioned (p. 91), and an important group is known under the name of ' the holy wedding ' In mythology it is represented as the wedding of Zeus and Hera, and its natural significance is seen in some well-known verses of Homer. Certain traces of the holy wedding are also found in the rite, but here, as in modern popular customs, the bride is the most important feature and sometimes appears alone. The rain pours down and fertilizes the lap of earth, an idea which Aeschylus has clothed in magnificent allegory. Earth is the All-Mother, but her personality, like her image —a woman whose lower limbs are hidden in the ground— was never separated from the element or took independent shape. Her cult is rare, and she is more an idea of Nature than a divinity.[1] Zeus himself as the giver of fertility becomes a god of the earth, a chthonic deity ($\chi\theta\acute{o}\nu\iota os$), which is not to be understood as a god of the lower world, ruling over the dead, but as the power which dwells in the earth and sends out of it the fruits of the field. Therefore Hesiod instructs the farmer, when he sets his hand to the plough, to pray to Zeus in the earth ($\chi\theta\acute{o}\nu\iota os$) and to holy Demeter, that the ears of Demeter's corn may be heavy and ripe. On Myconos, Zeus Chthonios and Ge Chthonie received a sacrifice in common, and two days previously a sacrifice was offered to Demeter, Kore, and Zeus Bouleus. Zeus seems here to have absorbed the Eubouleus who appears in the aetiological tale of the rite mentioned in connexion with the Thesmophoria (cf. p. 91).

Zeus thus enters into close relationship with the goddess of agriculture, Demeter, whose significance has already been discussed. At Phlya in Attica there was a common altar for Demeter ' who sends the gift (of the grain) ' ($A\nu\eta\sigma\iota\delta\acute{\omega}\rho a$) and Zeus the Acquirer ($K\tau\acute{\eta}\sigma\iota os$). In Homer and Hesiod Zeus is the giver of wealth, he is called in Sparta ' the wealthy ' ($\pi\lambda o\acute{v}\sigma\iota os$) and is sometimes described as $\acute{o}\lambda\beta\iota os$, which means the same thing. Wealth, under primitive conditions, consists in the supply of corn upon

[1] Accordingly I am unable to follow A. Dieterich, *Mutter Erde.*

which man must exist during the season of the year when Nature produces nothing. He who has nothing must starve ; he who has accumulated can help his needy neighbour. The god of wealth, Plutus or Pluto, therefore represents the supply of corn. In ancient Greece, as also to-day in many places in the south, this was kept in subterranean chambers or in large jars buried in the ground. Into these were placed after the harvest in June not only the supply intended to be converted into bread but also that which four months later in October would be sown to produce the next harvest. In Sicily the festival of harvest was therefore called Κόρης καταγωγή, ' the bringing down of the [corn-]maiden ', i. e. into the underground storehouse. Down there she was in the power of Pluto, the subterranean god of wealth, until at the sowing she was again brought up and united to her mother Demeter, the goddess of agriculture.[1]

From a natural fusion of the subterranean gods of the corn-supply with the gods of the lower world who ruled over the souls, and from the parallelism between the springing up and decaying of the crops and of human life, arose the religion of Demeter with which we are familiar. Demeter's daughter Kore was carried off by the ruler of the lower world and taken down to his kingdom. She spends a third of the year there, and two-thirds with her mother. The bald and not very profound origin of this myth is to be found in what we might call the religion of the household.

It is significant of the predominant position of Zeus and of his connexion with the crops that the gods of the household are identified with him. Zeus the Acquirer (Κτήσιος) protects the store-chamber.[2] A jar containing a *panspermia* is set out there for him. Originally he was the guardian

---

[1] F. M. Cornford, *The* Ἀπαρχαί *and the Eleusinian Mysteries* (*Essays and Studies presented to Sir W. Ridgeway*, pp. 153 et seq.).

[2] See above, p. 35.

snake of the house, and in the form of a snake he is represented far down into classical times. Strangers were not
allowed to take part in his cult and his altar formed the centre
around which the slaves of the household gathered. The
household gods often appear in the plural. They are then
called ' sons of Zeus ', Διὸς κοῦροι. Their symbols are the
same—two jars entwined with snakes. A similar figure is
' the good spirit ' (Ἀγαθὸς δαίμων), who at the end of the
meal received a libation of undiluted wine : he too was
represented as a snake. Besides him we hear of ' the good
gods ' (ἀγαθοὶ θεοί). Zeus Philios and Meilichios are akin to
Zeus Ktesios ; besides Zeus Meilichios we have θεοὶ μειλίχιοι,
' the gentle gods '. All these gods received theoxenia, that
is, a meal set aside for them on a table ; the household
deities received their food no less than the goblin or brownie
of later days.

The central point of the household and of its cult was the
fixed hearth in the midst of the large room where the family
lived, the ἐστία. The cult was not one of any image but of
the hearth itself and of the fire burning upon it. Consequently Hestia has often been only incompletely anthropomorphized ; the original conception shows clearly through.
The new-born child was received into the bosom of the
family by being carried round the hearth. Every meal
began and ended with a libation to Hestia, that is to say,
upon the hearth (just as in Rome the penates at every meal
received a portion of the food and drink, which was set
there in small bowls and afterwards emptied into the fire).
The sense of the proverbial expression ' to sacrifice to Hestia '
(Ἑστίᾳ θύειν) shows that no part of the offering upon the
hearth was taken away or given to others. In prehistoric
times this strict sanctity of the domestic cult was extended
even to the ashes of the hearth, which were buried within the
house.[1] The sanctity of the hearth is Greek, not Minoan,

[1] *ARw*, xvi, 1913, p. 315.

for in Crete the fixed hearth is wanting and there are only movable fire-pans. Here too, however, Zeus has gained admittance as the god of the hearth (ἐφέστιος).

The Greek house in olden times stood in a courtyard surrounded by a fence (ἕρκος). Within this the inhabitants felt safe, they were protected against the attacks of enemies and wild beasts. In the court stood the altar on which the sacrifices of the household were performed. It was dedicated to Zeus Herkeios and is often mentioned by Homer and in the myths. It is pointed out as especially terrible that Priam was killed by Neoptolemus at the altar of Zeus Herkeios. The obvious presumption is that a similar altar was found in every house. On the Acropolis at Athens the altar of Zeus Herkeios stood west of the Erechtheion in the Pandroseion, under the sacred olive-tree in the court of the old Mycenaean royal palace, and accordingly the same name is with justice given to the altar which stands in the courtyard of the palace at Tiryns. When the houses were crowded together in the towns the courtyards became contracted, and the conditions of life also changed. The altar of Zeus Herkeios is therefore mentioned less frequently in later times. Other gods protected the house : the herme on the street, the stone pillar of Apollo Agyieus, and Hekate's triple image, warded off witchcraft. Above the entrance was written : ' Here dwells the son of Zeus, Heracles the victor : no evil may come in.'

In a passage in Sophocles' *Antigone* Zeus Herkeios appears as the god of blood-relationship. It is quite natural that the god of the household and of the family should also become the god of the *gens*. Greek society was based upon the patriarchal family and the idea of consanguinity, and this idea had also to receive expression in the cult. Universal gods of kinship such as Zeus Patroös and Apollo Patroös are a later development, induced by the tendency to universalize deities. Originally every *gens* had its own gods and cults as distinct from those of others. Every *gens* too lived in its own district, so that its gods were often, though far from invariably, local gods. The cult was the property of the family, the members of which might admit strangers if they wished, but also had it in their power to exclude them. The Greek cults were to a very great extent originally hereditary ; they were the property of the *gens*. We need only look at the great Attic families [1] to see this, beginning with the Eleusinian priestly families whose private cult the mysteries once were and to a certain extent always remained. From the family of the Boutadai was chosen the priestess of Hephaistos and Athena Polias on the Acropolis, the Bouzygai carried out the sacred ploughing, the Lycomidai owned the mysteries at Phlya, the Euneidai the cult of Dionysos Melpomenos, and so on. Even as late as the end of the third century B. C., when Eurycleides founded a shrine to Demos and the Graces, the priesthood became hereditary in his family. Hence the knowledge of the cult came to rest with the great families, and the interpreters of the sacral laws (the exegetes) were therefore always chosen from the nobility. It is noteworthy that ephebes were permitted to appear personally in legal cases only in matters relating to inheritance and to a priesthood pertaining to the family. Herodotus says of Isagoras that he does not know his lineage but that his relatives sacrifice to Zeus Karios. The cult was a badge of the *gens*. Inscriptions show that the case was the same everywhere, not only throughout Athens. Nor must we forget the cult of ancestors, whose importance for the holding together of the family is obvious.

Ancient society was built up on the family and was intimately associated with the cult. Relics of this system were left even when the conquering democracy had broken the power of the great families and levelled their distinctions.

---

[1] J. Toepffer, *Attische Genealogie.*

Just as the family originated from a common ancestor and
worshipped a hero as its source, so ancestors were created
for the state as a whole ; every town had its eponym. Even
the new tribes which Cleisthenes created on a geographical
principle were named after heroes. It was a ruling idea
throughout antiquity that a community was composed of
consanguineous groups of people, even though the relationship might be only fictitious, and the cults in which any
social idea was expressed were therefore modelled upon the
cult of the family. As every house had its sacred hearth,
so now had every town, situated in the building where the
governing body had its seat and where its members assembled
for their common meal (the Prytaneion). Hestia therefore
became a city-goddess with the epithets ' of the Prytaneion '
and ' of the Council ' ('Εστία πρυτανεία, βουλαία). On the
hearth burned the sacred fire of the state, and when a colony
was sent out it took with it fire from the hearth of the mother-
city to be transferred to the hearth in the foreign land which
was to be the centre of the new city. Far on into the future
it was the custom to establish a common hearth as the ideal
centre for a confederation of states ; examples are the
common hearth of the Arcadians at Tegea and Hestia's
altar in the temple of Zeus Amarios at Aegion for the
Achaean League.

Hestia remained attached to the hearth ; she was only
incompletely anthropomorphized into a goddess. Zeus
is of even greater importance than she in the domestic
cult, and in the life of the state with its higher demands
he was bound to appear with still greater prominence. Just
as the father of the household is Zeus' priest, so Zeus himself
in the patriarchal monarchy of earlier times is the special
protector of the king and hence the supreme custodian of
the social order. Thus in Homer Agamemnon is under the
special protection of Zeus. The god was not dethroned
with the fall of the monarchy. As Zeus Polieus he is the

divine overlord of the city-state. Alongside of him appeared
the old Mycenaean city-goddess Athena, who received the
same epithet Polias. Zeus Polieus and Athena Polias stand
side by side in a great many cities. So closely connected
were they and so similar were their functions that it was
but natural for an age given to thinking in genealogies to
express the relationship between them genealogically, and
Athena became Zeus' daughter. These two divinities safe-
guard the existence and freedom of the city and Zeus is
therefore often called ' saviour ' (σωτήρ), and ' liberator '
(ἐλευθέριος). But they are universal deities, in contra-
distinction, for instance, to the Semitic tribal gods. In
Homer, certainly, Athena and Ares march out at the head
of the army ; in the civil warfare between the Greek cities
they could not do so, for often Zeus Polieus and Athena
Polias had their seats also upon the acropolis of the enemy's
city, and the feeling for identity was so strong that it
forbade, for example, Athena in Athens and Athena in
Thebes to appear as each other's foes. On the contrary the
tendency to universality showed its strength in the fact that
the city-goddess Athena ousted other city-goddesses, such
as Alea and Itonia. But men need divine patrons and
champions in battle who will take their part against all their
foes. This place was filled in Greece by the city-heroes.

The city needs protection not only for its political but
also for its material existence. The latter depended in
earlier times principally upon agriculture, but alongside
of this trades and professions gradually grew up. Here
Zeus and Athena part company. Zeus, as we have seen,
was the patron of agriculture. This function was only to
a limited extent transferred to Athena, certain vegetation
rites in Athens having become associated with her. She,
on the other hand, being a special goddess of the city as
opposed to the country, became the protectress of the
trades and handicrafts whose followers were collected in the

towns. As a woman she protected the feminine handicrafts, especially the art of weaving. The first specialized handicraftsman is the smith, who is already found in Homer and whose name (χαλκεύς, ' copper-smith ') shows that the calling originated in the Bronze Age. Athena became the patroness of the smiths, but in Greece as among other peoples the smiths had their mythical prototypes, like the dwarfs of Scandinavia—the Idaean Dactyloi and the Telchines. From Asia Minor came a fire-daemon, Hephaistos,[1] who lived in the fire which breaks forth from the earth. He quite naturally became the god of the smiths, and that fire became the fire rising from his subterranean forge. In the most important industrial town of Greece, Athens, Hephaistos and Athena therefore appear in close connexion, and they took over another of the most important industries of the city, namely, pottery.

The life of society depended in early times upon unwritten laws, and any friendly intercourse between peoples was always subject to these. Zeus protects the supplicating fugitive who prays for mercy and shelter. He is therefore called ἱκέτας and φύξιος. He protects the foreigner who strictly had no legal rights, but as a guest enjoys a protection hallowed by religion. Zeus is therefore termed ξένιος. In Athens, where many foreigners lived as aliens (μέτοικοι), they had a separate Zeus, μετοίκιος. The reason why a fugitive left his own people was often, in early times, that he had committed murder. The murderer must be purified before he could associate with other men. In later days Apollo took over the purifications as his domain, but there are various traces of the earlier state of affairs, in which Zeus as the protector of the fugitive was also the expiator of blood-guiltiness. The first murderer, Ixion, applied to Zeus to be purified ; Zeus is called ' the purifier ' (καθάρσιος), and as such had an altar at Olympia.

[1] L. Malten, *Hephaistos, A J*, xxvi, 1912, pp. 232 et seq.

That Zeus also protected the rights of the family and blood-relationship is a fact so natural and familiar as hardly to need mention. His consort Hera had as her principal function the same duties in relation to the wife and mistress of the household. She protected marriage and women's rights therein, and consequently the whole life of women. Her severe and jealous character bears the impress of her functions.

These functions grew up entirely upon the basis of primitive social life, but none proved capable of profounder moral development.[1] A better developed ethical sense elevated Zeus to an expression for the moral consciousness ; at his side was set Dike, Justice, as his daughter and assistant. The needs of social life forced these functions upon the old Nature gods. They are fundamentally in opposition to their character, for the natural powers have nothing to do with morality and never renounce their true origin. They could not be uprooted from the soil whence they had sprung. Hence there was introduced into the conceptions of the gods an element of strain and discord which more than anything contributed to the final dissolution of the Greek religion.

When political, social, and material existence has been assured the most important of man's needs are filled and his chief demands upon the gods are made. But his demands are not exhausted and of those which remain some must at least be briefly mentioned. The curing of diseases everywhere plays an important part and among primitive peoples lies in the hands of sorcerers and priests. There was in earlier Greece a class of seers and purificatory priests which in all essentials fulfilled this function. The art of healing consisted in magical ceremonies, purifications (cf. pp. 85 et seq.), and incantations. In later times these were usually called ἐπῳδαί, 'charms', but in earlier days they were certainly called ' paeans ' (παιάν), for Homer speaks

---

[1] L. R Farnell, *The Higher Aspects of Greek Religion.*

of the god of healing, Paieon, who takes his name from them. With the charm was blended the praise of the god, and thus the paean became a song of thanksgiving and eventually of victory. In later times Apollo has made the art of healing his own, and after him his son Asklepios took it over.

In the driving away of disease the prediction of the future is everywhere an essential part of the ceremony. The doctor-magician is therefore in many cases a seer at the same time. In other connexions also the prediction of the future is of great importance to primitive peoples. The methods vary, but in general the predictions, where they are not delivered in a state of ecstasy, depend upon omens and signs, which are connected with events through a system of arbitrary association of ideas.

In early times the greatest attention was paid to dreams, which seemed to be a message from the other world, and to birds, whose incalculable appearances constituted the most omnipresent and important of omens. Zeus sends the birds and also, as the second book of the *Iliad* shows, the dreams —those in which no figure of the dead appears. His was the sacred oak at Dodona, in whose rustling the future was revealed. At a later period Apollo came with a new method, the ecstatic prophecy, and became pre-eminently the oracle-god. From the condition of the sacrificial victim and the way in which it burned upon the altar it was judged whether the sacrifice was acceptable to the gods ; from this too a special oracular lore was developed.

In addition to these more or less rational needs, there is the claim of the life of instinct. It moves in the obscure depths and seldom reaches clear and conscious expression. We shall see how in Homer it is masked under the changing shapes of the *daimones* and personified in figures which have little to do with genuine religion and cult. Two of the most powerful instincts in primitive man took shape as individual gods, the sexual instinct in Eros, who is, however, seldom a god with a real cult but has more the character of semi-philosophic speculation or allegory, and in Aphrodite who came from the East. She may have been originally a goddess of fecundity, although she bears little of this character in Greece (cf. p. 120); nor has she anything to do with marriage as an institution of society. The second instinct—warlike courage in a form bordering upon Berserker frenzy—is personified in Ares, whose name may mean simply ' the Destroyer '.[1] No wonder that he was hostile to Athena, who represents ordered battle, which saves the city by courage combined with prudence and method. Whatever Ares and Aphrodite may have originally been, they represent for the Greeks hardly more than two powerful instincts. Their cults are few, especially in the case of Ares. Their mutual relationship has found expression in the myth about their amours.

Two great gods are absent from this survey, their names have been mentioned only in passing—Apollo[2] and Dionysos. Both are immigrants and both came into Greece in pre-Homeric times. Their importance lies upon a higher plane than the simple religion of needs which we have been following in this chapter, and appears in all its individuality in the greatest crisis through which the Greek religion passed, the rise of legalism and mysticism in the archaic period. We shall presently try to estimate their contribution by the merits of the new religious values which they were the means of introducing. It is a religious movement

[1] O. Kretschmer, *Glotta*, xi, 1921, pp. 195 et seq.

[2] Wilamowitz's theory that Apollo originated in Asia Minor (*Hermes*, xxxviii, 1903, pp. 575 et seq., and *Greek Historical Writing and Apollo*) is supported by details connected with the festivals (see my *Griech. Feste*, p. 102) and the time-reckoning (see my *Primitive Time-reckoning*, pp. 366 et seq.). It is significant that the Homeric epithet of Apollo, Chrysaor, only recurs in a Carian cult of Zeus (Zeus Chrysaoreus). The provenance of Apollo from Asia Minor has recently been disputed by E. Bethe, *Apollon, der Hellene* ('Αντίδωρον, *Festschrift für Wackernagel*, pp. 14 et seq.).

which one is tempted to call un-Greek. Certainly it did not pass without leaving deep traces, but on the whole it was an episode, after which the Greek religious sense returned to the more rationalistic course which the innate disposition of the people dictated.

A religion of a similar order, but more simple and primitive, existed, it is to be presumed, under the old patriarchal monarchy and domestic rule, a religion created by the simple material and social needs of the age. I have tried to sketch its outlines in the foregoing pages, and it is evident that Zeus there takes a still more predominant position in all the affairs of life than he does in the Greek religion as we usually know it. This is a welcome confirmation of our theory. For Zeus was the principal deity of the immigrating Greeks, the only one which upon linguistic grounds can be proved to belong to the Aryan race. The immigrants could not take their local gods with them, if they had any, but only gods and spirits of universal significance. Therein perhaps lies an explanation of the tendency to universal deities among the Greeks, though not, I would insist, by any means the whole explanation. The migration which left the local gods in the lurch was bound to contribute to the elevation of the deities which had a more general significance. In their new dwelling-places the people found gods which they recognized and worshipped according to the principles of polytheism : *cuius regio eius religio* ; I would translate : ' To the god who dwells in the country the worship is due.' Among them were both local and universal deities. Rites and forms of belief which the immigrants brought with them and others which they learnt became associated, as circumstances directed, with one god or another. Thus the Greek pantheon was formed by a fusion of the gods of two peoples, whose respective shares in the final result we can only very incompletely and uncertainly distinguish.

THE HOMERIC ANTHROPOMORPHISM
AND RATIONALISM

THE Homeric question is one of those which cannot be solved but only brought nearer to their solution : the means at our disposal are not sufficient. Yet the discussion has not been in vain. So much is clear, that the Homeric poems contain portions which originated at widely separated periods, from the Mycenaean Age down to the seventh century at least. Whether the creator of Homer as we have it—apart from obvious additions—was a mere editor or a poet of genius is of less interest for the history of religion ; what is of importance is that even if he was a creative poet he worked upon the basis of a rich and lengthy earlier epic tradition, which, as is proved by archaeological evidence in the poems, must have had its origin in the Mycenaean Age. When we seek to trace the origin and earlier stages of this epic poetry through the centuries of its course, it is not as though we could reach the earlier core by merely peeling off the outer coverings ; the more correct metaphor would be that of a mixture of various ingredients, in which old and new have become kneaded together and intermingled.[1]

The Homeric religion, like all other religions, grew up by a slow development, and it is to be presumed that traces of the intervening stages are to be discerned in Homer. But they cannot be demonstrated from external criteria ;

[1] K. F. Nägelsbach, *Homerische Theologie*, 3rd edition, 1884, can only be used as a collection of material, the fundamental views being derived from Protestant theology ; the more important material is also conveniently arranged by G. Finsler, *Homer*, 2nd edition, pp. 220 et seq. For the connexion with the Homeric question see the latter work and also P. Cauer, *Grundfragen der Homerkritik*, 2nd edition, pp. 306 et seq.

only on internal evidence can the history of the development
of the Homeric religion be discussed. This attempt must
necessarily be subjective and I shall not make it here, but
shall only suggest as occasion arises points which seem
to me to be least open to dispute. Homer exercised an
enormous influence upon the religious development of later
times—the famous statement that Homer and Hesiod
created the Greek gods is as early as Herodotus—and this
influence was exercised by the Homeric poems as a completed whole, not while they were in process of formation.
Hence the justification from the point of view of the history
of religion for treating Homer in the main as an undivided
whole, not forgetting the discrepancies which exist but
whose history cannot be sufficiently illuminated.

Erwin Rohde's book, *Psyche*, formed an epoch in the
development of our conception of the Homeric religion,
but it suffered the same fate as other pioneering research-
work. The method proved to be of greater validity than
the results, which in the effort after incisiveness and clarity
became too schematic and had to be revised. Rohde laid
stress upon ' survivals ', he showed traces of an older,
outgrown religious stage and found parallel traces among
foreign peoples. He showed that religious phenomena which
appear at every primitive stage—for instance, purifications
and expiations—and which therefore must also be supposed
to have been present in prehistoric times in Greece, and
actually appear in great force at the beginning of the historical period, play a part of decreasing importance in Homer.
He carried out his investigations principally in regard to
the cult of the grave and of the dead. For the strength
of these in the Mycenaean Age archaeology has given us
convincing proofs ; the importance of them and of their
offshoot, the cult of heroes, in the earlier historical period
need not be mentioned. In Homer the cult of the dead is
lacking, and the customs and ideas associated with it have

been pushed into the background and considerably reduced. Homer represents not a leap, but a break, in the development; the post-Homeric period joins on where the pre-Homeric period had ended.

Rohde drew the natural conclusion that Homer deviates from the main line of the general religious development of Greece, and follows a by-road. The Homeric poems were created among the emigrants in the colonies on the coast of Asia Minor. The emigrants could not take with them the graves of their ancestors, consequently they could not continue the grave-cult. It ceased of necessity, and thence followed a weakening of this important part of the religion. Its decline was furthered by the lack of introspection and the absence of tradition associated with life in the colonies, where every man was the shaper of his own fortunes; the tendency of the Greek temperament towards self-assertion and rationalism had free course. In the mother country the people lived on in their old traditions around the graves of their forefathers, and when the light of history falls upon them we find quite another state of affairs, which links itself on to pre-Homeric conditions.

Rohde has been reproached for his unhistorical isolation of Homer, but there is no doubt that he has historical right on his side. It is historically inconceivable that the rites of purification, which have their roots in primitive ideas of taboo, should have been an invention of the post-Homeric period. There are traces of them in Homer also. After the plague the Achaeans purify the camp and cast the refuse into the sea. Hektor will not make his offering to Zeus with unwashed hands, and when Patroklos goes out to fight, Achilles purifies the cup with sulphur and water before he pours out the libation for his success. After the slaying of the suitors Odysseus purifies his house with fire and sulphur. Under the circumstances we can hardly require more evidence.

It is far more important and profitable to examine the ideas about the dead which prevailed in the Homeric world and the conditions of their cult. One half of the old religion has lost its grip upon mankind : the old idea that the dead man lives on in the grave is found no longer. The grave-mound with its upright stone is mentioned not infrequently, but only as a mark of honour in memory of the dead. The burial customs continue—the burning of the dead man and his weapons, the hair-offering, the lamentation for the dead, the funeral meals and games—but they are all regarded as a final mark of honour, the only one that can be rendered to the dead. The words of Andromache after Hektor's death are significant of the total disappearance of the old understanding of the meaning of funeral gifts :

But verily all these things will I burn with devouring fire :
O yea, no profit to thee—they shall not swathe thee on the pyre ;
But to be for thine honour in Troy-town's sons' and daughters'
  eyes.

The continued cult of the dead man, the offerings upon the tomb, are not mentioned and seem no longer to exist. With the cessation of these the power of the dead over the living is broken.

In connexion with this change is associated a revision and a weakening of the ideas about that part of man which lives on after death, and about its existence. That which survives man is *psychè*, the soul, the shade : it is nothing more. It is true that the most important descriptions of the souls are contained in the two Nekyiae, which are later additions to the *Odyssey*. With a faint squeak as of bats—here the old idea of the bird-like appearance of the soul is seen—the souls of the murdered suitors follow Hermes, their guide, into the underworld. Odysseus three times seeks in vain to embrace his mother's shade ; she yields before his grasp. The ' impotent heads ' of the souls have neither flesh nor bone ; they flit away like dreams. Like a phantom the still unburied Patroklos shows himself to Achilles, in all things, even in size, resembling the dead man ; the vision draws from Achilles the significant cry :

O strange ! then even in Hades' homes—and I knew not this—
They have spirit and shape (ψυχὴ καὶ εἴδωλον), albeit in these no
life there is.

As in the Nekyia, the shade of Patroklos vanishes ' like smoke with a rustling sound '. In the Nekyia the prevailing idea, although it is not consistently carried out, is that the souls have no consciousness and can acquire this only by drinking the blood of the sacrificial animal, an idea which originates in the blood-offerings poured out upon the grave. The souls are shades possessing neither strength nor consciousness, and such figures there is no need to propitiate and worship. A continued existence of this kind is of no value to man.

Rather would I be a hireling to drudge in the fields all day
With a landless master, who sparely would feed me and niggardly
pay,
Than over the hosts of the dead which have perished a sceptre
to sway,

Achilles replies to Odysseus. The life after death becomes so pale and empty that it is not far from non-existent. The man who makes Death and Sleep twin-brothers and calls death ' a brazen sleep ' does not really believe in any future life.

The kingdom of the dead is modelled upon these ideas. There the detested Hades rules, the most odious of all gods to men, and his consort, the dreaded Persephone. His kingdom is dark and noisome. Its terror chiefly lies in the fact that the way back is closed to any who have once passed within its portals. Hades is the strong custodian of the gates ; his dog is mentioned in connexion with the Herakles myth. Pylos, where Herakles strove with Hades, is originally

nothing else than the gate of the realm of the dead. The
idea of a common kingdom of the dead is naturally much
older than Homer and recurs among most other peoples.
It arises of itself as soon as man, in order to depict the
life hereafter, makes use of the ever-present analogy with
human life. It generally exists without difficulty side by
side with the idea that the dead man lives and is active in
his grave, but in Homer it has completely prevailed and
may be said to be a kind of anthropomorphism. The life
after death has been brought closer to the life on earth
but has also lost its power and intensity. Instead of a copy
it has become a pale shadow.

The kingdom of the dead lies beneath the earth, for there
the dead are buried. During the battle of the gods Hades
springs up in terror from his throne, for he is afraid that the
roof over his head will fall in. Where are its gates ? In later
times grottoes and deep lakes were thought to be entrances
to Hades. The idea is certainly old, but for a seafaring
people, who naïvely imagined the earth to be a flat disk
surrounded by the Ocean, the world had an extreme edge,
and over this men passed into the realms below. On this idea
is based the famous description of Hades in the journey of
Odysseus to the underworld, but it exists also in the *Iliad*.
Patroklos exhorts Achilles to bury his body as soon as
possible, for the shades will not permit him to pass the river
which bounds the kingdom of the dead. This is a transposition to the Homeric world of ideas belonging to the old
belief that a man who has not been buried can find no peace ;
if his body does not rest in the ground he must wander about
unceasingly like a lost spirit. Accordingly Odysseus on his
visit to the lower regions meets the shipwrecked Elpenor
before any other shades ; for he has not yet been buried.

The bond between the two worlds of the living and of the
dead has been weakened but by no means severed, and the
doctrine that this bond was broken by the burning of the

corpse overstates the case. The poet certainly makes the
shade of Patroklos declare that after his burial he will never
come back, but this is merely an expression adapted to the
particular occasion and must not be erected into a general
theory. Homeric ideas are not without mutual contradictions. Passages have already been adduced to show that
burial was regarded as necessary, since without it the dead
man would not be admitted into the kingdom of the dead ;
but notwithstanding this it is declared in numerous instances
that the slain go down to the dwellings of Hades, and
Achilles himself says of the shade of the unburied Patroklos
that it dwells there. Cremation by no means originated in
a desire to be liberated from the troublesome claims of the
dead ; it is an old funeral custom alongside of which the
notion of the continued life and activity of the dead in
the grave can still exist and does exist in later times. In
the expression 'appease in the fire' (πυρὸς μειλισσέμεν) lies
neither more nor less than the old idea of burial as the
undisputed right of the dead, the same feeling that forbids
the Homeric warrior to refuse burial even to a dead foe.

The burial of Patroklos is familiar as a relic of the extravagant funeral-cult of earlier times. Achilles slays twelve
Trojan prisoners, four horses, two dogs, and oxen and sheep
in large numbers, but the poet does not understand the
custom, he does not know that such things were intended
to serve the dead man in another world. There are other
survivals than this. When, as often happens, the dead are
called ' corpses ' (νέκυες), we have a linguistic relic of the
old belief in *revenants*, which must go back to a period before
the introduction of cremation. On his visit to the lower
world Odysseus promises that after his return to Ithaca he
will burn a heifer and many valuable things in honour of the
dead. Homer's reverence for the authority of the gods is
seen in the fact that rites which really concern the dead are
referred by him to the rulers of the nether world. When

Althaia wishes to bring death upon her son, she strikes the ground and invokes, not her murdered brother's spirit, but Hades and Persephone. This development was arrested, and Hades hardly became a cult-god.

In the account of the funeral banquet for Patroklos, which took place before the burial, we are told that

' all around the corpse was the blood from bowls outshed '.

There is no reason for not taking the expression literally. This is the blood-offering (αἱμακουρία) afterwards so familiar in the cult of the dead : Odysseus, on his visit to Hades, brings the same offering. In this latter case, in accordance with Homeric ideas about the dead, the rationalistic explanation is given that the blood will restore consciousness to the shades. Upon the whole the Nekyia is not in so marked a contradiction with the rest of Homer as often seems to be supposed. Its surprising feature is indeed that it gives a detailed description of the realm of the dead. Odysseus' wanderings have the same climax as the labours of Herakles, they lead him even to the underworld. This undoubtedly implies an increased interest in the world of the dead, but also an increased interest in the folk-tale, which is the special characteristic of the *Odyssey*. Poetic economy took advantage of the fact that Odysseus' comrades in battle could in this way be introduced into the narrative, and the opportunity was even seized to add a list of heroines.

The last part, which describes ' the Culprits in Hades ', is considered to be a very late interpolation, originating in Orphic circles.[1] I am not fully convinced as to this latter theory. Minos here is not yet the judge of the actions of the dead, but, like Agamemnon and Achilles, he continues in the underworld the life he had lived upon earth ; he had been a peaceful king and lawgiver, and therefore he administers justice to his subjects. This is a primeval idea which has

[1] Wilamowitz, *Homerische Untersuchungen*, pp. 199 et seq.

nothing Orphic about it. The same applies to Orion and
Herakles. The three culprits are Tityos, Tantalos, and
Sisyphos. Originally these belonged to the upper world,
but they have been transferred to the world below. And
this is extremely important, for it is the beginning of that
very development fostered by the followers of Orpheus
which made the lower world the place of punishment. It is
not the only instance in Homer. In one place the Erinyes
are invoked, and in another ' those (masculine, and therefore
not the Erinyes) who in the under-world punish the per-
jured '. The spirits of vengeance were at one time the
spirits of the dead. It is this idea which has intervened and,
since the spirits of the dead belong to the lower world, has
also made this the place of punishment. Is not the final
cause of this transference probably to be sought in the sharp
contrast between the gay, vigorous life in the light of the
sun and the comfortless, empty existence in the realm of
shades which the Homeric poems bring out with such
merciless clearness ? Man in Homer has liberated himself
from the fear of the dead but not from the fear of death.
The tendency of feeling gave prominence not to the state of
nothingness, which may be a matter of indifference or even
a relief, but to the fear of nothingness. Feeling overcame
rationalism, and the ground was prepared for the development which was to transform the Homeric kingdom of the
dead into its very opposite.

But if the dead do not intervene in human life the gods
do so all the more effectively. The personal intervention
of the gods in matters great and small, sometimes indirectly,
often directly, is a well-known peculiarity of the Homeric
epic and is described by the technical term ' divine apparatus '.
The gods are human, in fact too human. Anthropomorphism
is the distinguishing mark of Homer and all later Greek
religion.

Anthropomorphism has its starting-point in animism.

The latter models the inner nature of a divinity upon that of man, though only in the broadest outlines of an unconscious individual psychology, and equips him with human will and feeling. The second source is the folk-tale, and the third the necessity of visualizing the gods. So long as gods are seen in animals and natural objects, anthropomorphism is not a necessity. But higher culture understands the difference between man and the animals and sets man above the animals ; then, if not before, anthropomorphism introduces itself and either conquers or, as in Egypt and India, blends with the conception of gods in animal and other shapes. Anthropomorphism is, therefore, partly external—in its manner of visualizing the gods—and partly internal—in the psychology and history of the gods, when mythology draws them into its sphere. Since the art of sculpture was of no account during the dark ages between the fall of the Mycenaean culture and the Homeric period— the time when the specifically Greek anthropomorphism must have been developed—it is to be presumed that the internal anthropomorphism was the leading force. But it is certain that the numerous Mycenaean representations of deities formed a starting-point and a stimulus for the development of ideas which the Greeks had brought with them.

Anthropomorphism, as developed from animism and the need for some visual presentation of the gods, is natural and exists among many peoples, indeed among all who have risen above the most primitive stage ; yet it does not hold absolute sway. The grotesque figures of deities from Africa and Polynesia are not merely the outcome of conventionalism and a lack of artistic skill. They mean something, no less than the Indian idols with their animal heads, multiplicity of arms, and other peculiarities. The idea of the superhuman power of the gods breaks through and seeks expression in art. To us the figure is grotesque, but not so to the devout negro or Indian. For we have been educated by the Greeks to a consistent anthropomorphism, and this is something specifically Greek.

In this consistent anthropomorphism lies a genuine Greek rationalism. The gods are anthropomorphic, they resemble man, and consequently they are neither more nor less than man-like. Anthropomorphism has, therefore, a characteristic limitation among the Greeks. If the visual form exists there is no anthropomorphism, but the development of the god is also arrested. The sun-god hardly became the real object of a cult in native Greek religion just because his visual form was limited to the disk of the planet. On the other hand he appears as a mythological figure in the *Odyssey*. The same applies to the rosy-fingered Eos and to the winds, and the process is seen very characteristically in the case of the natural powers which have a real cult—the rivers. Cult and conceptions are bound up with the object itself, the water of the river, even though now and again the river-gods are represented in human shape and Homer makes them take part in the assembly of the gods and gives them fathers and descendants. Offerings to them are lowered into the springs or into the water of the river. The power of the description of Achilles' fight with Skamandros lies in the fact that the river is regarded as an element—an inundation, a torrent—to which the hero is nearly forced to yield, until he is saved by the sending of another element, fire, against it.

It is said of Athena in one passage, in which she appears undisguised, that she was like a tall and fair woman. The gods form the highest anthropomorphic class; they are recognized by their appearance and behaviour, just as a prince or nobleman is recognized. When they appear in disguise they preserve, like a disguised prince, something of their superiority, and though they are easily recognized as they disappear, it is only then that the person to whom they show themselves realizes that there was anything peculiar about them or their appearance. Since tallness of stature was a mark of aristocratic beauty which the poet seldom omits to assign to his characters, and especially to women, it is given to the gods in a still higher degree. Thus, too, the naïve art of earlier times makes the gods larger than men. With a certain inconsistency, which yet is not difficult to understand, Athena in one place unveils the eyes of Diomedes so that he recognizes the gods in the battle.

Nevertheless it was sometimes difficult for the poet to keep his sense of the superiority of the gods within bounds. The old idea of the epiphany of the gods in the form of birds lived on, and, therefore, the rapid arrival or disappearance of a god is often compared with the flight of a bird. It is doubtless in accordance with the same idea that the tips of the branches of trees quiver under the feet of Hera and Hypnos, and that Hera glides over the highest mountain-tops without touching the earth with her feet. In other places we have instances of sheer poetic hyperbole, as when Olympus is shaken when Zeus nods or Hera moves upon her throne, or when Ares and Poseidon in battle cry out like ten or twelve thousand men. Here, as also when Ares, vanquished in the fight, covers seven roods, an almost burlesque touch is introduced. This last instance is an old folk-tale motif which the poet found useful and did not correct. The captive Tityos in the underworld covers nine roods.

From the beginning Zeus was the principal deity of the immigrating Greeks, and the immigration exalted him by letting other gods disappear or fall into the background. The immigrants found new gods in Greece and took over both the gods of the country and others which came to them from without ; they were all regarded as subordinate to Zeus. So Zeus, by reason of his original importance and of his development, became the foremost deity of all, the king of the gods. In Homer he takes an absolutely predominating position. This fact was of less importance in the cult, where the god who is being worshipped at that moment has an almost exclusive preponderance. Man directs his attention to one particular god, and the others are not immediately present to the mind. In the cult, therefore, there can scarcely be any question of relative superiority or inferiority among the gods. It is quite different in poetry, where the gods appear alongside of one another upon the same plane and as patrons of opposite camps. Here the consequences of anthropomorphism appear, which were concealed in the cult. The world of the gods is equipped with every human frailty. This point was reached by gradual stages during the development of the epic. The very working up of separate poems into one great epic must have involved a pronounced tendency in this direction. It has been said, perhaps not without reason, that the gods in the older portions of Homer are more independent of each other and that the divine community with its royal stronghold Olympus is a creation of the poet of the *Iliad*.[1] But our acceptance of this view will depend upon how much we are willing to ascribe to the creator of our present *Iliad*.

The divine community is a copy of the conditions of the age of chivalry. The seat of the gods is, therefore, an acropolis with its royal stronghold, Olympus. So much remains of the physical conception of Zeus' cloud-capped mountain that the top is represented as rising into space above the clouds. There Zeus sits when he wishes to be alone, as he sat before ; there he summons the council of the gods. Lower down lies the city of the gods, and all other buildings in it are outshone by Zeus' palace, the floor of which is laid with plates of gold. There the gods sit upon their thrones and drink wine like the Phaeacian princes at the house of Alcinoös. The palace is surrounded by shining

---

[1] Finsler, *op. cit.*, pp. 277 et seq.

walls, against which rest the chariots of the gods. Their horses eat ambrosia out of their mangers. Zeus and Hera have each their own thalamus just as Telemachus has. Round about stand the dwellings of the rest of the gods. Hephaistos, who has built all this splendour, has his workshop there. The city must be surrounded by a wall, since we hear of the gates which open of themselves and are guarded by the Horai. In a royal household there are many servants. The Horai are grooms to Zeus, Iris to Hera, Deimos and Phobos to Ares, even Poseidon on one occasion renders this service to his greater brother. Iris is the messenger of the gods (Hermes fills the position for the first time in the *Odyssey*), Hebe is their cup-bearer, Themis seems to attend to the meals. The trades are represented by Hephaistos, by Athena and the Graces who weave, and by the physician Paieon.

Life goes on much as in some royal house in which there is constant entertaining. We need not be too contemptuous of the idea : centuries later the blessedness of the other world could not be imagined under any other form. Zeus rules like Agamemnon over a troop of wilful and refractory vassals, each of whom is pursuing his own designs. On one occasion the gods revolted against him and were only subdued with difficulty. Old cosmogonic legends contribute to the completion of the feudal picture. Zeus has shared the world with his three brothers ; for his portion he has received the heavens and the clouds, but he rules over all in virtue of his right of birth. He has a will of his own and sometimes uses threats and violence in putting it into execution, but he has to have regard to the other gods, although sometimes with ill-concealed reluctance. In the *Odyssey* everything proceeds in a much more quiet and orderly—one might be tempted to say a more parliamentary —fashion. In the council of the gods the greatest harmony prevails, although advantage is taken of the absence of the irreconcilable Poseidon to decide in favour of the return of Odysseus to his home.

Like every noble family, the Olympians have their genealogical tree. The cosmogony in a genealogical form is of course older than Homer, to whom it is not unknown ; at least he speaks of Okeanos, the origin of the gods, and of their mother Tethys. Simple genealogical connexions, such as that a god had parents and a wife or that a human being was born of a god, naturally also belong to earlier times ; the Thetis myth offers an example from the folk-tale. These tendencies were developed by the genealogical interest and ambition of the nobility. Several passages in Homer show that the heroes loved to recount not only their own but also their horses' pedigrees. The ultimate ancestor is some god. In consequence, a more definitely established system was introduced into the genealogy of the gods. They were all united into one family. The old, vanquished gods of the country—for this is what the Titans may really be—were made the fathers of the ruling gods, and before them came the cosmogonic principles. Consequently there was introduced into the divine myth that domestic revolt in which Zeus hurled his father from the throne.

A comparison with later ideas concerning the attributes of the gods reveals certain limitations attaching to the Homeric deities, due to religious conceptions of an earlier age and not to Homer's anthropomorphism, although the latter with its usual consistency throws them into sharper relief. These limitations are suggested by the three words omnipresence, omniscience, and omnipotence, none of which qualities was ever fully possessed by the Greek gods. The gods are from the beginning localized to their customary haunts and the places of their cult. Their presence at the sacrifice has to be invoked. They are seen coming either in visible form floating down as a bird, as in the Mycenaean representations, or in imagination. Their presence is marked by visible signs, such as the nodding of the palm-tree in the hymn of Callimachus to Delian Apollo. Clouds gather around the mountain of Zeus and thunder breaks forth. Zeus comes from his mountain or from the sky, since Zeus means ' sky '. Zeus, in fact, dominated the Greek imagination. His mountain is called Olympus, but in Homer Olympus and the heavens are one. Therefore in their prayers men direct their gaze to the heavens, where Zeus lives, and the practice was transferred from the worship of Zeus to that of the other gods, those who in Mycenaean times were seen to reveal themselves as birds. The attention was probably directed merely to the fact of their coming, not to the direction from which they came. Finally anthropomorphism collected all the gods upon Olympus.

This does not prevent the gods from also having their separate dwelling-places; Zeus rules from Ida, where he had a shrine and an altar. Poseidon lives in the depths of the sea, where he has his palace at Aigai; Apollo dwells in Lykia or at his shrines at Chryse, Killa, and Tenedos. Ares and Phobos come from Thrace, the land of the Berserkers, and Boreas and Zephyrus also return to Thrace, the land from which they blow.

For simple people, who themselves spend their lives in the same place, the localization of the gods presents no problem. It is obvious to such people that the gods are to be found where they seek them in the cult, and equally obvious that they are not to be found in other places. But when the consequences of anthropomorphism are pressed home, as is the case in Homer, this localization is seen to be a human failing in the gods. Thetis cannot go at once to Zeus on her son's errand, for Zeus and all the gods have travelled the day before to Ethiopia to a banquet. Poseidon again is with the Ethiopians when the council of the gods is held at which the homeward journey of Odysseus is sanctioned. As the god returns he has a distant sight of Odysseus from the mountains of the Solymoi. Zeus from Ida has a view of the battle-field at Troy, and Poseidon from the top of Samothrake. The gods must, therefore, go from place to place, and here Homer employs a poet's licence. Poseidon requires four strides to go from Samothrake to Aigai and the gods' horses leap as far as the gaze of a spy can reach.

With genuine religious experience it is otherwise. This certainly presupposes its god to be localized, but it does not first inquire whether he is at home when it wishes to invoke him. It assumes that he will hear wherever he may be. The prayer of the wounded Glaucus is characteristic: ' Hear me, O Lord, whether thou art in Lykia or Troy ; for thou canst hear everywhere.' And he is immediately cured and made strong. Although the gods may not see everything, they hear all that concerns them, even in Homer. Hera, sitting upon her throne in Olympos, overhears Hektor's boastful speech, Poseidon hears the vauntings of the shipwrecked Aias, and Thetis, in the depths of the ocean, her son's lament for Patroklos. Anthropomorphism could not rob the believer of this conviction, but, as we shall see, it did partially modify its form.

It is sometimes said that the gods know all things, and of something quite uncertain it is said : ' That is doubtless known to Zeus and the other immortal gods.' But sometimes the gods reveal an extremely human ignorance as to that which very closely concerns them. Poseidon does not know that the hated Odysseus is on his way home until he sees his ship far out upon the sea. The omniscient Proteus does not suspect that Menelaos and his men have hidden themselves under seal-skins so that they may seize him and force him to reveal his wisdom. Lampetie has to inform the all-seeing Helios that Odysseus' men have seized his herds. Here the influence of the folk-tale, whose structure makes no demands upon consistency, is at work ; anthropomorphism has adopted its methods. There is an almost primitive

artlessness in the statement that Zeus, sitting upon Mount
Ida, has turned away his eyes and, therefore, does not
notice that Poseidon has come to the aid of the Greeks.

From omens and oracles men seek to know the future.
Oracles and omens come from the gods, and, therefore,
practical religion believes that the gods know the future.
This belief is found also in Homer. Thetis knows from Zeus
that her son will either live a short but glorious life, or else
will reach an obscure old age. The gods have warned
Aegisthos and revealed to him his fate. Circe tells Odysseus
what will befall him on his voyage home and after his
arrival at his house. But here, as on some other occasions,
Homer makes use of oracular sentences as a poetic device ;
through them he reveals his plot, as is done in the prologues
of tragedy.

Just as the Homeric man sometimes says that the gods
know all things, so he also says sometimes that the gods are
all-powerful. Like the former statement, this too must be
regarded from the standpoint of practical religious feeling.
When man wishes the gods to fulfil all his desires, it is
implied that they can do so. Otherwise he knows very well
that Nature goes her own course, and her regularity sometimes makes such a strong impression upon his mind that
he not only emphasizes it but sets it as a limit to divine
power. Thus it is said that not even the gods can ward off
death. Not even Poseidon could save Odysseus from the
whirlpool of Charybdis, says Circe. Odysseus cries out that
not even Poseidon, the giant's father, can restore the
Cyclops' eye. The standpoint is subjective and varies
according to the side from which the phenomena are regarded. The fancies of the folk-tale care as little for the
order of Nature as for consistency. For them it is a simple
matter to stop the sun and moon in their course. Anthropomorphism, which inserts the sun-god among the other
divinities, also finds it quite natural that Athena should

prevent the appearance of Eos in order to prolong the night for the reunited husband and wife, and that Hera during the battle over the dead body of Patroklos should send Helios below the horison against his will.

Of all the numerous characteristics which the gods carried with them from their primitive origin on their journey towards a higher religious plane, characteristics to which the Homeric anthropomorphism gave such clearness and prominence, none was more fateful than their lack of any connexion with morality. Power, knowledge, presence were not yet conceived in their abstract absoluteness ; the power of the gods, and not its limitations, was present to the religious consciousness. The absence of morality preyed upon the vital nerve of religious feeling. In proportion as the gods are Nature-gods, they have nothing to do with morals. The rain falls alike upon the just and upon the unjust. Animism implants in the gods human will and feeling, passions and caprices. At the earliest stage man's object is not to uphold morality but to obtain from the gods the fulfilment of his own desires—Autolykos had learned from Hermes to surpass all others in thievishness and false oaths—and this naïve point of view never disappears, even though man gradually learns that there are certain desires with which he cannot fittingly approach the gods. He seeks an authority for the practices in which the life of society has taken form, and he finds it in the gods. Public opinion then forces these customs upon the individual, even when they are at variance with his own desires.

The Homeric man has travelled some distance along this path. The bonds of society were weak, but the sanctity of the unwritten laws determining the mutual relationships of men was all the greater. Passions and will were of an intractable violence which often drove men to disregard these laws, but the transgression was severely judged as an act of insolence and presumption (ὕβρις, ἀτασθαλίη). In their appeal against the strong, men addressed themselves not only to the judgement of their fellows, to which the oppressor ought to submit, but also to the gods who enforce the unwritten law. Transgression of the latter brings down the divine indignation (νέμεσις). The suitors did not remember that their actions would incur the resentment of men, and Helen complains that Paris had no sense of this resentment. Submission to the ordinary moral code is called shame, modesty (αἰδώς) ; it urges on even the timid in the dangers of battle. The committing of outrage and a pious disposition, insolence and law-abiding conduct (ὑβρισταί—νόος θεουδής, ὕβρις—εὐνομίη) are placed in opposition to each other as contraries of which the gods are cognizant. But it is significant that these passages occur in the *Odyssey*. There is, however, a remarkable passage in the *Iliad*, in a simile, and, therefore, in one of the newest parts. We are there told how Zeus drives the autumn rain-storms over the earth in his anger with man, who pronounces vicious judgements, distorts the right, and does not respect the gods—a cry from the depths which announces Hesiod.

We are here in the presence of the still unwritten law. Elsewhere certain obligations appear, precisely those which make social life possible and are the foundation of the society of the day : offences against the gods, against parents, elder brothers, and refugees (naturally not upon the battlefield) are condemned, as well as perjury and breach of compact. Even the beggar, it is said, has his Erinyes. The story of the duel between Paris and Menelaos rests consistently upon the idea of the guilt of Paris, his crime against hospitality.

In opposition to this idea, which seeks to make the gods the guardians of law and custom, stands the old conception supported by the cult. When man turns to the gods he bases his appeal not upon his present frame of mind and the moral worth of his actions, but upon his divine descent and connexions with the gods, the favour they have formerly shown him, his offerings, gifts, and promises. In the cult the moral element falls into the background, for there man or the community is alone with its god ; the others are strangers or foes, in respect of whom moral considerations do not apply. It is quite otherwise in poetic story, where men or peoples are juxtaposed as equals. That which is right for one must be right for another. From the world of men human discords were introduced into the divine world, where they found points of connexion in the folk-tale.

Every one who sets out to battle believes himself to be under divine protection, in the Homeric world no less than in our own time. The simple solution that the gods stand over the combatants and decide the contest in accordance with a higher purpose, the fulfilment of their own will independently of man's, satisfied human demands upon divine assistance just as little then as now. During the recent war it was satirically remarked that God had been divided up into the god of the English and the god of the Prussians. The Greek gods were universal, and from this fact arose precisely the same difficulty, although it was not made the object of satire. The best evidence for the pre-dominating position of Zeus is that he really does stand above the combatants and fulfils his own designs. The Mycenaean period had city-goddesses, who were the special protectresses of prince and people. They were generalized, but not completely. Hera is the Argive national goddess, Athena ardently favours the Greeks, and certain heroes are under her personal protection.

The position of the gods as protecting deities need not necessarily clash with religious feeling. But that result does follow from the anthropomorphic picture of the conflict-ing parties given in the poem, where gods no less than men

are divided into two hostile camps. The spirit of partisanship affects all the gods except Zeus. Those who belong to
the Greeks stand on the Greek side with Poseidon. Apollo
and Aphrodite, who were admitted into the Greek pantheon
but whose foreign origin was not forgotten, take the side
of the Trojans, for these too must have their protecting
deities. The gods are partisans who pursue their ends by
every means, cunning and deceit not excepted. And if they
are partisans, it is a natural consequence that they will
themselves take part in the fray, not only indirectly but
also by direct interference. The account of the exploits of
Diomedes, where the hero with Athena's help wounds
Aphrodite and Ares, has a certain splendour about it which
recalls the age when the prince set out with the goddess of
his city and might meet in battle the protecting deities
of another town. But elsewhere this old-time feeling has
vanished. The consequence is that the gods also group
themselves into two conflicting parties, as in Book XXI of
the *Iliad*. The beginning borrows its grandeur from the
contest between the powers of Nature, but this is not sus-
tained. So much, however, the respect for the gods does
achieve—that they are not allowed to fall upon one another
in earnest. The total effect is therefore ridiculous, as Zeus
does not fail to see.

The partisan spirit is intensified by the fact that the gods
are protecting their favourites and sons. The Mycenaean
idea of the divine protectress of the prince has given way to
a purely personal relationship in which certain heroes are
under the patronage of Athena. Under the pressure of
anthropomorphism the religious idea of protection has
passed into one of human favouritism. This fact brings out
certain of the most striking features of the divine apparatus.
The sons of the gods come from folk-tale and genealogy,
and they accentuate the anthropomorphism, for it could
not but be supposed that the gods would resemble men in

favouring their own flesh and blood. Only Zeus is above this weakness and lets Sarpedon go to meet his fate.

It has often been said that the anger and favour of the Homeric gods—Hera's hatred of the Trojans, Poseidon's wrath with Odysseus, the persecution of Oineus by Artemis because he has neglected her in a sacrifice—depend, like those of man, upon personal motives, in which wounded honour and vanity play not the least considerable part. The gods are fickle, even treacherous. But this is not to be ascribed to anthropomorphism alone : it is also due to the fact that everything unexpected is attributed to the gods. To this point we shall return later. We have seen that the root of the belief is primitive, resting in the soil of the Nature powers and animism, but the fruits were over-developed in the atmosphere of poetic anthropomorphism, which makes the life of the gods a reflection of that of men. We have seen also that ethical demands were evolved and even superimposed themselves upon the gods : for an ethical creed requires the custodians of law and custom to practise what they preach. But anthropomorphism expelled ethics from the poet's description of the divine world, and set them in conflict with the religious demands made upon the gods in a more developed age. The problem of Job—the justification of that which is allowed by the deity to befall man—was present to the mind although it was unexpressed. Before the power which is unmeasurably superior man bows in fear and humility, without asking for justice, and on that ground the Nature-gods could maintain their position. But anthropomorphism had deprived them of their mysterious power. In an earlier form of religion that power must be a magic power, such as does not work with human means or in a human way. But magic is practically absent from Homer : there are only faint traces of it. This absence is a consequence of anthropomorphism, which was hostile to all that would not range itself under the banner of the human, to the wonders of magic no less than to gods in grotesque shapes. The gods became human, indeed too human, and were accordingly measured by human standards. Morality, justice, and mercy were required of them, but these demands they could not fulfil. Their nature was originally different and anthropomorphism places their defects in a strong light.

Homer's consistent anthropomorphism represents the gods as possessing every human need and weakness. Hermes complains of the length of the journey to the remote corner of the world in which Calypso lives. Hera washes her body with ambrosia before she goes to meet her lover, Zeus. Zeus rates the disobedient and threatens them with blows. Ares and Aphrodite are wounded. Zeus reposes, over-powered with love and sleep, while his son Herakles is tempest-tossed and while the Trojans are in sore straits. But rationalism reflects that there must be a distinction between gods and men, and a purely physical distinction too, since the gods are not subject to death like men. The answer is typically rationalistic. If the gods are immortal, it is because their food is different from that of mortal men. Not blood but *ichor* flows in their veins. Even their horses are immortal and eat ambrosia. Ambrosia can therefore also act as a preservative to protect the bodies of Patroklos and Hektor from corruption.

The immortality of the gods drew a clear line of demarcation which man could not pass. In other respects no such line exists. The gods are stronger, wiser, more powerful than men, but this is a mere question of degree. There is a significant word ' easily ' ($\dot{\rho}\epsilon\hat{\iota}a$) which constantly recurs in passages about the gods. They save or carry off a person ' easily, as a god does '; they live ' easily ', without the sorrows and tribulations which are the lot of man. Their life and demeanour are such that it has been said that Homer's descriptions of the divine world are a caricature of the life of the aristocratic circles of the age, or else that the Olympian scenes are a substitute for the scenes from family life which are necessarily lacking on account of the abnormal conditions of the camp.

In point of fact there are in Homer three anthropomorphic classes. The distinction between the two lower, the nobility and the people, is no less clear than the distinction between the two upper, the nobility and the gods. The lower distinction is mercilessly sharp. The words ' good ' and ' bad ' (ἐσθλός, κακός) already begin to be used as indications of class. There is a characteristic difference in the behaviour of Odysseus towards the people and towards the heroes when he tries to prevent the army from returning home. He addresses the heroes with convincing and eloquent words, he falls upon the people with abuse and blows. The scene with Thersites is one with which every one is familiar. In the accounts of battles the people pass altogether into the background. Courage is a noble virtue which does not belong to the vulgar. There seems to be something not unlike a conviction that the distinction is one established by Nature.

No doubt there were then, as there have always been, individuals who wished to pass beyond the boundaries of their class. What the nobility desires is only too evident. Again and again princes and princesses are compared to gods and goddesses. Idomeneus stands among his Cretans like a god ; the people of Lykia look upon Sarpedon and Glaukos as gods. Certain princes are called ' god-born ', several others ' god-nourished ', and the latter epithet is applied to the Phaeacian nobility in its entirety.

The boundaries between the classes are maintained by the unwritten laws sustaining the order of society. The disregard of these is insolence (ὕβρις) and calls down indignation (νέμεσις). The latter substantive is always used of the relationship between men, but the verb νεμεσάω,

' to be angry ', is employed of the gods as well. Hera
' is angry ' at Hektor's boastful speech, Apollo at the attack
of the Achaeans, Zeus at evil deeds. What would the man
of the people, had he striven to rise out of his own class
into that above it, have said about the opposition that he
met ? He would probably have applied to it the words
ἄγαμαι and μεγαίρω ; they properly mean ' to look upon
a thing as too great ', but were modified to a sense which
comes pretty near to ' envy ' The man of the people sees
from below what the nobility views from above. The
nobility in its turn views from below the class of highest
rank, that of the gods. And it is precisely of their relationship to man that the above two words are used. The thirst
for fame and an unlimited self-esteem urge the man of the
nobility forwards, and when misfortune overtakes him it is
described as the envy of the gods ; the gods regard his
success as beyond what human powers should achieve. The
explanation is constantly present : it is used when a bow-
string breaks in the fight, so that the foe escapes the shot ;
Calypso thinks that the gods grudge a goddess life with
a mortal man. The expression finally becomes stereotyped ;
Penelope says that the jealousy of the gods had prevented
her and Odysseus from living together. Thus anthropomorphism found in the settled order of society the ultimate
barrier between gods and men. The Greeks never lost sight
of the idea and the problem involved in it. Insolence towards the gods must be regarded by any genuine religious
feeling as the most deadly ethical and religious sin. That
it was not so regarded by the Greeks was due to their
anthropomorphism, which made the gods resemble men
and then measured them by the same moral standards as
mankind.

Actually, no living person has ever seen a god, and Homer
makes the gods associate personally only with favoured
fabulous peoples such as the Ethiopians and the Phaeacians.

But he is not consistent ; on rare occasions a god does reveal himself to certain heroes in an untransformed shape. Rationalism overcame the difficulty that the gods were so frequently supposed to intervene in human affairs and were yet nowhere to be seen by supposing that they assumed human shape. This device is characteristic of Homer's divine apparatus, and popular belief assisted it. There was thought to be something mysterious about the stranger, and it was upon occasion believed that a god was concealed under his form.

Religious experience had still less to say about the activities of the gods than about their epiphany. Many had doubtless experienced the intervention and influence of a god, but simple religious feeling does not ask how or by what agency this comes about. It sees something which it must ascribe to divine power, it knows its prayer to be answered ; with this it is satisfied and inquires no further. Rationalism succumbed to the temptation of representing the influence and intervention of the gods in a visible form credible to ordinary reason. Anthropomorphism by investing the gods with human shape had shown the way. What best accorded with reality was to make a god intervene in the disguise of a human being.

This became the normal fashion in which the gods are made to intervene, but there are certain distinctions. Zeus directs the battle from afar by means of his will and the messages he sends. He intervenes personally but once, when he hurls the lightning before the horses of Diomedes. Apollo strikes Patroklos with his powerful hand, and the armour falls from the hero's body. He goes before Hektor with the aegis and smoothes out with his feet the ditch around the Greek ships as easily as a child at play fills up a hole in the sand. But he never condescends to the office of a squire or to pure deception as Athena does. The intervention of the other gods displays still less of the divine power, is still more strongly humanized. Athena in the *Odyssey* becomes a familiar spirit, except that she is not invoked and compelled to appear but comes freely and spontaneously.

Another rationalistic explanation of the presence of the gods and of certain of their actions is the cloud or darkness which is always at hand when a god wishes to appear among men or to help and save one of his favourites. The gods sit upon the wall of Troy and descend to the fight hidden in a cloud. They withdraw heroes from the contest by wrapping them in a mist ; Athena covers Odysseus in the same way when he walks into the town of the Phaeacians, and also when he returns to Ithaca. Apollo protects Hektor's body with a mist. When a cloud lies spread over Olympus and when Zeus on Ida sits enthroned upon a cloud we have a reminiscence of visible Nature. At a later stage the cloud becomes a means of making invisible, resembling the helmet of Hades, the magic hat of our popular belief, and it is probably a rationalistic adaptation of this old popular idea. It is significant of the desire to visualize things that the cloud finally becomes a garment which the gods cast over their shoulders. The outstanding instance is that of Ares turning aside from the fight and sitting in a cloud against which he has leaned his spear. The converse notion of a cloud or darkness covering a person's eyes and preventing him from seeing seldom occurs.

At every point of human life Homer recognizes the influence of a divine power. The gods are the donors of physical and mental advantages, skill, and wealth. The prophetic eye of Calchas, Skamandrios' skill in hunting, Phereklos' art of ship-building, the house-wife's art of weaving, the sceptre of the Pelopides, the armour of Achilles, Pandaros' bow—all are the gifts of the gods. They are lords of the fates of men. They grant the fall of Troy, a safe home-coming, bride and children. The issue of the contest between Hektor and Achilles, the kingship in Troy, Penelope's hand, all these lie in the lap of the gods. They exalt and they cast down, they send prosperity and misfortune. Above all they are lords of life and death. The idea of an all-powerful conscious government of the universe has arisen, a government not according to a uniform plan but in accordance with a single will. It has been much disputed what is the relationship of the individual god's own will to this general idea. The question cannot be decided in the dogmatic fashion usually adopted in the discussion. We must appeal to religious experience, remembering that this finds no insuperable difficulty in allowing contradictory ideas to persist alongside of one another, and does so all the more easily the older and simpler they are.

Hitherto we have been principally concerned with the poet's own presentation, in particular with his divine apparatus. We have every reason to suppose that this form is adopted by the poet for the purpose of describing the relationships of the gods among themselves and to men, a description which is part of his poetic scheme, but that it does not accord with the Homeric man's real beliefs and expectations in regard to his gods. A means of distinguishing between the poetic presentation and the religious experience and belief has been furnished us in the observation that the gods are treated quite differently in the poet's own presentation and in the speeches which he puts into the mouths of men.[1] The divine apparatus belongs to the former, the speech of men does not make use of it. Where the poet can tell exactly which god it was that intervened, the human character, in reference to the same events, will speak quite vaguely about a *daimon* or some god or the

---

[1] O. Jörgensen, *Das Auftreten der Götter in den Büchern ι—μ der Odyssee* (*Hermes*, xxxix, 1904, pp. 357 et seq.) ; further developed by E. Hedén, *Homerische Götterstudien*, Uppsala, 1912.

highest god of all, Zeus. There is no mention of Athena in Odysseus' own story of his adventures ; in the poet's account she is the ever-present protectress. Exceptions occur, but they belong, characteristically enough, to the special spheres of activity of certain gods, originating in ancient cult and belief : a sudden death is ascribed to the arrows of Apollo and Artemis, the turmoil of the sea to Poseidon, the gift of artistic skill to Athena, the scourge of famine to Demeter's wrath. The king is under the protection of Zeus, but the personal protecting goddess belongs to the myth and therefore to the divine apparatus. With certain definite and easily determined exceptions, therefore, the people of Homer do not make individual gods responsible for all the experiences which they attribute to divine intervention. And these form a large element in their life.[1]

As is still the case to-day, there is no thought of the divinity in times of prosperity, while all is well and everything takes its usual course. But when things go amiss men turn to the gods, not, however, in Homer, to seek refuge and comfort, but to lay upon them the blame for that which has happened contrary to desire or intention. Even in the divine apparatus this idea finds expression in the common phrase : ' Now this would have happened . . . had not a god . . . '. The Homeric man is absolutely under the dominion of the emotion of the moment. When passion has subsided and the unhappy consequences begin to appear he says : ' I did not desire this ; hence I did not do it.' His own behaviour has become something foreign to him, it seems to be something which has penetrated into him from without. He lays the blame on some *daimon* or god, on Ate or on Zeus, Moira and the Erinyes, as Agamemnon does in regard to his treatment of Achilles. A kind of division of personality takes place within him, though not

[1] For the following compare my paper *Götter und Psychologie bei Homer*, *ARw*, xxii, 1924.

in the pathological sense of two different states of personality. Rarely do two contrary currents appear in the mental consciousness. The state of mind admirably described in Kipling's lines :

> (I've) stood beside an' watched myself
> Be'aving like a blooming fool

is not usual in Homer. Something like it may be found in Achilles in his quarrel with Agamemnon in the first book of the *Iliad*, but as a rule we find two different states of consciousness succeeding one another. The abrupt change from one state to the other cleaves the mind in two. The man becomes ' beside himself ', and when he comes ' to himself ' again his ordinary self refuses to recognize the effect of this derangement, and regards it as due to some force outside of him. The same cleavage takes place when man is overtaken by something unforeseen. An action may be disastrous in its results although it is undertaken not in the heat of passion but with calm self-control. Here too man says : ' I did not intend this ; hence it belongs not to me.' He regards it as something outside of him which has come into his life from without and crossed his designs. Here again he lays the blame on a higher divine power.

Hence comes the belief in the constant interference of the gods in human life. This belief applies to what has happened. As far as the immediate future is concerned, man knows perfectly well that the issue will depend upon himself, and he thinks and acts accordingly. This line of thought is egocentric and optional. Others know very well that a man himself bears the blame for his actions and their consequences, and they speak accordingly, unless they wish to make excuses, as when Priam declares to Helen that the gods, not she, are guilty of the misfortunes which the violation by Paris of the sanctity of hospitality has brought upon Troy. The individual usually wishes to excuse himself and therefore generally speaks about the gods, but he may also, when occasion serves and requires, lay the blame upon himself. Consistently carried out, this line of thought would deliver man from the responsibility for his actions and make him a puppet in the hands of the gods, but the Homeric man has too strong a sense of reality to draw this conclusion, even though he may come very near it when he has reason to disown the consequences of his actions.

The divine powers to whom all this is ascribed cannot be the ordinary specialized and anthropomorphized gods. These are therefore absent from the speeches which are put into the mouths of men and which reveal to us the Homeric man's real belief and religious experience. Instead of gods with personal names appear generalities : *daimon*, ' the gods ', ' some god ', ' Zeus '. The words δαίμων (' *daimon* ') and θεός (' god ') are often interchanged ; *daimon* may mean any whatever of the anthropomorphic gods, but it has its centre in the undefined, in power, whereas *theos* centres in the individual and personal. A *daimon* has no real individuality. Unlike a god, it acquires this only in the occasional manifestation of the divine power. Therefore in this sense we may find instead of *daimon* the indefinite ' some god ' (θεός τις) or the collective ' gods ' (θεοί), or the all-embracing deity Zeus, the highest god of all. An examination of the passages in which something is ascribed to a *daimon* will show that those are the most numerous in which the *daimon* brings or is the cause of bringing upon man something that is contrary to his will, purpose, or expectations ; in many other passages a sudden inspiration is attributed to the *daimon*. The adjective derived from the word, δαιμόνιος, has always an idea of blame more or less prominently attached to it and denotes something wonderful, incomprehensible, irrational.

Usener regarded the *daimon* as a momentary god. ' That which suddenly appears before us as a dispensation from above, that which renders us happy, afflicted, or overwhelmed, presents itself to the heightened emotion as a divine being.'[1] But the conception is not exhausted by these words and by the term ' momentary god '. A *daemon* has no real individuality ; an individuality is only conferred on it by the manifestation in which it appears, and is merely a mode of expressing the belief that a certain effect is produced by a higher power. The differentiation of the *daimones* depends not on the religious phenomena but on the phenomena of Nature and of human life. A god is developed by religious need and through the cult into a characteristic individuality, a *daimon* represents a portion, adapted to the accidental manifestation of the moment, of the supranormal power recognized by man in phenomena which he believes himself unable to explain from his ordinary experience. The power is in itself not differentiated ; therefore in each individual case it is made equivalent to the accidental manifestation of the moment. Without the general, however unconscious, conception of a power the detached conception of the expression of power is impossible.

The idea of ' power ' was living, although without a name, among the people of Homer ; it remained still living to the Greeks, and they afterwards coined abstract expressions, ' the divine ', ' the god-like ' (τὸ θεῖον, τὸ δαιμόνιον), to denote it. This conception alone could answer to the idea of a divine cause in all the details of human life and in the human heart ; the anthropomorphic gods could not do so, for the process of specializing and individualizing had set up narrow limits for them. We are here touching upon a primitive foundation, the first seed-ground of religion itself. In recent discussions on the science of religion this conception has been brought to the front. It is best known under the name of *mana*, but the Swedish people still preserves the belief in ' power ' (*makten*) and ' the powers ' (*makterna*), and the language still uses these words in this sense. In the

[1] Usener, *Götternamen*, p. 291.

Norse religion we find examples of how the belief in ' power ' was changed into belief in ' the powers ' and was connected with an anthropomorphic world of gods. The gods were given the epithets of *regin*, *bond* (' those who govern, who bind '), while *rå* (' those who rule ', *råda*) is still a common Scandinavian word for fairies and other such figures of popular belief. The Greek mind, with its concentration upon the individual and the concrete, did not consciously preserve the idea of ' power ' but only of its manifestations, in which a *daimon* revealed itself. Anthropomorphism and rationalism took possession of the gods, individualizing and specializing them. The conception of the *daimon* was certainly affected thereby, so that the word *daimon* could also be used of a god and the *daimones* were given a false appearance of individuality, but the contrast is plainly seen. The gods on account of their limitations could not be made responsible for the irrational in life, that very part of it in which human instinct most strongly felt the intervention of a higher power. The old belief in ' power ' therefore survived in this sphere, but was developed in a way peculiar to the Greeks.

The conception of the *daimon* sometimes receives a touch of generality which brings it near to the idea of Fate. The belief in Fate exists in Homer, although vain attempts have been made to explain it away or to solve the problem of the relationship between the might and free will of the gods, and Fate which determines all. It is not our task to enter upon a theoretical discussion of this point, but rather to try to understand how the conception arose and developed.

Man who has acted in passion or infatuation has become a stranger to his own action. Not always, when he is conscious of the intervention of a higher power, does he speak of a *daimon*, some god, or Zeus as the cause ; he very often uses the words ' infatuation ', ' share ', ' lot ' (ἄτη, μοῖρα, μόρος, αἶσα). These words cannot denote any concrete gods. Of Ate (blind folly, infatuation) we have two allegories in Homer which cannot be misunderstood. By the side of the substantives μοῖρα, μόρος stand the verbal expressions εἵμαρται, ἔμμορε. When Moira later became a mythological, anthropomorphized figure, the participles (εἱμαρμένη, πεπρωμένη) were resorted to in order to express the old sense clearly. Nor was any attempt made to turn into a god the word πότμος, ' lot ', which contains a similar idea. The appellative sense of the words is the oldest and the original one : ' portion ', ' share ', ' lot ', ' that which falls to the lot of any one '. When anything not intended, anything unexpected happens, man does not always invoke the gods or ' power '. He also speaks of his lot, that which falls to him, in things that happen, just as he speaks of his portion, his share, of a meal, and it is his ' portion ' also that everything does not always go as he would wish. The portion is the due and regular share, such as every man has, of reverses and misfortune, no less than of success and happiness. A man may even engross more than his share. From this simple point of departure comes the expression which so surprises us in its usual translation of ' over[ruling] Fate ' (ὑπὲρ μόρον, ὑπὲρ αἶσαν). With it is involved the similar expression ὑπὲρ θεόν, which is usually translated ' contrary to the will of the gods '. The expression has acquired this meaning because the myth, after the fashion of the folk-tale, allows men to fight with and conquer the gods. It was an example which appealed to the Homeric man's delight in his own sense of strength, and to which Apollo himself alludes on one occasion. On the other hand this expression serves to free the gods from the responsibility for human misfortunes and to lay it upon men themselves.

Man is most ready to look for the intervention of a higher power when his plans are crossed and misfortune overtakes him. This again is his share of human life, his lot, his *moira*.

The same circumstances are at one moment regarded as an outcome of 'power', at another as man's lot or share ; the point of view is only different in so far as a higher power is or is not looked for behind that which has happened. Man speaks of *ate*, which has blinded him. Blind folly (ἄτη), the result of being blinded (ἀᾶσθαι), becomes by a simple transposition the subject of the sentence, the cause, the agency, which has brought about the blindness. If we consider the matter more profoundly, it is the division of personality whereby man disclaims the responsibility for his own actions that has caused this transposition. In the same way the words that mean 'share', 'lot' (μοῖρα, αἶσα) are substantives. They may therefore appear as subjects, and since the two lines of thought naturally become confused and cannot be kept apart, the words are used to denote the 'power' and appear as agents, causes. In the sequel they become personified ; the beginning is seen in the phrase 'the strong moira'. From this origin comes the gloomy shade of meaning which is attached to the word. For in misfortune and above all in that last and inevitable portion, death, the conflict between man's will and his lot in life comes out most clearly.

Death is the certain lot of man, his portion and his regular portion in life above all else. Legend certainly tells of heroes who have conquered death and men who have become immortal ; Calypso promises Odysseus immortality. But the confident expectation of death exerts so powerful an influence that it is said that not even the gods can avert it. Death projects his deep black shadow upon the fair life of men ; the Homeric man is seized with terror when confronted with the empty nothingness of the kingdom of the dead. Therefore the idea of death as the certain lot of all the living, predetermined and assigned simultaneously with birth, grips him with violence. From this thought fatalism arises ; its root is the inevitability of death. Death is man's portion, but he has also another portion in life. As soon as the portion appears as the due and regular share—and this is implied in the very word *moira*—fatalism spreads farther and brings the whole of human life under its sway. Homer has already set out upon this path. He has got so far that men are sometimes relieved of the responsibility of their actions.

Here, however, we find once again the idea of the universal ' power ', even though in a disguised form, developed by the increasing tendency to reflection upon the destinies of human life. For the different events in life have not each a separate *moira* as they have a separate *daimon*. Just as the word is one, so also are events manifestations of one *moira*. The word is nowhere found in the plural except in one late passage, in which personification has already taken place.

This circle of ideas moreover was exposed to the influence of mythological conceptions, which in part contributed to anthropomorphize *moira* and in part to develop fatalism. Just as the *moira* of death is assigned upon the day of birth, so the idea arises that the whole course of life is predetermined at birth. We see it in the well-known image of the destinies that the gods or the powers spin and wind for men, as the spun thread is wound upon the distaff, destinies, that is to say, which the gods allow to come upon them. This predetermination arises from the folk-tale motif of the gifts which the gods bring men on their birthdays or wedding-days, gifts which are to serve them in life. The myths of Meleager and Herakles are examples of this motif. The developing idea of the portion, *moira*, laid hold upon it, and thus arose the notion that fate, the course of life, is determined at birth.

Moira and the *daimones* upon one side, and the gods upon the other represent two stages in religious evolution. The one is earlier and less definite, but has developed in a later

and peculiar manner ; the other is younger and is charac-
terized by individual and highly specialized anthropomorphic
figures. The latter are therefore incapable of appearing as
the causes of all the emotions, all the events in which man
feels the working of a higher power. The Homeric gods
were obliged on account of their special character to leave
one sphere of activity to ' power ' and ' the powers '. As
they themselves were to a great extent Nature-gods, this
sphere became first and foremost the life of man in so far
as it is not determined by Nature. The limits are neither
fixed nor clearly drawn. The word *daimon* also includes
' god ', and ' god ' can also be used indefinitely or collectively
to denote ' power '. As soon as ' power ' has gained sub-
stantival denomination, for instance, as *moira*, the tendency
to personification makes itself felt, and anthropomorphism
follows in the train of personification. One god, Zeus, is of
so universal and all-embracing a nature that his influence
can be traced everywhere. He rules destinies as Moira does,
because he, like her, is an expression for the all-embracing
' power '.

The two systems, that of the gods and of ' power ', stand
upon different foundations : the powers remain behind upon
the old foundation which the gods have abandoned. The
dispute as to the relationship between the gods and Fate is
from the point of view of the history of religion a dispute
about words. Simple faith has no difficulty in acquiescing
in such contradictions. But the two systems may come into
conflict with each other. Homer has left *naïveté* behind
and is a rationalist. Logic has, therefore, imposed a problem upon religion. Sometimes, with the simplicity of an
earlier time, the gods and *moira* are unconcernedly placed
side by side : sometimes *moira* is conceived as determined
by the gods and Zeus. Zeus feels himself able to correct
moira, and refrains from doing so not from lack of power
but upon the exhortation of Hera. One system is here

subordinated to the other. *Moira* is not taken seriously;
we have merely one of the customary conflicts between two
gods.   But as soon as the underlying sense of order, and
therefore of something determined by Fate, was taken
seriously, the conflict was brought to a head.   The problem
was momentous, for the very existence of religion was
ultimately involved in it.   Religion in the proper sense was
not strong in Homer, and this fact is in great measure due
to the powerful rivalry of the other system.

It sometimes happened that ' power ' received a name
adapted to its particular expression.   Ate (Blind Folly) is
one, but there are several : Strife (Eris), Fear (Deimos,
Phobos), Uproar (Kydoimos), in fact perhaps even Ares (the
Destroyer) himself, all belong to the same company.   These
powers are written with capital letters and are called gods,
but they are without personality and individuality because
they are each nothing but a power of a certain kind.   They
are personifications.   Personification is not an abstraction
belonging to a late and far advanced period, as is often
said ; it is the bastard descendant of ' power ' and the god.
In its train followed allegory, and of this too there are
elaborate examples in Homer.   In regard to religious
problems, he left a rich and fatal inheritance to later ages,
both positively and negatively.

A few words finally as to the myths.   It is a common idea
that they form the principal contents of the Homeric
poems.   To a certain extent this is incorrect : it depends how
much is included in the term ' myth '.   I have already
several times pointed out that anthropomorphism has one
of its main roots in the folk-tale.   In the folk-tale the
supernatural beings play a great part ; they are there upon
a level with the human figures.   So long as the tale is a
folk-tale merely and confines itself to what we call the
lower figures of popular belief, preserving its innate fantastic
character, the contradiction involved in placing the super-

natural on a level with the human passes without remark. But this contradiction makes itself felt when polytheism is developed, the supernatural beings of popular belief are exalted into gods, and the gods enter in place of these popular beings into the folk-tale, which now begins to develop into the myth. The myths are, as Professor Wundt has pointed out, a creation of the heroic age after the pattern of its own conditions. There is added in the case of the Greeks the inborn rationalism which swept away the fantastic and magical elements inherent in the folk-tale. By this removal the anthropomorphic character of the myths was heightened and made still more prominent. We do not know what was the pre-Homeric form of the myths, otherwise than by uncertain and subjective conclusions from later versions which seem to us unlike Homer. We are, therefore, restricted to an examination of Homer himself in order to judge of the effect which the Homeric lines of thought had upon the mythology.

In the case of the myths also there is a difference between the passages in which the poet himself is speaking and those which are put into the mouths of his characters. When the poet speaks in his own person myths are as a rule absent ; the mythological allusions are limited to a brief citation of names in the genealogical trees of the heroes. The genealogies would seem to present an opportunity ready-made for mythological digressions ; yet only one such digression is found in the *Iliad* in the poet's own mouth, that of the origin of the two Thessalian heroes Menestheus and Eudoros. In the *Odyssey* digressions seem to be less rare, the most noteworthy being that relating to the seer Theoklymenos and his family, and there are two others, but in such close connexion with the subject that they can hardly be reckoned here, one about the scar which Odysseus had received while hunting the boar and which leads to his recognition, and the other about his bow, the gift of Iphitos. Otherwise all the mythological digressions, for instance, the stories of the fates which befell the heroes on their way home, are put into the mouths of the personages introduced by the poet ; even the myth of the love-affairs of Ares and Aphrodite is attributed to the singer Demodokos.

Mythological stories, even mythological allusions where they convey something more than mere names, are put into the mouths of the persons appearing in the poems. They are most often adduced as examples, warning or excusing, comforting or exhorting, or else they serve to embellish the genealogy. In prayers they are introduced as a reason for the granting of the prayer. When Nestor so readily relates the story of his youthful exploits this is not only a stroke of characterization but is meant as an example to incite the young. The fact is really curious, for opportunities for mythological digressions were not wanting in the epic poem. Instead, Homer loves to talk in similes. Only once does he take a detailed simile from mythology, when Odysseus compares Nausicaa to the virgin Artemis. The similes, which are for us one of the most prominent characteristics of epic style, are really something new ; they reveal another, far more advanced side of life than the heroic portions.[1] Astonishing as it may appear, it is a fact that the mythology was regarded as almost out of date by the Homeric singers. It was an old inheritance which they took over, but their interest was beginning to follow other paths.

If we compare Homer's own presentation of his heroes and gods with the mythology elsewhere, it becomes apparent that he has modified the myths in an anthropomorphic direction. The contest between the gods in Books XXI and XXII of the *Iliad* comes to nothing—Ares alone is struck down by Athena—notwithstanding the solemn proclamation and the magniloquent opening. The poet no

[1] A. Platt, *Homer's Similes* (*Journal of Philology*, xxiv, 1896, pp. 28 et seq.).

longer dares to follow the myth and let the gods come to blows with one another. Even a contest between gods and men is rare, notwithstanding the active interference of the gods upon the battle-field ; the only example occurs in the account of the exploits of Diomedes, the distinct character of which is also shown by the fact that it is richer in mythological allusions than any other book in Homer. The gods, as has been remarked, associate personally only with fabulous peoples, the Ethiopians and the Phaeacians. In the original myths men and gods stand upon quite another footing of equality. In a myth related by Homer Idas uses his bow against Apollo and takes from him his bride, Marpessa. The contests with the gods are elsewhere consistently presented by Homer as deterrent examples. In the very midst of his anthropomorphism the poet's rationalism claims its due ; he cannot imagine that a god can be struck like a man—for that is something which has never been seen—nor yet that man will not be worsted in his struggle against the all-powerful.

It is the same with the gifts of the gods. With the exception of the arms of Achilles they are an inheritance ; only the legendary heroes are granted personal gifts by the gods. The legends are more brutal than the epic, and this is true not only of the divine but also of the heroic myths. This brutality is echoed in Nestor's words about the heroes of former days, who were themselves the mightiest and strove with the mightiest, the wild beasts of the forest. Homer's well-known words : ' We are worse than our fathers ' are due not only to the memory of the vanished glories of the Mycenaean Age but also to the mighty figures of the myths, which a less simple age could not imitate. It is significant that when the old crude motifs are adopted, they readily acquire a burlesque character.[1] We have instances

[1] W. Nestle, *Die Anfänge einer Götterburleske bei Homer*, *NJb*, xv, 1905, pp. 161 et seq.

in the scene at the end of the first book of the *Iliad* where Hephaistos appears as a cup-bearer in order to put an end to the strife between the gods ; in Zeus' threats at the beginning of the eighth ; in the outwitting of Zeus by Hera, into which the poet has worked, in a fundamentally blasphemous manner, an old cult-myth ; in the punishment of Artemis by Hera, who beats her about the head with her own bow as though she were a naughty schoolgirl.; and in the outwitting of Proteus, by Menelaos and his people, with the help of Proteus' daughter. Respect for the myths has almost been lost on account of their absurdities, and there is a tendency to turn them to ridicule. The worst example is the story of the love-affairs of Ares and Aphrodite. This is the reaction of anthropomorphism and rationalism against the myth, which they could not entirely overcome or transform.

Unfortunately most of the mythological stories are quite short, and above all we do not know the pre-Homeric form of the myth, so that we cannot by direct comparison judge the extent and nature of the transformation. But it seems to me certain that Homer not only transforms the myths in an anthropomorphic direction but also deepens their psychology ; this too is anthropomorphizing them in an internal sense. The process is already seen in the fact that the myths are not related for their own sake, out of an interest in mythology, but are made to serve as examples, as warnings, or as comfort and encouragement. Even Herakles, we are told, succumbed to Fate and the extreme anger of Hera ; this must be a Homeric alteration of the myth. This psychological deepening and humanizing appears clearly at the close of the myth of Bellerophon, who, hated by the gods, wandered along about the Aleïan Field, eating his heart out and avoiding the paths of men. He is not a mythical hero but an unhappy man, a tragic, not a mythological figure. And, therefore, Homer's finest tales, those which we admire for their masterly descriptions of men—the wrath of Achilles, Hektor's leave-taking, Priam's prayer—are undoubtedly the poet's own intellectual creation. The love of the faithful pair in the *Odyssey* is not a myth but a romance, and the devotion of the swineherd Eumaios to his old master is taken from life, not from mythology.

Homer humanizes the mythology, introducing human feelings and conditions in place of the brutal and fantastic elements of the heroic legends. The cosmogony takes the old, crude myths in quite another and a serious way. In one respect the humanizing of the myths had no great success. Interest in the stories themselves arose, and was directed towards collecting and rounding off the myths without making them psychologically more profound. The newly aroused interest in cosmic questions found its first expression in the cosmogony, the brutal and fantastic character of which rather led to speculation than to anthropomorphism. In another respect, however, the influence was greater than any one would have thought. The words of Aeschylus, that tragedy is composed of crumbs from Homer's abundant table, are true, but they do not apply to the myths, as is generally supposed. The tragic poets as a rule take their mythological material from other quarters than Homer. The legacy bequeathed by Homer to tragedy is the humanizing of the myths, the creation of real suffering and feeling men and women, instead of the unreal princes and supermen of the legends.

The fables of the *Odyssey*, the stories of the adventures of Odysseus, stand upon a different plane. The folk-tale is here seen once more breaking out, although it is a folk-tale of a different kind from the old, which had already become mythological. Life in the Ionian seaside towns, the first geographical voyages of discovery, as one might well call those first bold sea-voyages, indicated a means of satisfying the desire for stories. Out there in far-off fabulous lands there was room for the element of fable which anthropomorphism could not endure.

The Homeric age inherited gods with the weaknesses of primitive gods and myths with the fantastic and inconsequent characteristics of the primitive tale. It did not erect any religious system but it remodelled its inheritance in accordance with two predominating lines of thought, anthropomorphism and rationalism. The latter played into the hands of the former by removing all the element of the supernatural and the wonderful, and by refashioning the inherited myths in accordance with human standards. It went farther. Rationalism, combined with the Homeric man's self-assertive confidence in his own power, took the first steps towards the overthrow of religion. It substituted the eternal sleep for the other life and cast doubts upon the omens of the gods. ' The old man did not interpret the dreams for them when they went away ', the poet scornfully remarks about the sons of the soothsayer Eurydamas, who fell at the hands of Diomedes. ' One omen is best, to fight for one's country,' says Hektor ; this, according to all the conceptions of antiquity, is blasphemy against the gods. But these are only occasional sallies. A consistently developed anthropomorphism is Homer's legacy to a later age. It was a splendid but contradictory legacy which the religion never overcame and never could overcome. The attempt to set up an ethical boundary between gods and men was diverted by anthropomorphism into the idea of the jealousy of the gods, an idea over which the Greeks wearied their brains in vain, for religious feeling could never rest content with it. The belief in ' power ', which had to compensate for that which was lacking in the gods, was refashioned into the belief in Fate, which, consistently developed, would remove the gods from their thrones.

The humanizing of the gods penetrated deep down among

the people notwithstanding the resistance of popular belief. Homer's anthropomorphism gave rise to the first criticism of religion, and for the development of the Greek mind it had an importance the full extent of which has never been realized. For this humanizing of the gods served to ward off the conception of divine power as the magical, wonder-working agency which prevails in many religions, for instance, the Egyptian. Under this all-compelling magical power of the gods man bows in fear and terror, but from its fetters the Homeric humanization of the gods delivered the Greeks. They could henceforth of their own accord and by their own efforts find order and coherence in the world. From this origin came Greek science. The Ionian rhapsodist paved the way for the Ionian philosopher of Nature, the latter building up where the former pulled down. In opposition to this, Apollo alone succeeded in erecting something resembling a church and a system of religious laws, but he was only one of the Olympians ; his work was therefore involved in the general fate of the Greek religion.

VI

LEGALISM AND MYSTICISM

THE Homeric nobility, governing a rural population which was in great measure of foreign extraction, developed a sense of self-esteem which was also directed against the gods ; in the poems we can see the demand of the Greek temperament for perspicuity and a rationally comprehensible presentation of phenomena. When the light of history begins to dawn upon the mother country, we find powerful religious movements of an entirely different character, having associations with ideas and practices which the Homeric world had outgrown. In Greece itself the development had not been broken off ; there it was attached by all its roots, and not merely by a few fibres, to the old traditions. But the mother country, too, was passing through a period of unrest and transformation.

These changes were principally political and social. The nobility had overthrown the old monarchy and taken the authority into its own hands. Most of the land, and the best part of it, belonged to the nobility, and when trade began and money was invented to form a basis for the beginnings of capitalism the aristocracy was able to take advantage of this also. The humbler population found itself politically and economically in an oppressive state of dependence rendered still more vexatious by economic distress. The land seems to a very large extent to have been portioned out in lots so small that one of them could not even provide a scanty living for a single family ; debts increased and crushed the common people, while the laws of debt were pitiless. A remedy offered itself in vigorous emigration—this was the time when the Mediterranean was encircled by Greek colonies—but it brought only an alleviation, not a complete cure. The demand of the people for more reasonable laws and a share in political power was beginning to make itself heard, but the populace itself was still too little developed to take the power into its own hands. Its leaders accordingly exalted themselves into tyrants, but tyranny could only be a transitional stage, until the political conditions at the close of the archaic period were consolidated under democratic or more mildly aristocratic forms.

It is against this political and social background that the mighty religious movements of the period should be viewed.[1] Distress drives man into the arms of religion. It increases the tenderness of his conscience in regard to offences against the gods and transgression of their commands. In the heightening of religious feeling he seeks oblivion of the miseries of life and the worries of the day. These are the two main currents in the tide of religious feeling which dominated the early historical period. For the first of them we have contemporary testimony of the greatest value in the *Works and Days* of Hesiod. All that we now read in that poem is not due to Hesiod : certain portions were inserted later, especially the collections of maxims and taboo ordinances and the rules about lucky and unlucky days which form the conclusion. These are for us of the greatest

---

[1] The chief work on this period is Rohde's *Psyche*, but it deals with only the one side of the subject, viz. ecstasy, mysticism, and catharism, not with the legalism which completes the picture of the period. The just published book of A. le Marchant, *Greek Religion to the Time of Hesiod*, has not yet reached me. As to the mysteries and Orphicism the ground was cleared by C. A. Lobeck, *Aglaophamus*, 2 vols., 1829. A perceptible want is the absence of any full account of the religious history of Delphi ; T. Dempsey, *The Delphic Oracle*, is a good, but summary account. A necessary preliminary, which has not yet been undertaken, would be the collection of the many oracles, even though only a small part of them be of value. An excellent source for the history of religion, as well as for other matters, is H. Diels, *Die Fragmente der Vorsokratiker*.

importance. Though slightly later, they date from the same period—the Appendix of the *Days* is already quoted by Herakleitos [1]—and they were assimilated with Hesiod's poem on account of their affinity to it.

Hesiod has two passions : the demand for justice and the call to work. *Facit indignatio versum.* His poem is a sermon of rebuke to his brother Perses, an idler who by the aid of unrighteous judges had deprived him of his inheritance and wasted it in sloth. Into this poem he introduces his farmers' rules, to teach how work is to be done. The close-fistedness of the peasant, exaggerated by the hard times, comes out in his polemic against woman, who eats the man out of house and home, in his advocacy of birth-control—for what else is his advice that one son should be reared so that prosperity may increase ?—and in his recommendation to engage a middle-aged farm-hand, who will not be always wanting companions, and a servant-girl with no children. He has the liking for maxims, animal fables, and enigmatical periphrases which is characteristic of rustic wisdom ; the snail is called ' the house-carrier ' ($\phi\epsilon\rho\acute{\epsilon}o\iota\kappa os$), the thief ' the man who sleeps by day ' ($\dot{\eta}\mu\epsilon\rho o\kappa o\acute{\iota}\tau\eta s$ $\dot{a}v\acute{\eta}\rho$), and so on.

The demand for justice is opposed by the violence and arbitrariness of the age. The stronger governs in accordance with his whim, just as the eagle said to the nightingale : ' If I wish, I will let you go ; if I wish, you will be a dainty morsel for me.' The aristocratic judges receive bribes. This drives the poet to outbursts of despair. ' May neither I nor my son be just ', he exclaims, ' since the unjust ever prevails.' The description of the present time, the Iron Age, with its need and its offences, begins with the cry : ' Would that I had not been born in this age, but either before or after it ! ' To the injustice and distress of the age he opposes justice, to which he is constantly exhorting his fellow men, for in justice he has a firm belief. Under its

[1] In Plutarch, *Camillus*, ch. 19.

protection cities flourish. Possessions unlawfully acquired soon disappear, for the gods watch over justice. Zeus is all-seeing ; he has 30,000 watchmen who, wrapped in cloud, roam over the earth and observe men's judgements and misdeeds. His daughter Dike sits with him and complains of the wicked hearts of men, begging him to punish them. Justice is that which distinguishes man from the beasts. Perjury is revenged upon posterity. Zeus repays any one who wrongs a fugitive, a guest, fatherless children, or his aged parents—the old ideas appear with redoubled strength and intensity.

Work and justice are the fundamental institutions of the world. Hesiod pondered over justice, and he also thought much about work. In his day labour was too hard and yielded too little return. He does not know the inward satisfaction which work in itself can give, but it is to him a hard compulsion of necessity. Homer lets the gods live ' easily ', without sorrows or hardships, and the myth told of the Islands of the Blest, where the necessaries of life had not to be forced out of the ground by toil. So Hesiod was driven to inquire how toil, the harsh inheritance of man, came into the world. He had a tendency to think in mythical forms, and therefore he had recourse to the old myths. Many primitive peoples relate stories of the introduction of culture and its elements among men, and the Greeks too had similar early myths. The culture-heroes readily come into hostile relationships with the gods ; for they steal the elements of civilization from the gods and bring them to men. This was why Prometheus, the fire-bringer in the Greek myth, became the enemy of Zeus and was included among the Titans ; the idea that the human race in the morning of the world lived without hardships and sorrows has transformed the myth. Zeus, in his anger that Prometheus had deceived him, ' hid the means of subsistence ' from men, and also hid fire. Prometheus brought fire back ; Zeus then sent woman. The old myths are introduced as strokes and counter-strokes in a contest between Zeus and Prometheus. The fable of Pandora is a myth of the creation of woman, which the woman-hating poet has converted into Zeus' final revenge upon the human race. The story has a sequel—the box which the woman in her curiosity opens, thereby letting loose upon men misfortunes and diseases, hope alone remaining. It is true that this is an addition to the Pandora myth, but on the other hand this addition alone gives a full and complete explanation why the world has become what it is.[1]

The question so keenly interested the poet that he has yet another answer to give, the myth of the ages of the world. Its basis is twofold, first the perception that there was a time when iron was wanting and weapons and tools were made of bronze—to Hesiod should be given the credit of having discovered the Bronze Age—and secondly the mythological idea of the happy and easy life under the sway of Kronos. The ages of the world were given names and were graded according to the metals ; the present age became the Iron Age in contrast with that which preceded it, the Bronze Age, and the rule of Kronos became the Golden Age. The scheme necessitated the introduction of a Silver Age, although it is obviously only an expedient. The heroic myth forbade the representation of the age of the heroes as a time of mere degeneracy, and therefore the Heroic age was introduced as the fourth, between the Bronze and the Iron Ages ; but the colours in which it is painted are borrowed from the Bronze Age, which becomes devoid of substance.[2] What Hesiod has created is a mythical history of the

[1] The most recent treatment of E. Schwartz, *Prometheus bei Hesiod* (*Sitzungsberichte der Akademie zu Berlin*, 1915, pp. 133 et seq.), deals too rationistically with the myth.

[2] Compare Ed. Meyer, *Hesiods Erga und das Gedicht von den fünf Menschengeschlechtern* (*Genethliakon für Robert*, 1910, pp. 157 et seq., reprinted with some additions *Kleine Schriften*, ii, pp. 15 et seq.).

development of the human race, the first philosophy of history.

This questioning and meditative attitude in regard to the riddles of human life and the divine world is characteristic of the age. The cosmogony, which had previously existed in scattered myths, was worked up into a connected whole. Hesiod does not share Homer's repugnance to the old crude myths in which the cosmogony abounds ; on the contrary he has an undeniable liking for them, as well as for fabulous monsters, which he introduces into his genealogies. He is himself conscious of the opposition to Homer ; in his invocation to the Muses he makes them say that they can sing many lies which resemble truth, but can also, when they wish, sing of the truth itself. Hesiod lays claim to be the prophet of the truthful Muses.

Like all primitive cosmogony, that of Hesiod proceeds on the assumption that there was something existing from the beginning. The world was not made out of nothing, but creation consisted in the moulding of the primitive substance into definite forms. Accordingly Chaos is placed at the beginning, after which arose Gaia, Tartaros, and Eros (Love). It is commonly said that Hesiod, without following it up, has propounded a deep thought, that of Eros as the generating principle, the driving force in development. The truth is that Eros is described by the ordinary Homeric epithets, while everything that follows is but a series of physical conceptions. The description of the development of the universe by the method of generation, the only form of development comprehensible to the poet's age, shows clearly enough what Hesiod means by the place he has given to Eros. In the trace of a cosmogony which is to be found in Homer it seems to be water, Okeanos, that is the first principle, and this agrees with the ideas of many peoples. Hesiod goes farther back, but his first principles are very largely speculative philosophical conceptions,

notwithstanding the fact that they are now written with
capital letters as though they were personified. From Chaos
arose Darkness and Night ; of these were born Ether and
Day.   Gaia gave birth spontaneously to Heaven, the
high Mountains, and the Sea, and with Heaven she gave
birth to Okeanos. Hesiod has now reached the point at
which Homer began. The mythological names are a transparent covering for the first natural philosophy. The
latter has its origin in the mythical cosmogony and long
preserves the mythological names for its principles. This
is the case in Pherekydes and even far later in Empedocles,
who calls his four elements Zeus, Hera, Aidoneus, and
Nestis, and gives to the driving forces of development the
names of Love and Strife. Here Greek rationalism has done
the work that was to be expected of it. The mythological
explanation of the universe was transferred to the realm of
philosophy and finally compelled even to discard its mythological dress. Mythology was once more relegated to its
proper sphere. Hesiod, however, is still chiefly a mytholo-
gist : he relates in detail the crudely primitive cosmogonic
story of the mutilation of Uranus, and gives long lists of
personifications—Moros, Ker (Fate), Momos (Blame), Oïzys
(Distress), &c.—which he inserts in his genealogies.

The portions of Hesiod's *Works and Days* which are later
additions show how the demand for the observance of
justice is extended from the relationships of men with one
another to their relationships with the gods. Piety is
inculcated. Men should sacrifice according to their ability,
and should pray and pour out libations both at rising and
at bed-time. Even in the farmers' rules we find the direction
to pray to Zeus and Demeter when the hand is laid to the
plough to begin the work of autumn. Religious devotion
takes possession of daily life in a fashion which is otherwise
unknown in Greece.

This condition of mind helps to explain the superstitious

injunctions contained in the concluding part of the work. Some are purificatory rules concerning sexual life and the performing of the natural functions, which are always especially associated with taboo. The prohibition against pouring libations with unwashed hands is as old as Homer. Reverence for the rivers, which filled an important place in the Greek cult, is inculcated by further commands. Others again embody popular ideas of taboo, for which parallels can be found both among primitive peoples and in modern folk-lore.[1] The finger-nails must not be pared at a sacrifice, just as is now forbidden on a Sunday ; the ladle must not be placed across the mixing-vessel, just as it is still considered unlucky to cross knife and fork. Children, who are particularly susceptible to evil influences, must not sit upon a tombstone; a man must not bathe in a woman's bath, &c.

The strict observance of these ritual ordinances was taken up by men who considered themselves to be something better than others. We are accustomed to regard the Pythagoreans as a philosophical school, but they are just as much a religious sect. Several of Hesiod's taboo ordinances are found again among the so-called Pythagorean precepts ; their number was augmented by others, but these, too, are derived from popular ideas of taboo,[2] for instance, the prohibition against breaking bread, against picking up crumbs which have fallen under the table, against stepping over a broom or the beam of a balance. Others refer to the cult ; a shrine must be entered from the right and quitted from the left, the worshipper must be dressed in a clean garment in which no one has slept ; at sacrifices he must be barefoot, he must not blink when pouring a libation, must not pluck the leaves from a wreath, must not even kill a louse within the sacred precincts. More peculiar to the

[1] E. E. Sikes, *Folk-lore in the ' Works and Days ' of Hesiod* (*Class. Review*, vii, 1893, pp. 389 et seq.).

[2] F. Böhm, *De symbolis Pythagoreis*, Dissertation, Berlin, 1905.

Pythagoreans is the development of special rules concerning diet, which conclude with the well-known prohibition of animal food.

A great many of these decrees are based on well-known popular ideas, but in Hesiod they are on the way to becoming laws as to ritual purity, enjoining certain ablutions at a sacrifice or when crossing a river, certain occasions when sexual intercourse is forbidden—in short, legalism bids fair to seize upon human life. The great mass of the people were exempt from these bonds, while the Pythagoreans, who took them upon themselves, were sharply distinguished from the crowd ; nevertheless the beginning of a codification of ritual laws exists in Hesiod. Nothing was wanting but their systematic development and their presentation as decrees of the gods binding on mankind, and the fetters of legalism would have been fastened on the whole of life. But it is to the esteem of men and not to the gods that Hesiod looks for the enforcing of his precepts. The anthropomorphic gods of the Greeks did them the service of not troubling about the minor affairs of life provided that the simple and easy demands of the cult were complied with. Nevertheless the ritual law was not far off.

Further evidence for this is given in the very last part of Hesiod, the *Days*. All peoples have observed the varying phases of the moon and have reckoned in months, and so also did the Greeks. During this period the Greek time-reckoning was regulated, by the aid of Delphi, in accordance with lunar months.[1] The observance of certain days of the month thereby acquired increased weight, the old festivals becoming associated with certain fixed days of the month. In particular they were assigned to the days of full moon, which are everywhere considered the most lucky.

---

[1] See my *Die Entstehung und sakrale Bedeutung des griechischen Kalenders* (*Lunds Universitets Årsskrift*, xiv, 1918, no. 21), pp. 43 et seq.

The people took kindly to this regulation by the sacral calendar ; it agreed with popular belief that everything which was to grow and increase should be carried out under the waxing moon, while that which was done when the moon was on the wane should diminish and decline. The twelfth day of the moon-month is the best for general business as well as for festivals. Hence arose a long list of lucky and unlucky days for various tasks and under-takings ; upon the reasons for their distribution it is vain to speculate. The superstitious regulation in accordance with the days of the month took the place of the practical regulation of agricultural work by the stars. The calendar regulation undoubtedly emanated from Delphi and it might have been expected that Apollo would take the choice of ·days also into his charge. But he did not do so ; the days are said by Hesiod to originate in ' Zeus the Counsellor ', who is the supreme protector of all law. Apollo was a god, and he thought more of the gods than of men. The desire for ritual standards for life, which existed among the masses of the people, found no support in a divine authority.

The establishment of the civil law proceeded on parallel lines with the development of the sacral and ritual laws, and in fact the recording and development of the law was the great concern of the age. This was the period of the great lawgivers, Charondas, Zaleucus, Draco, and Solon, who rather codified the existing unwritten laws than created new ones. Thus law was a prominent interest both in pro-fane and religious life. Profane law (as well as religious law) had been placed from time immemorial under divine pro-tection. Zeus watches over law and justice, and even after men had begun consciously to shape and alter the positive laws, Zeus sees that justice takes her proper course. For all primitive peoples law has divine sanction and authority, and this idea was not yet forgotten. It was, therefore, only natural that the legislative activity of the age should seek to invest the law with divine authority. The method employed was to learn the will of the gods from their oracles. The ancient traditions of the support and help of Apollo in establishing the civil law are in harmony with the temper and requirements of the age.

It matters little whether the figure of Lycurgus is purely mythical or conceals a germ of historical truth ; the important point is that in public opinion the laws of Sparta were supported by the authority of Delphi. Herodotus says that, according to some, the Delphic oracle revealed the laws to Lycurgus ; in Sparta it was said that he got them from Crete. The latter is the more scientific explanation, which is based on the great resemblance between social conditions in Sparta and in Crete. Tyrtaeus does not know Lycurgus as the founder of the Spartan order of society, but for him, too, it is derived from the god at Delphi. Demonax of Mantinea was sent by the oracle to Cyrene as a lawgiver ; according to another story he went to Delphi before beginning his work.[1]

The legislative activity in Athens is the best known. The connexion with Delphi is here less prominent, but there are nevertheless unmistakable and very real signs of it. Draco instituted laws dealing with murder and homicide ; that these did not come into existence without the co-operation of Delphi is clear. We shall return to this point farther on. Again, when Cleisthenes overthrew the old basis of state organization by establishing his ten phylae, the oracle was called upon to choose the ancestral heroes of the new phylae. Solon's connexions with Delphi are mere anecdotes ; but notwithstanding this we are on firm ground in regard to the sacral legislation. The ancient accounts divide his

[1] The controversies as to the existence of Lycurgus and the date at which Tyrtaeus lived must be left on one side. For Demonax see Herodotus, iv. 161, and the epitome compiled by Heraklides Lembos out of the writings of Hermippus about the legislators, Oxyrhynchus Papyri, xi, no. 1367.

work into the civil and the sacral laws. The cult was one side of the activity of the state, and its regulation formed one half of Solon's work. Part of the sacral legislation was concerned with the regulation of festivals, of *fasti*. The festivals of the gods had to be celebrated at the proper times ; the importance attached to this can be seen from the choosing of special days. The festivals were appointed for certain particular days in accordance with the lunar calendar, and hence arose a systematic calendar which was also of use in civil life. The connexion with Delphi here becomes apparent. The luni-solar calendar comes from Delphi and is under the special protection of Apollo. Further evidence of this is furnished by the instructions which Plato gives in the *Laws*, and which rest upon the tradition formed during the period of Delphi's greatness. Plato lays it down as the duty of the legislator, with the oracle's help, to regulate the festivals and determine what sacrifices shall take place and to which gods they shall be offered. In another passage he enumerates all that falls within the province of the oracle— the founding of shrines, sacrifices, the cults of the gods, *daimones*, and heroes, the graves of the departed and the manner of appeasing the dead—and he instructs his law- giver to apply for assistance to ' the ancestral exegete ', Apollo. The passage is especially important for its invoca- tion of ancestral custom, which the Delphic ordinances were meant to follow.

In order rightly to adjust their relations with the gods, men needed a divine court of appeal, some divine authority which would tell them what was fitting and right. Here was a limit to the sovereignty of the people. Neither a majority in the popular assembly nor the civil legislator could decide in respect of what related to the gods. Apollo was ready to help, either by means of his oracle or through his deputies, the ' interpreters ' (exegetes). The exegetes were no doubt originally men of special experience in the sacral system and its traditions, but they had come under the influence of Delphi and leaned upon its authority because the new problems embraced more than ancestral custom could decide. In Athens there were two kinds of exegetes, those elected by the people and those appointed by the oracle. The latter seem to have been the more important ; they attended to purifications, the interpretation of the oracles, the calendar, and so forth—anything which appertained to the particular province of Apollo. There were exegetes in other states also. Thus Apollo secured representatives who spread his ideas and worked for him, but they were citizens of their own particular states, just as the priesthood in general was, and not the bond-slaves of the god. Herein lay the structural weakness of his religious organization, and this in turn was due to the relation between state and religion inherited from earlier generations. Apollo always enjoined upon his followers to worship the gods according to ' the law of the city ' or according to ' ancestral custom '. Ancestral custom was well known and in ordinary cases there was no uncertainty as to what had to be done. But disputes might arise which the exegetes could not settle, and then Apollo must be applied to for authoritative advice. There might also be important occasions when the advice and help of the gods was more urgently needed than at other times. Thus, the Athenians turned to Delphi before the battle of Plataeae and were informed that they must sacrifice to the seven local heroes of the place. In the myths the constant reason why resort is had to Delphi is some national disaster, famine, or plague, in which the wrath of the gods is revealed, and such calamities occurred likewise in real life. Ancestral custom was on such occasions insufficient. In particular it was inadequate when a cult was to be reorganized, or new cults were established and new gods arose with claims to men's worship and to influence over human minds. Thus Cleisthenes of Sikyon asked counsel of Delphi when he wished to be rid of the cult of Adrastos. The god insisted upon the ancestral custom and reprimanded the tyrant, but the latter, as was the way of tyrants, achieved his purpose in a roundabout manner. When the pious Xenophon founded a shrine to Ephesian Artemis at Elis, he bought for the purpose a piece of land situated where the Delphic god directed.

This was the great age of emigration, during which Greek colonies were founded all round the shores of the Mediterranean. The protection of the gods had to be sought for the numerous bands of emigrants, just as Xenophon, when he was about to join in the expedition of Cyrus, asked Apollo to which gods he should sacrifice in order to come safely back. The cults of the new city had to be arranged. The emigrants took some gods with them from the mother country, others they found in their new homes. I am inclined to think that herein lies the starting-point of that undeniably great and much discussed influence of Delphi upon the Greek colonization.[1] When the Phocaeans, for instance, set off to found Massilia, they were advised to take Ephesian Artemis as their guide, and her cult consequently became the most important in the new city. Men had always been accustomed to inquire of the gods, even in regard to their own purely worldly concerns, and it was only natural that those who hoped to find new dwelling-places in foreign lands should do the same. Apollo could give good advice ; for into Delphi poured people from all quarters of the Greek world, as well as from foreign lands to which Greek influence had reached—Lydia, Etruria, tradition said even Rome. Here was amassed a knowledge of the world such as no other place could offer. It is, therefore, no wonder, that the oracle is represented as the leader of colonization.

[1] The most recent treatment is that of A. S. Pease, *Notes on the Delphic Oracle and the Greek Colonization* (*Class. Philology*, xii, 1917, pp. 1 et seq.).

No other religious movement took so powerful a hold upon men's minds as the Dionysiac ecstasy. It was something new, something in conflict with ancestral custom. That Apollo managed to bring the ecstasy under control by the force of legalism, to fit it into ancestral custom and himself to derive new vigour from it, is the strongest proof of his power. This will require detailed exposition later on.

The sense of duty towards gods and men was extended also to the world of the dead. It is partly due to this sense that the hero-cult flourished during this period. Among the heroes there lurked local deities, and new and less important cults readily took on the form of the hero-cult, for the heroes were not, like the gods, a company limited in numbers by ancestral tradition. It had not been forgotten that a mortal after death might join the company of the heroes. But the divine authority had to decide when a cult of this kind, having arisen, was to be recognized, when a dead man could lay claim to a cult not only among his relatives but among all his fellow citizens. It was to Apollo that men turned for the decision ; he canonized the heroes. Apollo has been blamed and accused of raising into heroes men who had gone mad and committed outrages. But it is forgotten that he stood upon the ground of ancestral custom. Kleomedes of Astypalaia had certainly done these things, but his death, the disappearance of his body, showed that there was something supernatural about him. The hero-cult is more than any other apotropaeic ; it is designed to appease the mighty dead, who are by no means slow to wrath. This should not be forgotten when the interference of Apollo in the cult of heroes is criticized. It is the rule, even in historical examples, that the hero's wrath sends disasters, plague, and famine, and that he is appeased according to the instructions of Delphi. When famine and pestilence broke out in the town of Kition in Cyprus, the oracle ordered its inhabitants not to forget Kimon, the victor at Salamis in Cyprus. Ever after-

wards his grave there was worshipped with honours befitting
a hero. A typical example is the story told by Herodotus
of the shipwrecked Phocaeans who had landed at Agylla
(Caere) in Etruria and had been stoned by the inhabitants.
Men and animals who trod upon the scene of the crime fell
down dead or became crippled. The oracle ordained that
the dead should be appeased by sumptuous offerings and
games. This is the honour paid to heroes, although the
fact is not expressly stated.

Here the connexion between the cult of heroes and the
expiation of blood-guiltiness, one of Apollo's best-known
functions, is very clearly seen. With blood-guiltiness is
associated the primitive custom of vengeance for blood. That
both are wanting in Homer is an illusion : in the mother
country they survived. The important point is that Apollo,
who was the god of purifications and expiations—all ancient
ceremonies of the kind were converted into Apollo festivals—
took special charge of the expiation for blood. The force
with which the problem of vengeance seized upon men's
minds is shown in the myth of Orestes, which according to
a general assumption was elaborated in a Delphian epic.
Who is the avenger, when the wife has killed her husband ?
The son, hers and the murdered man's, is the logical answer.
Apollo drives him to perform the duty of blood-vengeance
but also purifies him. And this is sufficient ; for the son
has only done his duty according to the decrees of ancestral
law. The god approved of this logic, but human feeling rose
against it, as is shown by the version of the myth in Aeschylus
and Euripides.

Hand in hand with the sacral regulation of purification
from blood-guiltiness went the state regulation of vengeance
for blood. Apollo must have seen how advantageous it was
for him that the state should take vengeance into its own
hands and make it impossible in practice for a son to be
involved in the same clash of duties as was Orestes. The

state cancelled the old right and duty of the murdered man's kinsmen to exact blood for blood, regardless of whether the blood had been shed with criminal intent or by accident; it took the punishment into its own hands and meted it out in accordance with the intention. A man who had unintentionally caused the death of another went free, but he must be purified, and until that was done he was cut off from all association with the gods or his fellow men. Every house was closed to him, no one dared to come near him, the mere contact with his clothes, indeed the very sight of him, rendered a person unclean. It was a hard but wholesome lesson, which Apollo pressed home. The destruction of a human life could not be taken lightly, as it had been during the Homeric period. By insisting absolutely and without exception upon this demand, which harmonized with the feeling of the age in favour of ritual purity, Apollo gave emphasis and gravity to the claim that human life should be respected. He himself set a good example. Even after killing the dragon Pytho he had subjected himself to a thorough purification. First and foremost he was inculcating even in this matter respect for the sanctity of the gods. At Sybaris the people had killed a zither-player at Hera's altar. When men from Sybaris came to the oracle, they were driven away. The victor at Plataeae, Pausanias, had been caught plotting against his city and had taken refuge in the temple of Athena Chalkioikos. The Spartans barred the doors of the temple and let him starve to death. The oracle forced them to make amends. Blood-guiltiness which is not expiated falls upon the whole people and city. It is related that when a metragyrt, a begging priest engaged in propaganda for the cult of the Great Mother of Asia Minor, came to Athens about the year 430, the Athenians flung him into the barathron, where he died. Thereupon the great plague overtook Athens. The oracle commanded that his death should be atoned for and that a temple should be built to the Great Mother.

This purification was entirely ritual, an external rite, but its importance should not be underestimated. It gave a definite form to the fear of the dead man's vengeance. It heightened the respect for human life and supported the state in its efforts to do away with the practice of the vendetta and substitute its own judgement. In other cases, again, Apollo intensified the purity of the cult. It will be sufficient to mention the purification of fire, for even fire could be contaminated. After the battle of Plataeae pure fire was fetched from Delphi in order to set alight the sacrifice for victory. The Athenians brought pure fire from Delphi in a brilliant procession ; [1] ' fire-bearer ' is the name of certain functionaries in the cult of Apollo to whom there are many references.

Apollo's standpoint was ritual, but his doctrine was capable of refinement and undoubtedly paved the way to a higher morality. Many are inclined to exaggerate this influence, and it is an exaggeration to compare the Apolline movement with the contemporary prophetic movement in Israel. Hesiod could better support the comparison. Apollo did not understand the profundity of Hesiod's demand for justice : his was the external ritualism. The inward state of mind has its importance for him also, but the right state of mind consists in not exalting oneself and in following the commands of the gods and the customs of one's forefathers.

Later sources quote certain remarks of the god as to sacrifices from which it has been concluded that Apollo held the view that the widow's mite was the most acceptable offering to the gods. But the point is not that a small offering given with a devout mind is the best : the rich Magnesian too is devout, while the poor man from Hermione, who has offered a pinch or two of flour, becomes obnoxious when he pours out the whole sackful. The point is rather that pride in making large and costly gifts to the gods is to be

[1] A. Boëthius, *The Pythais*, Uppsala, 1918.

condemned.[1] Man is not to exalt himself even in his piety. The type of the Apolline piety is Clearchus of Methydrion, who performed all the monthly and yearly rites as well as he was able. The ritual law should so have entered into a man's blood that he will perform almost instinctively, as the Hermionensian did at first, that which ancestral custom enjoins in regard to the gods. Religion enters into daily life in the way that it does in Hesiod ; this is the great and important point of contact between him and Apollo. Apollo sets himself against self-exaltation in religion and cult and teaches obedient submission to the decrees of the gods.

A similar idea undoubtedly underlies Apollo's opposition to the tyrants, for instance, to the Peisistratidae in Athens and the Orthagoridae of Sicyon ; this attitude is not adopted merely in compliance with the politics of Sparta, but the matter is one that touches the god's own heart. In spite of their detestation of the tyrants, the Greeks could not help admiring them as ' the equals of the gods ', who, like the gods, could permit themselves to do whatever they pleased. But Apollo inculcates μηδὲν ἄγαν, ' no excess ', ' do not exalt thyself '. Man should know himself to be in subjection to the gods ; he should submit to the decrees of the oracle. Several legends were remodelled in this direction under Delphic influence. Sentences such as these : ' For the righteous one drop is sufficient, but a wicked man not even the ocean with its currents can wash clean,' or, ' Purity consists in a devout frame of mind,' are not met until much later.[2] As an illustration of Apollo's demands for a higher purity of purpose the story of Glaukos in Herodotus is often quoted. Glaukos inquired of Delphi whether he might by perjury acquire property that had been entrusted to him. The god answered : ' Swear, for even the upright must die ; but the oath has a son which will root out the perjurer's

---

[1] Th. Plüss, *Phidyle*, *NJb*, iii, 1899, pp. 498 et seq.

[2] But compare Hesiod, *Opera*, v. 740, κακότητ' ἰδὲ χεῖρας ἄνιπτος.

race, while the children of the upright shall be rewarded with blessing.' Significantly enough, this crime, perjury, is one whose punishment has from time immemorial been regarded as quite specially belonging to the gods, but we have here something really new. Even the criminal intention is punishable, or rather the attempt to induce the god to sanction it. The oracle replied to the repentant Glaukos: ' To tempt the gods and to do what is evil is all one.' Apollo never reached higher, although even this is not the ethics of the prophets.

Advice was sought and obtained from the oracle on the trivial details of daily life and in worldly troubles. What it did to lighten guilty consciences in the minor affairs of every day escapes our knowledge. It gave advice to statesmen and colonists, but all this does not explain the predominating position of Apollo in the intellectual and religious life of the age. The explanation may be given in a word : his task was to secure peace with the gods. It was an age of political and social unrest and distress, with which came religious disturbance and need. Men felt their consciences oppressed by conscious and unconscious transgressions of the god's commands, their souls seized by a new religious longing and aspiration. In the midst of all this they sought a fixed centre and a sure path. Laws were drawn up and the life of society was regulated. In the religious sphere men longed for the same things. While demanding justice which should deal evenly with them, they were ready to grant the gods also their due. The anger of the gods was revealed in the disasters of the period : here human authority was not enough. The laws of men were supported by divine authority, and still more was that authority needed in questions that involved the relations of men with the gods.

These are the grounds for Apollo's influence over the souls of men. He was the authority who restored and maintained peace with the gods. His task was not to arouse consciences,

as the prophets did, but to calm them. He was not a
religious revolutionary, hardly even a reformer. He built
upon an old foundation, or, to change the figure, planted
new and wild shoots in the old ground. He regulated
festivals and cult. He adopted the old demand for ritual
purity, especially in that expiation of blood which penetrated
so deeply into the life of the community. He regulated the
worship of heroes. He tamed the Dionysiac ecstasy and
led the cult of the god into the accustomed paths of the
Grecian cultus. But his limitation lies in the fact that he
was one of the Olympians. He stood on the same foundation
as the ancient gods and could, therefore, create no new
religious values. His advice is constantly ' according to the
law of the city ', ' according to ancestral custom '. There
were things which were beneath his dignity, the taboo
ordinances of Hesiod and the Pythagoreans, which, systema-
tically developed and sealed with the stamp of divine
authority, could have placed not only a sect, but the masses
in general, under the bonds of ritual law. As it was, these
ideas lived on as superstitions among the people or within
a sect, and died away. Neither had Apollo any means of
subjugating human life to rules. For that a sacred book
would have been necessary, whereas he was content with
refashioning the old legends in the spirit of Delphi. He
would further have required a priesthood which was ex-
clusively in his service ; but his representatives, the exegetes,
were citizens of the state like other men. Their dependence
on Delphi was a voluntary subjection. The Apolline
tradition lived and spoke through the mouths of Pythia
and the exegetes when its counsels were needed.

Apollo had only glimpses of a higher ethics. The great
ethical demand of the age, the cry for justice which rises to
meet us from the pages of Hesiod, did not reach him. Hesiod
appeals to Zeus, the patron of justice. Apollo represented
himself as the mouthpiece of Zeus, in that capacity acting

also as a loyal member of the Olympian family of divinities. The consequence was, however, that the position of Zeus as the protector of the order of society and the upholder of justice was arrested in its development ; his overshadowing authority was weakened. The rivalry of his son thrust him into the background, with every expression of filial devotion. With other means, but with the same result, Dionysos exercised his rival claims upon the minds of men. We no longer find that strict subordination of the many gods of polytheism to one supreme god, superior to all not only in power but also in moral force, of which evident traces are to be found persisting in Homer. Many-headed polytheism, assisted by the particularism of the Greek states, carried the day.

The depth and nature of the religious movement upon which Apollo erected his power is only fully understood when we consider other movements of a kindred nature. It is also instructive to see in what respects these went farther than Apollo and what the latter rejected, and to note how and where connecting threads lead to Delphi.

Pythagoras occupies a place in the history of philosophy ; he fills an equally notable place in the history of religion. In him the sense of formal law was so strongly developed that when he discovered the regularity of the mathematical laws of number he laid them down as the basis of existence. In religious matters his school was a sect which taught a new doctrine of the greatest importance, the transmigration of souls. This doctrine affected the popular ideas of taboo that had been adopted to the extent that these were finally made to include the prohibition of animal food. The characteristics of a sect, which we here meet for the first time, are significant. The Pythagoreans knew themselves to be something more than others and, therefore, shut themselves off from the surrounding world. They show close affinity to the Orphics but their connexions with

Delphi were also quite plain to antiquity. 'Pythagoras' means 'mouthpiece of Delphi'; it sounds like a *nom de guerre*. At Croton Pythagoras was identified with Hyperborean Apollo, and tradition said that he had obtained most of his ethical maxims from Delphi. This shows what men, at least in certain circles, would gladly have received from Delphi had Apollo given it.

There are curious figures in Apollo's company. Pythagoras was said to perform miracles. Hermotimus of Clazomenae, who was later made one of the philosopher's previous incarnations, had the power of causing his soul to leave the body for long periods, during which it roamed about in far-off lands and experienced occult things, while the body lay as if dead. On one such occasion his enemies seized the opportunity and burned his body. Aristeas of Proconnesos had the same power. Once, Herodotus tells us, upon entering a shop in his native town, he fell down dead, but at the same time a traveller far away had met him and spoken to him. His dead body vanished, and not for six years did he reveal himself again. At Metapontum he ordered the building of an altar and the erection of a statue to Apollo; the god was to appear accompanied by Aristeas himself in the form of a raven. He is said to have written an epic about a legendary people far to the north, the Arimaspians. Both Aristeas and Abaris are mentioned by Pindar. Abaris too had connexions with Apollo and the fabulous northern races which played so great a part in the Apolline legend. He is said to have been a Hyperborean who carried the god's arrow about in different countries, and took no food. Plato mentions him and also a certain Zamolxis—a Getic god who had been admitted into this company and made a disciple of Pythagoras—as authors of charms against sickness. Somewhat later it is said that he had learned oracles from Apollo and on the occasion of a great plague had come to Athens and delivered the world by means of certain sacrifices.

In these figures appear two curious characteristics of the Delphic religion of Apollo : the ecstasy, in which the soul leaves the body and roams about independently, and the mission, as the apostle of which Abaris travels about the world. The religion of Apollo differs from all other Greek religions in having a missionary character. The Greek cults are usually bound to the particular locality, and especially those in which the god is named after the place ; but the Pythian and Delian Apollo are found everywhere in Greece. Wherever these epithets are met, they testify to the missionary activity proceeding from Delphi and Delos. Apollo himself was a migrating god. In all probability he came from Asia Minor, bringing with him rites of purification and the beginnings of a regulation of the calendar. The epiphany plays an unusually important part in his cult. To Delphi he comes from his devout Hyperboreans, originally upon his feast-day, the seventh of the month of Bysios, the only day on which in ancient times oracles were given. The epiphany became a means of uniting all the various places of his cult.

The most famous of all these miracle-workers, seers, and purificatory priests is Epimenides of Crete. He is certainly an historical figure, but legend has spun her webs about him and created insoluble difficulties. According to Aristotle he was brought to Athens to expiate the blood-guiltiness incurred in the suppression of Kylon's attempt to make himself a tyrant. Plato says that he came to Athens ten years before the Persian wars, and in the fragments ascribed to him some have found an allusion to Athens at the time of Cleisthenes' alteration of the constitution. The legend is especially important as an illustration of the mental atmosphere of the age. It relates that he fell asleep in a cave and woke after fifty-seven years. He lived on certain wild plants, and his soul could leave the body for considerable periods. Several poems were also ascribed to him.

All these figures have in common a certain resemblance

to the sorcerers of the nature peoples. They fast and fall
into hypnotic trances while their souls wander about in
far-off lands. The arts of purification and of prophecy are
in them combined with ecstasy as they are in the primitive
sorcerers. They are seers and purificatory priests. From
them, and not, as is usually stated, from Dionysos, Apollo
learned the art of ecstatic prophecy which his priestess at
Delphi practised. But they belonged to an advanced
culture, and worked for their ideas through poetry. To
these men is ascribed an abundant literature of poems about
the origin of the gods and the world, about distant, pious,
fabulous peoples, about purifications—a literature which
was in great measure a refashioning of earlier epics for
purposes of propaganda. We may include in the same class
of writings the numerous collections of oracles which were in
circulation. Bakis is the collective name for the male
prophets, and Sibylla for the female. Heraclitus already
speaks of the sibyl who, urged by the god, utters with foam-
ing mouth words naked and unadorned, and whose voice
reaches through the ages. How much of what was subsequently associated with the sibyl is to be traced back to this
period we cannot tell. Her mere name is valuable as an
evidence of the tendency of the age to ecstasy and prophecy.

The reverse side of this disposition of mind is the fear of
the spirit-world, in fact, belief in ghosts. The goddess of
ghosts and of purifications, Hekate, to whom apotropaeic
gifts were offered with averted face at the cross-roads on
dark, moonless nights, comes from the south-west of Asia
Minor. She must have been introduced into Greece during
the earlier archaic period. The oldest evidence comes from
Miletus and dates from the sixth century.[1] Propaganda for
her cult appears in the literature of the time. One part of
Hesiod's theogony praises her as almost the chief of all the

---

[1] My *Griech. Feste*, pp. 397 et seq. ; Dittenberger, *Syll. inscr.
graec.*[3], no. 57, line 25.

gods. It is certainly an interpolation, but an old one, as is shown by the hymn to Demeter, in which Hekate plays an important part. That she was identified with Artemis is due not only to the external resemblance but also to a certain affinity with Apollo. Her activities as a purifier are to some extent a caricature of his. The image of Hekate was set up, like Apollo's stone pillar before every house, so as to avert all evil.

These instances show how the mystical and ecstatic elements of religion found expression in association with prophecy and purification. In reality it was an epidemic of psychopathic religiosity which seized upon mankind, similar to that with which we are familiar in our modern faith-healers and speakers with tongues, and in the sorcerers of the nature peoples. Ecstasy is infectious, and so it was during this period. It may not only serve prophecy and purification but may also minister to that dormant longing which exists in every man, however humble his station, to enter into communion with the divine, to feel himself lifted up from the temporal into the spiritual. This form of ecstasy found its herald in the god who, with Apollo, impressed himself most strongly upon the religious feeling of the age—Dionysos. Not every man can be a miracle-worker and a seer, but most are susceptible to ecstasy, especially as members of a great crowd, which draws the individual along with it and generates in him the sense of being filled with a higher, divine power. This is the literal meaning of the Greek word ' enthusiasm ', the state in which ' god is in man '. The rising tide of religious feeling seeks to surmount the barrier which separates man from god, it strives to enter into the divine, and it finds ultimate satisfaction only in that quenching of the consciousness in enthusiasm which is the goal of all mysticism. The desire is felt by the most cultivated, no less than by the most primitive peoples. The origin of the cult of Dionysos is primitive, the well-known methods by which his devotees induced ecstasy. Their wanderings in the desert and giddy dance in the light of torches brought the maenads to the point where they had visions, saw milk and honey flowing out of the ground, and heard the bellowing of bulls. The god revealed himself in animal form, ' raging with taurine feet ', as is said in an old cult-hymn. The maenads saw him in animals, which they seized and tore to pieces and whose flesh they devoured raw. This sacramental meal is the supreme mystery, through which the worshippers received the god and his power into themselves. Like all primitive cults this one had originally a practical purpose, which evident indications show to have been the arousing of the fertility of Nature. Phallic rites are therefore so inevitable a part of the worship of Dionysos that the symbol of generation was brandished by the maenads and borne about in all processions at his festivals. However, it was not this external purpose that prepared the way for the victorious march of the Dionysiac religion : cults of fertility of an ecstatic and phallic character existed before and may have furnished a point of connexion for the new cult. It was rather the ecstasy itself and mysticism as a religious movement.

Homer knows the myth about Lycurgus who, unluckily for himself, persecuted Dionysos and his ' nurses ', and the maenad was so universally known that the despairing Andromache is likened to her. The victorious march of Dionysos had already begun, although the Ionian poet and his rationalistic and courtly circle cared little for what was going on among the masses of the people and in the mother country. The movement spread in the form of a violent psychical epidemic, almost like St. Vitus's dance, more particularly among women, since they are specially susceptible to this kind of infection. It is no wonder that it aroused the disgust of those who were not affected by it, and that attempts were made to suppress it, in the last resort, by force. But an epidemic of such a kind cannot be restrained by force and violence. The traces of the severe struggle by which Dionysos prepared the way for the ecstatic cult have been converted into myths.

Euripides, in his most remarkable drama, the *Bacchae*, in which the problem-poet, to some readers' surprise, shows that he understands even the psychology of religious ecstasy, has made the myth of Pentheus famous. The latter opposed the Dionysiac frenzy, and having climbed a tree to spy out the maenads fell into their hands and was torn to pieces by his own mother Agave. The poet has described in a magnificent manner the power of the god to infatuate men ; Pentheus himself falls a victim to his visions. Boeotia was a centre of the cult of Dionysos. This is also the scene of the myth of the daughters of Minyas, who stayed at home over their weaving and disdained to accompany the other women to the orgies, until suddenly ivy and vine-runners twined themselves about their looms, and milk and honey dropped from the ceiling ; they caught up one of their little sons, tore him in pieces, and hurried to the mountains and joined the maenads. The myth is designed to show how the ecstatic thought may develop subconsciously until it breaks forth with a violence all the greater for the delay, and sweeps away the resistance of the will.

Similar myths are found in other quarters. In Attica the story was told of the daughters of Eleuther, who mocked at the epiphany of Dionysos ; they were seized with madness, and in order to appease the god the cult of Dionysos Melanaigis was instituted. The cult legends give a similar reason for the introduction of the phallic cults into the service of Dionysos. In the myth of the daughters of Proitos the seer Melampus appears, and delivers the women from their frenzy by means of certain purificatory rites Melampus, we are told, was especially dear to Apollo. Much later, in an inscription from Magnesia on the Maeander, we learn how the oracle is consulted in consequence of a Diony-siac epiphany, a cult is established, and maenads are brought from Thebes to organize it.

It was Apollo who overcame the epidemic, not by working against and suppressing it, but by recognizing and regulating it. A regulated ecstasy has lost its germ of danger. This is what the Apolline institutionalism managed to accomplish, and the fact is sufficient testimony of the extent to which it had become engrained in the people. A red-figured vase-painting from the end of the fifth century shows Apollo and Dionysos extending hands to each other before the omphalos at Delphi, surrounded by the train of Dionysos, satyrs and maenads. The sculptures on the gable-ends of the temple of Apollo at Delphi tell the same story. On the eastern pediment stood Apollo, surrounded by the Muses, on the western Dionysos, surrounded by the Thyiades. These groups confirm the information given by Plutarch as to the connexion between the cults of Apollo and Dionysos at Delphi. During the three winter months the paean of Apollo was silent and the dithyramb of Dionysos was sung instead. Apollo returned with the spring ; the old day for his epiphany, the seventh of Bysios, falls in the first month of spring (in Athens Anthesterion). If we reckon three months back we come to the first real winter month, which in Athens took its name from the winter storms (Maimak-terion). At Delphi it was named after the torches swung at the orgies of Dionysos, and was called Dadaphorios. This name is evidence enough for the age of the cult of Dionysos at Delphi. The names of the months were doubtless regulated in conjunction with the calendar in the seventh century.

Still more important for our understanding of Apollo's influence upon the Dionysiac cult are the accounts of the kind of orgies celebrated at Delphi, or rather on the peaks of Parnassus. In the midst of winter the Thyiades roamed about among mountains and snow, swinging their thyrsi and torches in orgiastic frenzy. But these Thyiades were not a band of ecstatic women which could be joined by any one who was seized by the spirit. They were a body specially elected for this cult. With the Delphian band of Thyiades was combined another which came from Athens, at least in Plutarch's time. This body is certainly no new-fashioned institution, but it illustrates the method by which Apollo managed to control the ecstasy. When the orgies of Dionysos were introduced into Magnesia on the Maeander, the Theban maenads introduced three maenad communities. In Sparta we hear of eleven Dionysiads and in Elis of ' the sixteen holy women about Dionysos ', who sang an interesting old-fashioned cult-hymn to Dionysos and had also other duties in connexion with the cult.[1]

We may take it for granted that this restriction of the orgies to official communities of maenads was the means by which Apollo curbed the ecstasy and brought the cult of Dionysos into line with ancestral custom. It is more difficult to decide whether this cult contained anything more than the visionary and ecstatic raptures in which men in the rites above mentioned believed that they received the divinity into themselves. Our best source for the Delphian cult of Dionysos is Plutarch ; he was a close friend of the leader of the Thyiad community, Clea. But Clea had also been initiated into the mysteries of Osiris. It is to be feared that later times had added new rites and ideas. Above all we should like to know whether the ideas of life and death, germination and decay, belonged to Dionysos from the beginning and gave his cult a deeper significance. Plutarch speaks of a mysterious sacrifice in Apollo's temple ' when

---

[1] L. Weniger, *Ueber das Collegium der Thyiaden von Delphi*, Program, Eisenach, 1876, and *Das Collegium der Sechzehn Frauen und der Dionysosdienst in Elis*, Program, Weimar, 1883.

the maenads awake the god in the winnowing-fan (Λικνίτης, the infant Dionysos) '. Are they then old, this rite and this idea of the new-born divine child ? Their antiquity seems to me to be confirmed by our oldest witness, Homer. For why should he call the maenads the nurses of Dionysos unless they had the new-born divine child to tend and care for ? And Dionysos lay dead and buried in Delphi ; Philochorus speaks of his tomb in Apollo's temple, though he is a comparatively late witness. Orphicism provides a stronger proof. It was associated with Dionysiac mysticism, and the death and re-incarnation of Dionysos were from the beginning one of its main doctrines.

The ideas of birth and death, germination and decay, derived from Nature's changes, form the foundation of the cult of Dionysos. Upon this foundation mysticism rested, but like all mysticism it was pushed into the background in the official cult, whereas in the Orphic sect it had free course and became a central feature. With these facts is associated the view that the belief in immortality in the proper sense was introduced into Greece by Dionysos. This would seem to be doubtful. The revival of the cult of heroes and of the grave had more to do with the increasing strength of the belief. In Orphicism it goes hand in hand with the mystical Dionysiac religion, but that does not prove that it was also introduced by Dionysos. In the general cult of Dionysos more cannot be seen with certainty than that the god established a connexion with ancient festivals of souls. All Souls' Day in Athens, the Anthesteria, became a Dionysos festival, and the Agriania, a Dionysos festival in Argos, was also a festival of souls.

What we call the hope of immortality is rather the desire for a better existence after this, and the idea filled an important place in the religious life of the time. We can trace how it springs up and comes to flower in a cult which is more famous than any other in Greek religion, the Eleusinian mysteries. We have here an old source of information, the Homeric hymn to Demeter, which was composed in Attica in the time before Solon, before Eleusis had yet lost its independence and become merged in Athens.

The Eleusinian mysteries arose from an original pre-Grecian agrarian festival, which was the private property of certain families of Eleusis. The strength of the mysteries lay in the fact that they possessed no dogma, for dogma is the part of religion which perishes most easily in religious changes. Instead, they had certain sacred acts, which aroused religious feeling and into which every age could put the symbolism it desired. They had a myth which touched the deepest chords in human nature and was free from the usual ballast that encumbered the Greek myth. The rites show that the mysteries were originally a feast of fertility and purification, having reference to the autumn sowing which was immediately at hand. The hymn to Demeter is in great measure an explanatory tale deriving the practices of the cult from the myth. Hence Demeter, with her grief and her search, becomes a prototype of the *mystes*.

An inscription relating to the tithes for the goddesses at Eleusis orders that three subterranean granaries shall be built in Eleusis for the garnered corn, in accordance with ancestral custom. Herein lies the key to the explanation. The mysteries were to a certain extent a parallel to the Thesmophoria ; both were secret festivals, the one a woman's festival and the other celebrated within an exclusive circle. Both concerned the promoting of the fertility which was to emanate from the seed soon to be laid in the ground. The subterranean granaries were opened, the corn-maiden was led up from her subterranean dwelling in the halls of Pluto, god of wealth, and was re-united to her mother.

To this set of ideas, which has already been touched upon (cp. p. 123), was joined, doubtless in early times, another

which was not far distant from them, that of the gods of the
nether world in the ordinary sense.   The descent of Kore
into the earth was regarded as a descent to the realm of the
dead.   She herself was identified with a presumably pre-
Grecian mistress of the kingdom of the dead, Persephone
(the name is unexplained, and the Attic form Phersephassa
is still more obscure), and Pluto was identified with Hades,
and to them was transferred an idea which is common both
in ancient and modern times, that of Death fetching his
bride.   Hades carried off Kore to the lower world ; there
she becomes Persephone.   The agrarian cult was thus brought
into connexion with the realm of the dead, and the myth
thereby acquired a deeper meaning.   In the hymn old and
new stand side by side.   The last verses praise the happy
man whom the goddesses love, for to his house and hearth
they will send Ploutos, who gives men riches.   A few lines
above we read : ' Blessed among men upon the earth is he
who has seen these things ; but he that is uninitiated in the
rites and has no part in them has never an equal lot in the
cold place of darkness.'

The Homeric idea of the empty nothingness of the kingdom of the dead had never succeeded in driving out the
older, more vigorous ideas of the mother-country in regard
to the life after death.   A time of so much religious emotion,
in which grave-cult and hero-cult flourished, could not
escape the problem of the other world.   It was only natural
that during this period it should be developed and should
come to occupy perhaps the most important place of all.
In the Eleusinian mysteries the ideas of the lower world
played an important part.   They became all the more
concrete because the worshippers in their rites suffered and
rejoiced with the mother in her search for the daughter
carried off by the ruler of the nether world.   In the *Frogs* of
Aristophanes we find what the initiated of his day thought
of their lot in the other world.   Only for those who had been

initiated and had led a pious life does the sun shine in the world below ; they tread in Persephone's meadows the sacred choric dance of the mystery festival. Here the ethical demand for a pious life has been added, but it is not sufficient of itself ; the initiation into the mysteries is equally important. Diogenes, with his usual cynicism, said that it was absurd that the thief Pataikion should have a better lot after death than Epameinondas, just because he had been initiated into the mysteries. He hit the nail on the head, for such was really the case, and the belief shows the antiquity of this idea of a better lot in the world below. There is no reason to suppose that it originated in the fifth century—far from it. The life after death is to all primitive minds a repetition of the present life. As it is for Minos and Orion so is it for the initiated. They will continue their old life, they will go on celebrating the mysteries in the lower world ; therein consists their blessedness. The depth of the impression which the mystery festival produced can best be measured by the strength of this idea, which in its turn lent to the mysteries a new profundity and a new power over men's minds.

It has been said that the idea of immortality in the Eleusinian mysteries is borrowed from Orphicism. Upon the grounds which I have sought to make clear, I cannot but think it more likely that the same idea grew up independently in two different quarters. Orphicism is a combined religious movement in which all the different elements which we have hitherto seen scattered in various quarters are brought together in one mighty current.[1] Unfortunately it is extremely difficult to form an idea of Orphicism during the period when it arose. The most prolific sources date from late classical times. The dispute as to whether one of

[1] Of the numerous recent works on Orphicism may be mentioned Jane Harrison, *Prolegomena to the Study of Greek Religion*, chs. 9–12, and O. Kern, *Orpheus* and *Orphicorum Fragmenta*.

the main creations of Orphicism, the so-called rhapsodic theogony, goes back in fundamentals to the sixth century B. C. or belongs entirely to far later times is not yet settled, although the former theory seems to be gaining more and more ground.[1]

The ' famous Orpheus ' is mentioned for the first time by the poet Ibycus shortly before the Persian War. The oldest evidence is the frieze on the Sikyonian treasure-house at Delphi, dating from shortly before the middle of the sixth century ; there Orpheus is represented with the Dioskouroi on board the Argo, with the zither in his hand. From this we may conclude that at that time he had already been brought into connexion with the voyage of the Argonauts, perhaps that here we already have one of those Orphic Argonaut voyages which are afterwards mentioned in such great numbers. There is a rich Orphic literature which is ascribed to the sixth century, but extremely little of it has been preserved. Among the poets several take the name of Orpheus. Most of them belong to Sicily and Greater Greece. These lands too were for long a centre of Orphicism, and therein is shown the relationship of Orphicism to the doctrines of Pythagoras. A Pythagorean also, Kerkops, is mentioned among the authors of Orphic poems. The other centre was Attica. There Orphicism seems to have been favoured by the Peisistratidae. A famous Orphic poet, Onomacritus, was engaged at their court, until he was caught forging oracles of Musaeus and was driven away by Hipparchus. Pindar and Polygnotus, whose painting of Hades at Delphi is of great historical importance, belong to a period which extends even beyond the Persian Wars. In the clear atmosphere of the fifth century Orphicism sank to the level of a despised, popular sectarian superstition, and as such it

[1] O. Kern, *De Orphei, Epimenidis, Pherecydis theogoniis*, Dissertation, Berlin, 1888 ; O. Gruppe, *Die rhapsodische Theogonie, NJb* 1890, Suppl., pp. 689 et seq.

figures in Aristophanes ; but the profound thoughts which lay beneath its grotesque forms had the power of gripping the highest minds, those of Pindar and Plato. It is with Orphicism as with the Eleusinian mysteries : the mystical belief which we find in the period between the Persian Wars and Alexander was probably not created in that period but originated in the time of the great religious crisis. As far as possible, however, we should check our conclusions by the few notices which go back to the archaic period itself.

Here for the first time in the history of the Greek religion we meet a founder of a religion who is also a man, even though a mythical hero, one who dies as a martyr to his faith, torn to pieces by Thracian women. Orpheus was a singer in the myth. This means that he was regarded as the source of the sacred poems in which Orphicism couched its doctrines. Attempts were made to invest these poems with the authority of antiquity—Orpheus is said to be earlier than Homer—and the Orphics appropriated the earlier epic by refashioning it to suit their own purposes, a process which we meet once more in the religious upheaval of late antiquity. Orphicism is a book religion, the first example of the kind in the history of Greek religion. Orpheus himself as a mythological person is probably a comparatively late projection of his sect.

At the head of the cosmogony stands a new, more abstract principle, ' Time which never grows old ', and only after this come Chaos and Ether. The idea of Time as the origin of all things is to be found also in Pherekydes, who is usually reckoned among the philosophers, although his philosophy is in a high degree mythical and mystical. At the beginning he places Zeus—he gives the word an unusual form which is intended to mean 'that which lives'—, Time, and the Earthly. After that, Time, according to the Orphic cosmogony, formed a silver egg in the divine Ether. In the Greek myths we otherwise only find that certain mythological

personages are born out of an egg ; but the creation of the
world from an egg recurs in the cosmogonies of so many
peoples that we need not entertain a moment's doubt as to
its primeval origin. From the egg proceeded the first god,
Phanes, the creator of the world. In Aristophanes he is
called Eros, elsewhere he has also the curious name of
Erekapaios. The Orphics praised Zeus as the beginning,
middle, and end, but Zeus had acquired his greatness by
devouring Erekapaios, just as he devoured Metis. He
claimed his place as ruler, but he belonged to a later generation of divinities. So the old folk-tale motif was used, and
he was made to incorporate the creator of the world with
himself. All this is but a further development of old and
well-known cosmogonic motifs ; the only original feature is
that Time is made the first principle. Whether this idea
originated among the Persians, as some have maintained,[1]
I am not able to judge.

In the myths and also in Hesiod there are only feeble
attempts at inventing an anthropogony in addition to the
theogony. It is here that the Orphics made their most
original contribution to mystical religious speculation. By
Persephone, the queen of the lower world, Zeus had a son,
Dionysos-Zagreus. Zeus intended the child to have dominion
over the world, but the Titans lured it to them with toys,
fell upon it, tore it to pieces, and devoured its limbs, but
Athena saved the heart and brought it to Zeus, who ate it,
and out of this was afterwards born a new Dionysos, the
son of Semele. The Titans were struck by Zeus' avenging
lightning, which burned them to ashes. From the ashes man
was formed, and he therefore contains within himself
something of the divine, coming from Dionysos, and something of the opposite, coming from his enemies, the Titans.
In its essential features this myth goes back to the sixth
century. An old epic, the Alkmaionis, already calls

[1] R. Eisler, *Weltenmantel und Himmelszelt*, pp. 392 et seq.

Zagreus the highest of all the gods ; Aeschylus calls him
the son of Hades ; Onomacritus had already mentioned the
Titans as the authors of the crime against Dionysos. Plato
speaks of ' the Titan nature ' much as we do of ' the old
Adam ', in a way which clearly points to the Orphic teaching.
The aphorism of Herakleitos : ' Time is a child who plays
and moves the pieces, the lordship is to the child,' first
becomes fully comprehensible in the light of this teaching.

The myth of the Titans' crime against Zagreus might be
taken as an aetiological tale intended to explain the central
rite in the Dionysiac orgies, the tearing to pieces and devouring of the god personified in an animal, but with this rite
Orphicism indissolubly associates the myth of man's origin
from the ashes of the Titans, in which particles of the divine
Zagreus were also present. Man has a twofold nature,
good and evil ; this is the necessary basis for the doctrine
which is built upon it. For this, as for everything original,
it is difficult to find a genetic explanation. We may suggest
that the feeling for justice generated the sense of guilt when
the demands of justice were applied to the individual
himself ; we may suggest that the religious ecstasy, the
sense that the god made his dwelling with man, divided
man's nature into a divine and a human part ; or finally
we may point to the doctrine of the transmigration of souls,
and the tendency to asceticism which it brought with it.
All this gives the environment in which this idea might be
born, but does not explain its birth. It was the creation of
a religious genius, but it took place among a people whose
psychology permitted them to react very little to the sense
of guilt, and was enveloped in a mythology which could not
but be repulsive to that people's clear processes of thought.

Like the *mystes* initiated at Eleusis, the Orphic expected
a better portion in the other world. The thoughts of the
mystes took their direction from the mystery festival ;
those of the Orphic followed another direction. His god,

Dionysos, had already become the god of wine, and wine played a certain, though quite inconsiderable, part in stimulating the enthusiasm of the devotee. Thus the Orphic imagined the life of the blessed in the other world as a banquet of the holy or, literally translated, as a ' carousal '. It is easy to mock at this conception—Plato already paraphrases it as ' an eternal intoxication '—nevertheless it appeals so readily to the natural man that we meet it still on the walls of the catacombs.

It proved disastrous that the Orphics formed a sect from which the rest of mankind was excluded, and that they believed themselves to be better and more devout than others ; for they had also to experience the scorn and hatred of the world, and what they had to suffer here, they avenged in the next life. I do not doubt that the important place which the description of the fate of the unblest occupies in the Orphic teaching is ultimately due to their feeling of antagonism and ill will towards their unconverted neighbours. Here, too, the starting-point is the same old belief in the other life as a repetition of this. Purifications played a great part in Orphicism ; those who were admitted into the sect were purified in the ordinary ways, which included rubbing with meal and mud. Those who had not been purified and initiated lived in their uncleanness and continued to do so in the other world. Hence comes the stock expression as to the lot of the uninitiated, that they lie in the mire (ἐν βορβόρῳ κεῖται) ; ' mire in plenty and everflowing slime ', says Aristophanes in the Frogs. The popular ideas about the lower world were also included in the conception, abysses and expanses of water, snakes, monsters, and ghostly apparitions. These things were too closely in keeping with the kind of lower world which the Orphics contemplated for their adversaries—and the adversaries were all the uninitiated—not to be adopted.

The most important witness to the Orphic ideas of the

lower world is Polygnotus' great picture of the visit of
Odysseus to the world below, painted in the hall of the
Cnidians at Delphi and described in detail by Pausanias.
It contains more than the Nekyia of the *Odyssey* and is
also quite different in character. Orphic influence is recogniz-
able. We know the titles at least of Orphic descriptions
of journeys to Hades, and it is from one of these that
Polygnotus has taken his images. Here popular figures
meet us : the old ferryman Charon, who ferries the shades
over to the kingdom of the dead ; Oknos constantly weaving
his rope in vain, for an ass stands behind him and eats up
the rope as fast as he can twist it ; Eurynomos, half black
and half blue, like a bluebottle, sitting on a vulture-skin
and showing his teeth with a grin as he picks the flesh from
the joints of the dead, leaving only the bare bones. This
corpse-eating demon gives a concrete horror to death such
as nothing else conveys ; Kerberos no doubt once fulfilled
a similar function. The artist was deeply saturated in the
tide of mysticism. He includes founders of mysteries
among his figures—Orpheus, Thamyris, and Kleoboia, who
introduced the mysteries of Demeter into Thasos. The
fate of the uninitiated he brings before the eye in two
groups : they are carrying water in broken pitchers. Plato
mentions it as an Orphic conception that the unrighteous
had to carry water in a sieve. The origin of the idea can
easily be understood. The man who has not been purified
in this world cannot be purified in the other ; he is for ever
bearing water to the bath of purification and it is for ever
running away from him out of the broken pitcher or the
sieve. The repetition becomes a punishment.

In Plato it is not the uninitiated but the unrighteous
who has constantly to bear water in vain. In him Minos
appears for the first time not as the king who judges his
people, but as the judge of the lower world, deciding the
fates of men there. When man's lot in the world below was

made to vary according to his life on earth, a judge became necessary to balance the account. The myth presented the figure of Minos and the change came about of itself. It seems to me to be doubtful that it was already Orphic. In Orphicism the judgement was really pronounced here upon earth. The sense of human guilt is the original feature in the Orphic myth about the creation of man, and the sense of guilt must lead to an attempt to rid oneself of that guilt ; the Orphics had a tendency to asceticism and, like the Pythagoreans, abstained from killing animals. Morality is therefore added to ritual. In their lives the Orphics felt themselves to be not only more devout but also more righteous than others. In them the demand for ritual purity was actually exalted into a demand for moral purity, whether or not the demand was fulfilled, and therefore they assigned to the lower world not only the ritually unclean, the uninitiated, but also the morally unclean, the criminals. In so doing they were able to incorporate old conceptions and we have seen how the idea had considerable influence in the fifth century. Polygnotus painted not only the mythological criminals known already from the *Odyssey* —to them he added Theseus and Peirithoos, who tried to carry off the queen of the world below—but also a man who has done his father a wrong and in the lower world is being strangled by him, and one who has committed sacrilege, and into whom, as a penalty, a woman is pouring poison. It is a simple *ius talionis* in harmony with popular ideas, but the important point is that all this takes place in the lower world. Hence arose a fatal idea, that of the world below as the place of punishment, as hell.[1]

The problem of justice and retribution was in the air. The Orphics also demanded justice ; they felt themselves to be better and more righteous than others and yet they were rejected and despised by the masses. In the common

[1] A. Dieterich, *Nekyia.*

conception retribution was a problem which concerned not only the individual but the family. The heir had to take over not only the material and physical but also the moral inheritance of his forefathers. The race of the unjust and the perjurer falls into misfortune and is rooted out, but that of the righteous persists and flourishes. The avenging and equalizing hand of justice does not always overtake the offender himself, but his race cannot escape. This solution of the problem of the correspondence between moral guilt and punishment might satisfy an age for which the individual merely existed as a link in the chain of the family, but all mysticism is individualistic. Only the individual experiences the blessedness of union with the godhead, a man is initiated and purified for himself alone, not for his forefathers and descendants. Mysticism had to break with the old conception of the responsibility of posterity for the sins of its fathers; it had to lay the punishment where individualism demands that it shall rest, upon the criminal himself. If retribution did not overtake him in this life, it did so in the next. And when it was noticed how often the unjust man prospered in this life, the demand for justice made its contribution to the conception of the lower world as a place of punishment. The idea found support among the people, as we can see from Aristophanes.

This law of retribution may have sufficed for the people and indeed also for the simpler souls among the Orphics themselves, but Orphicism taught something more, the transmigration of souls, its most obvious point of resemblance to the doctrines of the Pythagoreans. It is found in the Orphic texts upon the gold leaves which, in the third century B.C., were laid in the graves of the dead in Southern Italy as a passport for their journey to the other world.[1] A far older piece of evidence is a remarkable ode of Pindar

---

[1] Collected by Jane Harrison, *op. cit.*, Appendix, and A. Olivieri, *Lamellae aureae Orphicae* (Lietzmann's *Kleine Texte*, no. 133).

to Theron, the ruler of Akragas, dating from the year 472.
' In the presence of gods high in honour, whoso took delight
in keeping oaths has his portion in a life free from tears ;
while the others endure pain that no eye can look upon.
And all they that, for three lives in either world, have been
steadfast to keep their soul from all wrong-doing, travel
by the high-way of Zeus to the Tower of Kronos, where the
Ocean airs breathe about the Islands of the Blest. . . . '
The circle of births is not eternal ; there is an end when
the righteous have been tested sufficiently and pass into
eternal bliss. This is doubtless in fact a compromise between
the doctrine of soul-migration and the idea of the kingdom
of the blest, but the content and depth of the conception
are in no way diminished by the fact. This doctrine forms
the very summit of Orphicism, man's final liberation from
his Titanic inheritance by means of the observation of strict
purity. Therein lay the higher meaning of the purifications
and the asceticism to which the Orphics submitted ; like
the Pythagoreans they extended their asceticism to the
abstention from animal food. But this way of life could not
be followed by every one. Orphicism had to remain a sect,
and what is more its imperishable religious ideas could only
be the property of the highest minds. It is little wonder
that a Pindar or a Plato should feel himself drawn to them.

Orphicism is the combination and the crown of all the
restless and manifold religious movements of the archaic
period. The development of the cosmogony in a speculative
direction, with the addition of an anthropogony which laid
the principal emphasis on the explanation of the mixture
of good and evil in human nature ; the legalism of ritual
and life ; the mysticism of cult and doctrine ; the development of the other life into concrete visibility, and the
transformation of the lower world into a place of punishment
by the adaptation of the demand for retribution to the old
idea that the hereafter is a repetition of the present ; the

belief in the happier lot of the purified and the initiated ;—
for all these things parallels, or at least suggestions, can be
found in other quarters. The greatness of Orphicism lies
in having combined all this into a system, and in the incon-
testable originality which made the individual in his relationship to guilt and retribution the centre of its teaching. But
from the beginning Orphicism represented itself as the
religion of the elect ; others were repelled by the fantastic
and grotesque mythological disguise in which it clothed its
thoughts. The age took another direction ; the demand of
the Greek mind for clarity and plastic beauty carried the
day. In the clear and rarefied atmosphere of the period
of great national exaltation which followed the victory over
the Persians the mists and the figures of cloud were dissipated.
Orphicism sank to the level of the populace, but it persisted
there until Time once more wrought a transformation and
the overlordship of the Greek spirit was broken after more
than half a millennium. Then Orphicism raised its head
again, and became an important factor in the new religious
crisis, the last of the ancient world.

VII

THE CIVIC RELIGION

MYSTICISM sought to raise mankind to the level of the divine and to surmount the barrier which ordinary Greek ideas set between gods and men. Legalism felt itself everywhere encompassed and threatened by the supervision and anger of the gods ; the Greeks called the feeling *deisidaimonia*. Both tendencies have popular roots and both were in opposition to Homer's anthropomorphic conception of the gods, which had also been impressed upon the popular consciousness ; these gods set up the impassable barrier which man must not seek to transcend, but they were not omnipresent and were content with the routine of the cult carried on in accordance with ancestral custom. ' Moderation is best ', says a proverb which expresses a distinctive trait in the Greek character. The genuine Greek demand for moderation was brushed aside during the struggle for new religious values, but it was never forgotten. Its cause was pleaded during this period by wise men who administered the affairs of the states, and whose whole efforts were directed towards finding a middle way and preventing the extremes from dismembering society. Often they seemed to speak to deaf ears—Solon's work was upset almost immediately—but they were by no mean without support among the better and more thoughtful portion of the people. In the end, too, their efforts were successful ; calmer political, and better social conditions supervened. An important contributing factor to this result was the improved economic position in the most advanced states, which is with reason associated principally with the rule of the tyrants. The decisive change came with the heightened national enthusiasm and the enlarged political status which were a consequence of the victory over the Persians.

In the religious domain [1] we know no more of these wise men than that they instituted a state regulation of the cult ; Solon was certainly not alone in founding a sacral legislation. For a later age they represented a whole period, ' the period of the Seven Sages ' ; properly speaking, they do not form a special period of time but rather express one aspect of the period and its aspirations. Among the Seven Sages were statesmen, as well as the first philosopher, Thales. It was said that they couched their wisdom in aphorisms such as the above, ' Moderation is best '. These aphorisms lived upon the lips of the people and the god at Delphi adopted them. In his temple some of the best known and most expressive maxims were inscribed : $M\eta\delta\grave{\epsilon}\nu\ \mathring{a}\gamma a\nu$, $\Gamma\nu\hat{\omega}\theta\iota\ \sigma\epsilon a\upsilon\tau\acute{o}\nu$, ' Nothing overmuch ! ' ' Know thyself ! ' ' Nothing overmuch ! ' was the guiding principle of these men in the struggles of the community, and it was also their religious programme. Still more clearly is the principle expressed in the famous $\gamma\nu\hat{\omega}\theta\iota\ \sigma\epsilon a\upsilon\tau\acute{o}\nu$, into which we, with Socrates, import an exhortation to self-knowledge. The words really mean : ' Know that thou art (but) a man ! ' It was an expression of the idea of the insurmountable barrier between gods and men, the inculcation of which was one of Apollo's most important tasks. But those who coined the maxim built upon less puerile grounds than Homer's anthropomorphic doctrine could supply. They were raised above popular *deisidaimonia* and had pondered

---

[1] K. F. Nägelsbach, *Nachhomerische Theologie*, 1857, is only to be used as a store-house of material. There are numerous works on the religious views of the Greek writers, especially the tragic poets ; I mention L. Campbell, *Religion in Greek Literature*. The only attempt at a modern general view is Wide's chapter, *Geschichte der Religiosität*, in Gercke and Norden's *Einleitung in die klassische Altertumswissenschaft*, ii, 3rd edition, pp. 215 et seq.

upon the way of the world and the varying fates of men ; it was evident to them that they were under divine guidance. But, looking at the vicissitudes of Fate, they found more of misfortune than of happiness in life. Even the mightiest was not exempt : indeed the greater his happiness, the greater his misfortune.[1]

A typical example is the ode of consolation which Pindar sent to King Hieron of Syracuse during his illness.

‘ For one blessing, the Immortals give to man a double portion of sorrow. Fools cannot bear it off with a brave show, but only the noble heart, by turning the fair side outermost. . . . Well may that mortal man who keeps in mind the world’s true course, have comfort of the fair lot that falls to him by heaven’s grace. But the winged winds of the height blow changefully with changing time. Man’s fortune voyages not far unshipwrecked, when its burden is too deeply laden. As are the days of great and small things, so will I be great or small. With due observance, as I may, my heart shall wait upon the spirit that guides my destiny from hour to hour.’

This is an objective view of life. What life brings, man must endure. It comes from the gods and they are under no obligation to give an account to man. He must know his weakness and resign himself to their decrees. The same idea recurs in the two oldest of the great tragic writers. Aeschylus gives it an individual turn by laying special emphasis upon the omnipotence of Zeus. Sophocles has given the clearest expression to the idea. His Oedipus, who from the height of happiness is hurled, through no fault of his own, into indescribable suffering, offers the most striking and lofty example of human impotence and of destiny ordered by the gods. The poet extends this point of view to the state, which is under just as little obligation as the gods to render account to the individual. Antigone sets the decrees of religion above those of the state, but

[1] A. B. Drachmann, *Hovedtraek av Graesk Religiösitet* (*Udvalgte Afhandlinger*, 1911, pp. 38 et seq.).

nevertheless she too must suffer the penalty which the state imposes on her. This was the doctrine of Socrates, and he put it into practice in his death.

The conception was one adapted to the wise and thoughtful. Such resignation can hardly have been popular, except at most as a half-unconscious submission to religious and political necessity. It is significant that along these lines of thought we hardly ever hear of any definite god, but of ' the gods ', ' the god ', ' the divine ', ' the *daimon* ', or of Zeus, whom Aeschylus in particular is wont to bring into the foreground. Anthropomorphism had robbed the gods of that fullness of power before which man bows in the consciousness of his insignificance. The idea of the divine power lived on in the conception of the inevitable destiny of man and found expression in the words ' the godhead ', ' the divine ', ' the *daimon* '. It might be exalted to the inaccessible height which this point of view involved, an abstract notion of the gods. The gods have complete happiness, complete power. The transgression of the boundary line is always called ' insolence ' ($\H{v}\beta\rho\iota s$) ; man must not be so presumptuous as to strive to raise himself above his mortal lot. ' It is best to seek from heaven things fitting for a spirit that is mortal,' says Pindar, ' knowing what lies before us at our feet, and to what portion we are born. O my soul, set not thy desire upon the life of an immortal, but use to the full the power that is within thy compass.' $\Gamma\nu\hat{\omega}\theta\iota$ $\sigma\epsilon\alpha\upsilon\tau\acute{o}\nu$. Remember that thou art man, and especially in times of happiness, for man is then most prone to forget the lot of mortal life. When bliss is at its height, disaster is closest at hand. It is the highest peaks that the lightning most often strikes. Man must not rise too high, too near the gods, as did the tyrants. They or their race ended in ruin.

There is no question here, any more than in earlier times, of any ethical foundation for joy or woe. These things come from the gods, and the gods owe to man neither explanation nor reckoning. But the sense of justice, at least of the formal justice dispensed by the law of compensation, makes its influence felt. It is the source of the idea of Nemesis. Those who rise highest are overtaken most speedily and most cruelly by disaster. To each measure of joy answers the same measure of woe. This lesson is taught by the course of history. The age finds in Croesus, Poly-crates, Xerxes, all great and splendid princes, all overtaken by the heaviest blows of fate, examples to illustrate its favourite theme. But this is also a departure from the objective mood which takes the world as it is and the changes of Fate as they come.

The legislators of the archaic period sought to apportion social duties and obligations in accordance with justice. It was towards justice that their efforts were directed. It could not be denied that the good man often had to suffer innocently while the wicked man died peaceably in possession of his unlawfully acquired goods. For an age which had not emancipated the individual from the chain of the family the answer was simple : posterity had to take over not only the material and physical, but also the moral inheritance of its forefathers ; it had to suffer for their crimes. This is incisively expressed by Solon : ' The one must pay the penalty at once, the other later ; or else his innocent children or his kin must afterwards pay the penalty.' But a word has slipped in almost unnoticed which betrays the growth of a feeling that this doctrine was unjust : ' his *innocent* children '. Theognis desires that Zeus will so arrange it that the punishment overtakes the guilty and the misdeeds of the fathers are not visited upon the children. Aeschylus emphasizes justice with especial force. ' It is an ancient saying that he who has done wrong shall suffer.' Justice is with him avenging justice : Zeus is its source and guardian. But Aeschylus' idea of justice is none the less bound up with the ancient tradition ; as in the past, it is especially aimed at insolence (ὕβρις) and at crimes against the gods. In one well-known passage in the *Agamemnon*, however, he protests against the commonly accepted opinion. Disaster is not a consequence of happiness, he suggests, but crime fosters crime ; a house where justice is honoured always flourishes. A curious concatenation arises. The punishment for a crime consists in a fresh crime, which in its turn gives birth to another. This is family guilt as conceived by Aeschylus.[1]

It is not surprising that a philosophy such as that of the Seven Sages should foster quietism. If the thunderbolt most often strikes the highest peaks, then it is best to dwell down in the valleys. Hipponax mentions that Apollo had declared Myson to be the most discreet (σωφρονέστατος) of all men ; he was afterwards placed among the Seven Sages. The anecdote makes Solon seek him out ; he discovered a poor peasant, engaged in mending a broken plough. Myson reminds us of another of Apollo's favourites, Clearchus of Methydrion. Both were living expressions of the subordination which Apollo required. The famous conversation between Solon and Croesus in Herodotus inculcates the same doctrine. In the story of the Athenian Tellos, who saw flourishing troops of children and grandchildren and at an advanced age fell in victorious battle for his country, we may still discern the Greek ideal of citizenship. But it is no wonder that men drew the logical conclusion from the philosophy which makes one joy be counterbalanced by two sorrows ; in that case it is best for man not to be born, and next best to find while young a gentle death. Theognis puts this clearly ; Herodotus makes Solon give an example in the story of Cleobis and Biton. Their mother prayed the gods to reward them for their filial devotion by granting them the best that could befall man. They fell gently

---

[1] Drachmann, *Skyld og Nemesis hos Aeschylus, op. cit.*, pp. 9 et seq.

asleep in the temple and never woke again. Their statues
have been found at Delphi and bear an archaic inscription
referring to the legend about them. This is the profound
pessimism of the Greeks which cast its shadow over the
healthiest epoch of their national life. That it should have
developed from the view held of the gods and the destinies
of life is not surprising ; but it involves the Homeric conception of the kingdom of the dead, and not the more vigorous
popular beliefs regarding the dead and their continued
existence.

Such a philosophy is but a meagre wisdom. It could
exist only because man did not live in accordance with its
teaching. It did not prevent the Greeks from enjoying
to the fullest extent the beauty of life. Sophocles did so,
and he gave clearer expression than any one else to the
conception. He was a poet, while the Seven Sages were
involved in the practical business of the statesman. As in
the poet's narrative of the moving fates of heroes, so in
the statesman's hours of weariness, when he cast up accounts
with life and was filled with a sense of loathing at its devastat-
ing contrasts, there was manifested a sense of resignation,
the unconditional submission to the caprice of Fate. How
little even highly educated men could maintain a consistent
view of life is shown by the comprehensive work of Herodotus. He believes in omens and oracles as firmly as any
member of the populace. He believes that the gods punish
crime, at least in a later generation if not earlier. He believes
in the special Greek sin of insolence ($ὕβρις$), but it is changed
into a conception of the envy of the gods. The gods are
envious and vexatious. (Drachmann has well called this
an anthropomorphizing of the idea.) He is led to the cruel
belief that the gods beguile men into insolence in order to
punish them in the interests of the moral order of the
universe. But on the top of all this he has attacks of Ionic
rationalism, he criticizes the myths, rejects the intervention

of the gods, and entertains the idea of causal connexion. Herodotus was a receptive nature in whom are reflected all the contradictory moods of the age. Therein lies his charm and his importance.

The wisdom of the Seven Sages too was but a meagre wisdom. Man seeks not only the fear of God but also God's grace and help. ' The divine ' (τὸ θεῖον) was inaccessible to prayers and sacrifices. Grace and help had to be sought from the anthropomorphic gods, from rivers, stocks, and stones. For the purpose of practical religion this wisdom has little meaning ; it was at most an admonition to man to know his own place in relation to the gods as also in relation to the state, an inculcation of the traditional submission to the divine and human order. It was easy for the intellectual criticism of the sophists to make short work of this feeble religiosity. Its foundations were already shaken, as we can see from Sophocles' eager defence of it.

The movement here described was associated with the most highly cultivated circles, with those who accepted the world as it was, but also pondered upon life ; who accepted the traditional religion, especially as developed in the Homeric poems, which were already the basis of culture, but felt repelled by its most glaring anthropomorphic blemishes. Accordingly, as men searched for the power which governs the world, the anthropomorphic gods gave place to the abstract ' divine ', or else, as in Aeschylus, we find the position of Zeus still further exalted. A religion of Zeus has even been spoken of. In practice these men were concerned with the ordinary gods, and their practical piety consisted in maintaining the cults. It was the only way of testifying to their reverence for the power which governed the world. Here, as elsewhere, they stood upon the ground of ancient tradition. The movement harmonized admirably with the efforts of the statesmen to set up a stable social order. What was needed for this was precisely what its philosophy enjoined—submission to the gods and to the state.

The key-note of life became resignation, and its sum the observance of the traditional cult and obedience to the behests of the state. Such a political doctrine is an expression of the solidarity of state and religion. The individual forms of religion which had manifested themselves in the movements of the archaic period knew no political bounds ; the Greek religion, on the other hand, was from the beginning a religion of the community. As Greece split up into small states, it became a religion of particularism. The Homeric poems had given the Greeks a universal conception of gods and the world, and the enormous popularity of the poems implanted this conception in the national mind. Alongside of these more universal beliefs the particularist cults and the local gods could indeed exist. Legalism could also at need be reconciled with them. But upon the whole the mighty religious movements of the archaic period, and especially mysticism, which gives pre-eminence to the individual, were a protest against particularism in religion. In the minds of men a struggle was being fought out, at least unconsciously, between the universal and individualistic, and the political, local, and particularistic religions. The strengthening of political authority, with the appearance of calmer social conditions, and the increase of national enthusiasm after the Persian wars, was not the least important factor in contributing to the suppression of the individualistic religious movements of the archaic period and to the triumph of the official religion, with particularism as its basis and with its Homeric dress.

The archaic period was the time when constitutions were formed, when the states were consolidated and their limits fixed, and when the constant wars between neighbouring cities established the distribution into minor states. In the fights between the cities men needed divine help and support. The Athena of Athens could not take the field against the Athena of Thebes, as the god of Moab, Chemosh, could against Yahweh, God of Israel, for in men's minds she represented the same goddess in each case. The states needed divine champions, and the heroes seemed to have been created on purpose to satisfy particularist demands for champions of the kind. The city represented in theory a blood-relationship, and the heroes were the citizens' ancestors, who helped them and no one else, just as kinsmen support their kin. They were tied to their mortal remains and to the soil wherein these rested: they rose from the grave and helped their own people, their posterity. The flourishing of their cult is associated with the development of particularism and of the conception of the state.

The heroes go out to fight for their people and enter into the struggle in person. The Tyndaridae accompanied the Spartan kings into the field; when one of the kings stayed at home, one of the Tyndaridae stayed at home also. The Persian wars abound in legends of heroes. At the battle of Marathon there fought in the ranks of the Athenians the hero Theseus, rising from the ground in which he rested, the local hero Marathon, and Boutes, the ancestor of the ancient family of the Boutadai. In the battle there appeared a man in the dress of a peasant, who killed many Persians with a ploughshare. When the battle was over, he disappeared ; thereafter the oracle commanded the Athenians to honour the hero Echetlos. A ship was sent to Aegina to fetch the Aeacidae, Telamon, Aias, and others, to the battle of Salamis. Before the battle of Plataeae the Athenians, acting under the instructions of the oracle, sacrificed to the seven local heroes of the district. At Delphi the heroes Phylakos and Autonoos marched out against the foe, as two hundred years later Hyperochos, Laodikos, and Pyrrhos marched against the Celts. Those who fell at Marathon and Plataeae themselves became protecting heroes and were worshipped. It is not surprising that the Greeks themselves said of their victory : ' Not we, but the gods and the heroes have achieved it.' Visible intervention is ascribed only to the heroes. Before the battle of Leuctra the armour vanished from the temple of Herakles ; he was arming himself in order to march against the Spartans. In a rich group of figures, which the Tarentines erected at Delphi out of gratitude for their victory over the native tribes, the heroes Taras and Phalanthos were represented by the side of the combatants. However artificial may be the heroes of the tribes which Cleisthenes created, an orator could nevertheless turn the conception to account by representing each as exhorting his tribe to bravery. A relief, depicting a scene from the hero-cult, bears the inscription ' the leader, the chief ' (ἡγεμὼν ἀρχηγέτης). At Tronis in Phokis a hero was worshipped as leader (ἥρως ἀρχηγέτης) who was of great assistance in time of war. Some said that he was Xanthippos, others called him Phokos ; and this is significant. Men turned to their ancestors, to the dead. Often no one knew what they were called, but any name which served was given them. An empty, eponymous name such as Phokos was adopted, or one was chosen from the long array of heroes' names offered by Homer and the myths.

Sometimes attempts were made to gain the favour of the heroes of the land which it was desired to conquer. Thus the Athenians, by the oracle's advice, fenced off a shrine for Aiakos before beginning operations against Aegina. A city could send its heroes to help its friends. In the struggle between Croton and Locri Epizephyrii the Locrians, on the score of their relationship to the Opuntian Locrians, called Locrian Aias to their help. The Spartans sent them the Tyndaridae. When the Thebans came into conflict with Athens shortly before the Persian wars, they asked the Aeginetans for aid. These sent the Aeacidae, but when the war went against the Thebans the latter sent the Aeacidae back and asked for men instead.

The heroes are tied to their graves and their mortal remains. No doubt through Homer not only the divine but also the heroic myths became common property, but the gods were common to all in quite another way than the heroes. A hero is bound in the cult to a single place, his grave. If several are attributed to him, a dispute arises as to which is the real grave ; in regard to the places of the divine cults any such doubt would be absurd. If the hero is not local, he is made so. Who knows how many heroes, who were originally unattached legendary figures, were given graves in this period ? Oedipus was given four.

How living the belief was is shown by the anecdote that Solon's ashes were strewn over Salamis in order that his remains could not be separated from the soil of the island, but would always remain there and preserve for Athens the land which he had conquered. If the heroes rested in foreign soil, they could not be present to advise and help when called upon. So if their bones had been carried afar they must be brought home. They were sought out and moved like relics of saints. The Spartans were told by the Delphic oracle that they must discover Orestes' bones and take them away from Tegea before they could conquer the Arcadians. The Athenians carried home the bones of Theseus from Skyros and established a splendid cult to their national hero.[1]

The gods behave quite differently. It was said that they abandoned a conquered town and left their temples and altars ; the heroes, on the other hand, were indissolubly associated with the soil in which they lay. It was not until long afterwards, at a time when the old religion was already breaking up, that the Homeric idea was revived, according to which the gods marched out to battle at the head of the army,

[1] F. Pfister, *Der Reliquienkultus im Altertum, RGVV*, v.

as Poseidon did at the battle of Mantinea in 249 B.C., and Asclepios, according to Isyllus, against Philip of Macedon when the latter attacked Sparta in 338 B. C.

We can realize how sorely the assistance of the heroes was needed by the Greek states and can understand why the flourishing of the hero-cult belongs to the time when they were being formed. We can see, too, that the canonizing of new heroes and the regulation of the hero-cult would provide an extensive field of activity for Apollo, the mouthpiece of divine authority. Even the emigrants who settled in foreign lands, to which they could not carry ancestral graves, felt the necessity of providing themselves with heroes. They met the need partly by resorting to the well-known figures of mythology, and it is to this fact that the myths which told how the heroes of the Trojan war wandered about the coasts of the Mediterranean are indebted for their popularity. But these heroes were not sufficient, and so at last it became the established custom for the leader of a new pioneering enterprise to be buried in the market-place of the colony and honoured after death as its protecting hero.

In the light of particularism and against the background of the struggles by which this was established it becomes easy to understand why the hero-cult flourished so vigorously. Particularism, too, needed religious expression, and this feeling was so strong, so intimately associated with the ideal of the Greek people, that it defied Homer, Apollo, and Orpheus.

The heroes were regarded as ancestors. In the legends they were princes, like Aias in Locris and the Aeacidae at Salamis. Their deeds were the early history of the people ; this was obvious and the Greeks never doubted it. And therefore the claim of the people to their land and its soil depended ultimately upon the heroes, unless the people were content with the actual possession without seeking to establish any legal title. And such a title was needed in the disputes about boundaries. Wars between cities found their reflection in the myths, and were carried back to the mythical period. Thus the struggle between Athens and Eleusis is reflected in the mythical struggle between Eumolpus and Erechtheus, in which the daughters of Erechtheus sacrificed themselves for their native town, a widespread legendary motif.

There is consequently a political mythology. In ancient Greece it played much the same part in the aspirations of the states to territory as the claims to nationality play in our own century. The influence of politics upon mythology was not small. The great legendary cycles were already established, but they could be altered in detail, and it is in the mythological padding, the genealogies, that this remodelling and alteration for political ends is seen most clearly. Athens and Megara both laid claim to Salamis and took the Spartans as their judge. The latter assigned the island to Athens because the Catalogue of Ships in the *Iliad* makes Aias place his ship alongside those of the Athenians. Solon is said to have pointed out to the judges that the sons of Aias, Philaios and Eurysakes, had obtained Athenian rights of citizenship, and lived at Brauron and Melite. Against the method itself no objection was raised, but it is significant that the Megarians, in order to refute the arguments of the Athenians, afterwards declared that Solon or Peisistratus had interpolated the said verses in the *Iliad*. Athens tried to incorporate Megara, too, within her territory. She succeeded for a short time about the year 460, but a similar attempt had been made much earlier. Peisistratus conquered Nisaea, the harbour town of Megara. To this state of things corresponds the legend that King Pandion of Athens, when dividing his kingdom among his four sons, handed over Megara to one of them, Nisos, who is the eponym of Nisaea. The assault of the Pelasgians upon Attic maidens related by Herodotus constitutes the justification of Miltiades in occupying Lemnos, where Pelasgians lived. Indeed the main theme of the history of Herodotus, the struggle between Greece and the East, is based upon the mythical struggles connected with Medea and Helen.

Herakles became a special Dorian hero, much more as a basis for the political position and claims of the Dorians than as a representative of the Dorian ideal of manhood. Homer relates that Zeus had promised him the lordship over all the neighbouring peoples, but that Hera had by cunning transferred the promise to Eurystheus. The conquest of Peloponnesian country by Herakles and his descendants reflects the Dorian conquest of the Peloponnese and at the same time provides the conquerors with a title for their occupation. Originally the legends were associated with Herakles himself. A whole series of legends depart from the ordinary Herakles myths, in which the hero performs his exploits by his own strength. In this series he is placed at the head of armies, conquers countries, and sets up kings. The myth about the struggle at the gates of the kingdom of the dead is transformed, in virtue of the resemblance between the words, into the struggle for the town of Pylos ; Herakles killed all the sons of Neleus except Nestor. By this is obviously meant the later Pylos in Messenia, which belonged to Sparta. After that the hero took the field against Sparta, killed Hippokoon, who had driven away his half-brother Tyndareus, and reinstated the latter. Then he turned against the Eleans, who had supported Sparta, and there set up Phyleus as king. But when the mythological chronology came to be arranged, Herakles himself could not be brought into play, for he belonged to the period before the Trojan war. The year of the fall of Troy is the point from which events are dated in the legendary chronology. But the Dorian invasion took place after the Trojan war, and was accordingly ascribed to the descendants of Herakles in the third generation. The predominating position of Argos in the earliest period is reflected in the legend that the eldest of the Heraklidai, Temenos, became king of Argos. Otherwise the legend was chiefly elaborated in Sparta. The myth which relates that the second of the Heraklidai, Cresphontes, through unfair dealing in the allotting of the conquered country, obtained the best piece, Messenia, for himself, while Aristodamus had to be content with Laconia, is an attempt to create a justification for the Spartan conquest of Messenia.

Another similar myth-formation falls well within the historical period and expresses the newly awakened national feeling of the Arcadians when, thanks to Epameinondas, they had been freed from the yoke of Sparta after the battle of Leuctra. They erected in Delphi a group of statues in which appear the progenitress of the Arcadians, Kallisto, her son the eponym Arkas, and his sons, Elatos, Apheidas, and Azan, eponyms of the three great Arcadian tribes. But besides these appears another son of Arkas by a second wife, Laodameia, the daughter of Amyclas. He is called Triphylos and is simply an eponym for the coastal district to the west, Triphylia, whose inhabitants were related to the Arcadians and gravitated to them, although they had long been subject to Elis. After the battle of Leuctra they became independent and combined with the Arcadians against Elis. Triphylos is otherwise mentioned only by the Arcadian Polybius of Megalopolis. The Arcadians had therefore introduced him into the genealogy of their heroes in order to strengthen their own claim to the district and to repudiate the claim of Elis.[1] Under the Roman dominion, when the disputes had to be fought out with words instead of weapons, the old arguments reappear. When Lacedaemonians and Messenians disputed before the Roman senate,

[1] H. Pomtow, *Ein arkadisches Weihgeschenk in Delphi, AM*, xiv, 1889, pp. 17 et seq.

in the time of Tiberius, about a district in Taÿgetus, the Messenians supported their claim by referring to the old distribution among the descendants of Herakles.

In later times it was in the main the genealogies alone that could be refashioned. This was done in the interest not only of the states but of families. When the Elean seer, Tisamenus of the famous prophetic family of the Iamidae, became a Spartan citizen and settled at Pitane, near Sparta, the heroine Pitane was made the first ancestress of the Iamidae.[1] The Hellenistic rulers used this convenient method of embellishing their pedigrees. When King Pyrrhus wedded a daughter of the tyrant Agathocles of Syracuse, named Lanassa, his royal historiographer, Proxenus, gave Herakles a new daughter of the same name. She was made to be the wife of the ancestor of the royal house, Neoptolemus-Pyrrhus, and ousted the old wife, Andromache.[2] The best example of the application of mythology to the service of political interests is the way in which the Romans made use of the legend of their Trojan origin as a political point of connexion, first in Sicily and then in Greece. When the senate intervened in the year 250 B. C. in favour of the Acarnanians, it reminded them that they alone of all the Greeks did not take part in the expedition against the mother city of Rome. In the peace with Macedonia in the year 204 the Romans allowed the inconsiderable town of Ilium to take its place by their side in the treaty.

There were exceptional cases in which particularism did not win a complete and entire victory. It might happen that smaller places were combined into a larger state. Thus the largest single state of Greece, Athens, arose from a combination of the many, once independent, smaller towns of Attica. In Attica we can still discern how religion and cults were

---

[1] Wilamowitz, *Isyllos von Epidauros*, pp. 162 et seq.

[2] M. P. Nilsson, *Studien zur Geschichte des alten Epeiros* (*Lunds Universitets Årsskrift*, vi, 1909, no. 4), p. 30.

made to help in welding together the united larger state.[1]
The cult of Apollo seems to have been confined chiefly to the
east coast. The sacred ship which was sent out to Delos
sailed from Prasiae, on the eastern shore of Attica, even
after Athens had taken over the sacred mission ; this was
the ancient starting-point. At Brauron there was a famous
cult of Artemis ; it had a branch on the Acropolis of Athens,
and every fourth year a ceremonial procession marched from
Athens to Brauron. The Athenian Thesmophoria were
enlarged by a festival at Halimus, which was reckoned as
their first day. When Eleusis was incorporated with Athens,
the Athenian state took charge of the mysteries and placed
them under its own protection. The minor mysteries of
Agrae, a suburb of Athens, were associated with them and
the cult was given a branch in Athens itself, in the Eleusinion,
below the Acropolis. The sacred objects were carried to
Athens, and then back to Eleusis, in the great Iacchus
procession. The god of tragedy, Dionysos Eleuthereus, was
taken to Athens from Eleutherae when this neighbouring
Boeotian town was incorporated with the metropolis. The
list of cults which were transferred from the smaller places
to Athens or were given branches there in order to set the
seal of religion upon the work of unification is not exhausted
by these examples. During their period of greatness the
Athenians tried to raise their position by making the
Eleusinian cult into the common cult of Greece. They
exhorted all Greeks to give tithes to the goddesses of Eleusis
as they themselves and their allies did. The myth that
Demeter had sent out Triptolemos to spread agriculture
and the blessings of a civilized life over the world always
expressed for them the idea of that leading position in
civilization to which they had well-founded claims.

The same kind of thing occurred elsewhere. The town of

---

[1] Wide, *op. cit.*, 2nd edition, pp. 217 et seq. (the passage is omitted
in the third edition).

Patrae arose through a combination of the three places, Aroë, Antheia, and Mesatis. At the Dionysos festival images of Dionysos Aroeus, Antheus, and Mesatis were carried to the temple of Dionysos Aisymnetes in the town. Artemis Triclaria, the Artemis of the three country districts, takes her name from the union. It is said that the people of Cyzicus, when by force of arms they had compelled the inhabitants of Proconnesos to unite with them, carried off an image of Meter Dindymene. The process was repeated in the year 370, when a number of small Arcadian towns were united into the ' Great City ', Megalopolis. A shrine was instituted there to Zeus Lykaios, which, like the summit of Lykaion, was not to be trodden by human foot. A bronze statue of Apollo Epikourios was taken to the city from his famous temple at Bassae near Phigalia. Pan Sinoeis was worshipped in the neighbourhood ; he, too, was taken to Megalopolis. Pan Scoleitas was moved from a hill of that name. It is perfectly clear from these examples how attempts were made to concentrate and confirm the formation of the state by concentrating the cults. By the time Megalopolis was founded the device had already lost a great deal of its ancient power, but in the consolidating of Attica it answered its purpose well. We cannot refuse our admiration to the unknown statesmen who, with the aid of the cult, acquired for Athens a greater area of territory than any other Greek state was afterwards to possess, and thus laid the foundations of her future greatness.

No such unity as we find in Greece between state and religion has ever existed elsewhere. The individualistic religious tendency, which does not recognize state supervision and is not concerned with territorial boundaries, tried to break down this unity, but failed. It was too deeply rooted : state and religion were one, and the fact is explained by their origin. Their unity was an ancient inheritance, and this was all the more perceptible since the Greek states were small. The state was built up on the idea of kinship and family. Every state had its mythological ancestor whose posterity its citizens were supposed to be ; hence comes the number of insubstantial eponyms, especially in mythological genealogies. When the population was redistributed into new groups on a different basis, a fictitious blood-relationship was imported into these. Cleisthenes, for instance, gave his new and entirely artificial *phylai* (tribes) Attic heroes as eponyms and ideal ancestors. The cult in which the idea of the state is most clearly expressed, that of the state hearth in the Prytaneion, the assembly-hall of the state authorities, contains a direct imitation of the central point of the family cult, the hearth of the house.

The oldest order of society was the patriarchal monarchy. Under primitive conditions the king was also the chief priest, the supreme guardian of religion in his state, as the father was in the family. The royal house, too, had its family cults, but there were also other cults which devolved upon the king in his capacity as head of the state. When the monarchy was overthrown and its place was taken by republican officials, either elected or chosen by lot, these took over both the sacral and the civil functions of the king. Religion is always conservative, and therefore the name of king was given even in historical times to the highest sacral official of the state, not only in Athens, where the second archon had the name of king, but also in a number of other cities. But this so-called king was an ordinary servant of the republic. Thus the cult practised by the king passed into the hands of the republican state, and the customary organ of the state, the ecclesia or popular assembly, exercised the right of control over it. A couple of examples show that a special order of procedure was established for sacral matters. In Athens such questions were dealt with by the last two ordinary assemblies of the month ; and there is reference to a popular assembly for sacred matters at Argos.

Not only the religious functions which belonged to the king as head of the nation but also his family-cults were taken over by the organ of the republican state. The state inherited the claims of the family upon the individual both politically and religiously. The strengthening of the power of the state in the archaic period was achieved by the suppression of the arbitrary rule of the nobility, that is to say, of the great families. They must—for instance, when the minor towns of Attica were united into a single state—have had to submit to restrictions in regard to their power over the cults no less than in other matters. Just as the knowledge of the then unwritten legal traditions governing civil life had once been the exclusive possession of the nobility, so originally the knowledge of cult and religion, of the sacral laws, rested with them alone. But here the prerogative of the nobility survived the democratic upheaval. The interpreters of the sacral laws in Athens were always members of the nobility, whether they were elected by the people or appointed by Delphi.[1]

Alongside of the ancient houses, in which the old sense of the family, its traditions and ideas, was kept alive, new elements of the population grew up which were without these old family traditions. During the archaic period they acquired a share in the government and in later times occasionally ruled the state. The clouds were gathering, and broke in the first political struggle for religious privileges.

The populace had no pedigree, no inherited cult ; in the opinion of the nobility it had no gods either, because it had no family cults. In religious matters the common people were the dependants of the noble houses ; like the slaves, they were permitted to take part in the family cults of their masters, but this permission could be given or withheld at the discretion of the nobility. The latter could likewise

---

[1] A. W. Persson, *Die Exegeten und Delphi* (*Lunds Universitets Årsskrift*, xiv, 1918, no. 22).

exclude all outsiders if they wished. It was so, for instance, with the private cult of the Eumolpidae, the Eleusinian mysteries, but we have here a secret cult exceptionally developed from family rites which once were limited to a certain circle according to the discretion of the family The privileged position of the noble families in the matter of cult and religion was broken down by the democratic reforms of Cleisthenes. The basis of the old family-state was the *phratria* ; the *phratriai* were combined into four *phylai* (tribes), at the head of which were *phyle*-kings (φυλοβασιλεῖς), chosen from the nobility. In later times different *phratriai* had different internal organizations and different cults. A *phratria* was afterwards divided into cult-communities (θίασοι). In the period before Cleisthenes it consisted partly of a noble family, forming its kernel, and partly of a section of the people, associated with the family as participators in its cult (ὀργεῶνες). The first step was now to make it obligatory for the *phratria* to admit both the members of the family and the *orgeōnes* (sharers in the cult), the religious dependants of the family.[1] The populace was thus assured of its share in religion and cult and could no longer be excluded according to the caprice of the noble families. Cleisthenes went farther ; he brushed aside the very foundation of the old order by breaking down the predominant power of the nobility in the elementary organization of society. He let the *phratriai* remain, but only as a kind of ecclesiastical community, which was required to carry out certain cults and keep the lists of citizens. It was naturally a condition of this arrangement that no citizen might be excluded from the *phratriai*. The civic community was built up on a newly created basis, the *deme*. A *deme* was formed like a municipality. Membership of it depended upon residence within its area, and thus the difference in privilege between the nobility and the people

---

[1] Law quoted by Photios, s.v. ὀργεῶνες.

was obliterated. The *demes* were combined into new *phylai*, ten in number, which were named after Attic heroes. But the idea of the community as a blood-relationship dominated antiquity. The geographical principle was applied only in the first formation of the *demes*; subsequently the right of membership in them depended not on place of residence but upon birth, so that the descendants of a man who in the time of Cleisthenes had lived, let us say, at Eleusis, would for hundreds of years belong to the *deme* of Eleusis, wherever they might live.

Democracy could not permit any one to remain outside the state organization of the cult. It took over or broke down the old family cults and transformed in a democratic spirit the old cult-organization which had rested on the family. This phenomenon was so common that Aristotle in his *Politics* describes as one of the customary reforms tending to promote democracy the creation of several *phylai* and *phratriai* and the amalgamation of the private cults, that is, of the family cults, so that they should be fewer in number and accessible to all. As illustrations he adduces not only the reforms of Cleisthenes, but also the establishing of democracy in Cyrene. The tyrant Cleisthenes of Sikyon, who seems to have belonged to the suppressed native population, mockingly named the three Dorian tribes after animals (swine, asses, and pigs); his own tribe he called ' chiefs of the people ' ('Υᾶται, 'Ονεᾶται, Χοιρεᾶται, 'Αρχέλαοι). Inscriptions from Argos have taught us a number of names of *phratriai* which evidently belong to a democratic transformation.[1] Some seem to be local names; here, too, division on a geographical basis has been used as the democratic device for breaking down the rule of the families. It is curious that in Agamemnon's old kingdom three *phratriai* are named after Odysseus and his race, which has no connexion with Argos.

---

[1] *Bull. de corr. hellénique*; xxxiii, 1909, pp. 171 et seq.

The struggle between the families and the state in regard to the cults often ended in a compromise : the cult became state property and was accessible to all, but the charge of it remained within the family ; the priest or priestess was chosen from the family whose property the cult had originally been. In Athens it very often occurs that the holders of the priestly office for a certain cult are restricted to a certain family. Thus, for example, the priestess of Athena Polias and the priest of Poseidon-Erechtheus were taken from the ancient family of the Boutadai. It is a very tempting supposition that the family whose inherited possession is the priesthood of the old city-goddess of Athens, and of the mythological representative of the Mycenaean kings, was once the ancient royal house of Athens, although the royal house of the legend is another. In other cults again, newly established or rearranged, we may find the priest appointed by the people. Thus, for instance, the document describing the ordering of the cult of Athena Nike in the middle of the fifth century prescribes that the priestess shall be elected by the popular assembly from among all the women citizens of Athens. In matters pertaining to the cult, even more than in other matters, the Athenians showed the moderation for which they were famous. They did not dissolve all the bonds of tradition attaching them to earlier times, and this was a source of strength in the sphere of religion.

In other quarters there was much more radical tendency. In the Ionian cities it was the custom to let out the office of priest to the highest bidder ; we have, for instance, from Erythrae a list of about forty priests appointed in this way. The priest might have considerable perquisites, according to the popularity of the cult ; certain fees for every sacrifice and certain parts of the sacrificial animals, such as the skin, fell to his share. By the renting of the office the state diverted a considerable portion of these emoluments into its own treasury. It might indeed imagine that it was acting wisely and perhaps equitably in so doing, but in reality it showed that it had lost all respect for religion when it used its control of the cult as a means of acquiring pecuniary profit for itself. This was the final phase of the Greek state religion : it was secularized and profaned in the interests of the state. To the human heart with its longings such a religion had nothing to offer.

The efforts to democratize the cult were early directed with deliberate vigour against that section of it in which the noble and wealthy families made it a point of honour to display the greatest possible luxury—funeral customs and the cult of the grave. The so-called Dipylon vases from Athens, sepulchral vases from the eighth century, depict the sumptuous funeral processions of the period. The dead man rests upon a carriage spread with carpets and is followed by troops of men and female mourners. Games formed part of the funeral ceremonies : rows of racing chariots testify to these costly amusements. The finds in the graves of this period are of no great importance ; this is quite natural since the funeral gifts were burned with the corpse, but costly materials formed the dead man's shroud and were consigned with him to the flames. The sense of honour and position, which drives men to make the greatest sacrifices, gave rise to extravagant display, such as only the rich and great families could afford. It is not surprising that the people regarded it as a proof of their insolent pride, and compared this extravagance with their own poverty. The discreet legislators had to agree that it was an unnecessary and harmful waste, upon which great sums were expended that might have been put to a better use.

The restriction of this extravagance in funeral customs began early. Enactments in this direction are ascribed to most legislators—Lycurgus, Charondas, Pittacus, Diocles of Syracusae. Of Solon we have more detailed information. He forbade the ancient custom by which the female mourners lacerated their own bodies. It was the custom for singers to perform the funeral dirge, in which the dead man was extolled. A technical form for the dirge had been developed ; we already have an example of it in Homer, when singers are called to Hektor's bier. This too Solon forbade. An ox must no longer be sacrificed as a funeral offering and the dead man must not be wrapped in more than three shrouds. Solon's laws show that it had formerly been the custom for women mourners to sing dirges at the funeral beside the monuments of other members of the family ; he forbade this practice also. This last decree was a blow directed against the grave-cult handed down from ancestors to posterity, in which the family feeling of the nobility expressed itself. Similar decrees are found in an inscription from Delphi of about the year 400 B. C. We find here also a prohibition against repeating the dirge on the day following the burial, on the tenth day after it, or on the anniversary of the burial. Only the nearest relatives must take part in the dirge at the burial-place, and the funeral procession must pass along in silence.[1] There are preserved in inscriptions various later laws which by still stricter regulations inculcated simplicity in the burial rites. The philosophers followed the example in their ideal legislation, and when one of them, Demetrius of Phaleron, governed Athens shortly after the time of Alexander the Great, he put these precepts into practice. By so doing he gave the death-blow to that costly elegance which the Athenian families took pleasure in displaying in their funeral monuments, the works of art which we may still admire on the burial-ground at Dipylon. Demetrius forbade the expending of any more labour upon a grave than ten men could perform in three days. The decree was obeyed, backed up as it was by increasing poverty in the town. All later funeral monuments are plain and simple.[2]

[1] Compare my article in *NJb*, xxvii, 1911, pp. 618 et seq.
[2] A. Brückner, *Der Friedhof am Eridanos*.

The ancient cult of the dead persisted in the cult of heroes. To them was sacrificed an animal, whose blood was caused to flow down a hole into the ground to moisten the dead man's ashes ; games and races were held for them as formerly at the funeral of a nobleman ; in some cases the funeral dirge was repeated for them, on a fixed day in each year. The cult of the heroes was the public cult of the state ; in it the old forms were preserved, but private individuals were required to abstain from these and restrict themselves to a democratic simplicity, which in Athens, nevertheless, during her period of greatness, was ennobled by works of art. It is characteristic that in one other case the state intervened and gave the burial a ceremonial character : this was the case of those who had fallen in battle for their country. Those who fell in the fight against the Persians were regarded as heroes and were worshipped as such. It was certainly not so in later times in Athens ; it is not said that other than the usual grave-offerings were made to the fallen, but the state honoured them and encouraged patriotism by giving them a state funeral. Their remains were taken home and kept until the great common burial, when they were deposited in the common grave, an enormous mound covered with white stucco, the foot of which was encircled by many monuments of the fallen.[1] The chief mark of honour was the memorial speech which one of the most prominent of the citizens was deputed to make. The most famous example is the speech which Thucydides puts into the mouth of Pericles on the occasion of the beginning of the Peloponnesian war, a lofty and unsurpassed expression of the ideal programme of Athenian democracy, the patriotism of its citizens, and their pride in their city.

The new state had broken down the old family state, but

---

[1] S. Wenz, *Studien zu attischen Kriegergräbern*, Dissertation, München, 1914 ; P. Wolters, *Eine Darstellung des attischen Staatsfriedhofes* (*Sitzungsberichte der Akademie zu München*, 1913, no. 5).

had at the same time inherited its claims. In the family organization the individual himself was of no account ; he counted only as a link in the chain of his race. The family gave him his religion, his privileges, and his responsibility. The state originated in an idea of blood-relationship, and if this relationship was in reality broken in order to find room for the populace, ' who had no forefathers ', yet the idea of the state as a blood-relationship was a compelling thought throughout antiquity. The state inherited both the political and the religious claims of the family organization. The individual himself now counted only as a member of the state : if he did wrong, the consequences came upon the state to which he belonged. The gods sent disaster upon the country in their anger at the crimes of the individual. Even in the diplomatic fencing which ushered in the Peloponnesian war the opponents used similar weapons. The Spartans challenged the Athenians to expiate the blood-guiltiness which the Alcmaeonids had incurred in the suppression of Cylon's attempt to make himself a tyrant, and the Athenians replied by demanding that the Spartans should expiate their crime against the gods when they let the victor of Plataeae starve to death in the temple of Athena Chalkioikos. So prevalent still was the feeling of the state's responsibility for the crimes of the individual ; the individual in his turn was responsible to the state for his actions.

From this source arises the demand of the state for the maintenance of its cults. This was the political and particularist element of the religion. The general element, as regards its greatest and most important part, consisted in the ideas and myths about the gods, especially in so far as Homer had made them common property. In these the particularist state, which merely followed its own ends, took no interest. It has often been remarked that the Greek might say and believe what he liked about the gods so long as he respected the cults. This fact is due to the different attitude of the particularist state to the state-cults on the one hand, and to the ideas and myths about the gods on the other. It followed of necessity from this conception that the citizen should seek in the cult not first and foremost his own personal interest, but that of the state, the general good. In his private concerns he might naturally turn to the gods or omit to do so as he pleased, but above all he must not by his actions endanger the relations between the state and the gods. He must not neglect, despise, or oppose the state cult. He must first of all adhere to the cults which his fellow citizens practised, the cults of the state. Reverence for the gods prevented the state from forbidding the old private family cults. Many were brought under state control, but many were also allowed to persist as private cults, apart from the numerous local minor cults of trees, springs, rivers, and so on. These fell, in point of importance, below the predominating position of the state religion, but they stubbornly persisted and proved ineradicable. The struggle against the private cults is illustrated most clearly in the case of the cult of the dead. The cult of ancestors was more than any other bound to the family ; here the claims of the family to an independent position alongside of the state appeared most plainly. Accordingly the dead of the great families were reduced to the level of the ordinary unimportant dead, by restrictions in regard to grave-cult and burial customs. It was only for the dead whose cult was public and the property of the state, that is, for the city-heroes, that it was permitted to maintain the grave-cult in its ancient forms. The family was to have no separate interests which raised it above the rest of the citizens and divided it from the state. The scheme was successful. The Homeric kingdom of the dead, with its ineffectual shades, was impressed upon the mind of the people. The practice of heroizing individuals does not emerge until late classical times, when the life hereafter demanded stronger colours, and the state had attained such dimensions that the idea of it had lost its compelling force.

It has been said that in the Athens of the fifth century all splendour and magnificence were reserved for the state, since it was only in relation to the gods that it might be displayed. This was the time for the building of the Parthenon, the so-called Theseion, the temple at Sunium, the temple of Athena Nike, and finally the Erecththeion. The individual, it is said, lived plainly and simply, and it was not until after the changes of the period of the sophists that any considerable luxury was developed in the habits of the private citizen. This statement, however, is subject to reservations. The wealthy Athenians of the period preferred living in the country to living in the crowded city. What sort of a life they lived there we hardly know, but Kimon, for instance, lived like a *grand seigneur*. Still there is an approximation to this democratic simplicity in private life, whereas it had been otherwise under the rule of the nobility. The statement is true, however, in so far as it relates to the cult, for the state festivals were celebrated in brilliant fashion. Here too the rule of Pisistratus laid the foundation for the coming development. He deliberately used the festivals as a factor in his levelling, democratic policy. To him is generally ascribed, although it must be admitted that the grounds of the ascription are not particularly strong, the founding of the two most brilliant festivals of Athens, the Dionysia and the Panathenaea ; it would perhaps be more prudent to say the great Panathenaea, with games and contests, held every fourth year. The democracy completed his work.

To every festival belonged a festival procession, which gave occasion for the display of all the pomp and magnificence possible. The preparations were on a grand scale. An inscription from Piraeus mentions that the streets along which the procession was to pass were to be repaired. In Athens there was a special building at Dipylon where the processions were equipped and from which they started. On the frieze of the Parthenon we see the procession at the great Panathenian festival—demure maidens ; men and youths with sacrificial animals, censers, and sacrificing implements ; chariots which were to take part in the contests belonging to the festival ; and the flower of Athenian youth, the ephebes, on horseback. This is a typical example which must stand for all, even the less brilliant, but the processions were made as splendid as possible. At festivals of which contests formed a part the pomp was increased by the fact that all who had entered for the contests took part in the procession. In later times schoolboys and girls had their special place in it. At the great Dionysia we hear of persons who carried baskets, doubtless containing what was needed for the sacrifice—bread, wine-skins, vessels for the sacrificial meal, and water. Everything that was needed for the great sacrificial banquet was therefore included in the procession, as well as the sacrificial animals, not only implements and vessels, but also bread, water, and wine.[1] Certain feasts were celebrated on a very large scale, the state entertaining the citizens, and the sums expended were by no means small. In later times the state sold the skins of the animals sacrificed in order to make a little money, and we have a number of accounts of the income thus derived. In the year 334–3 it amounted to 5,549 drachmae. An ox at that time would no doubt cost about two hundred drachmae ; what the skin would fetch we do not know, but the figures are in any case eloquent. The distribution of the flesh of the victim was carefully regulated, and the portions of honour assigned to officials and to those taking part in the procession.

The great festivals, as is the case with Easter in modern

[1] E. Pfuhl, *De pompis sacris Atheniensium*, Berlin, 1900.

Greece, were the only opportunities which the man of the people had of enjoying roast meat. The democracy provided the funds in the name of the gods. At the great Dionysia an entrance fee was levied to help in covering the expenses. But the drama too was a part of the cult, from which no one was to be excluded on the score of poverty. The state therefore distributed money to the poor citizens, so that every one might be able to buy a theatre ticket. When the democracy degenerated, this practice was abused and became a mere distribution of doles, which ate into the finances of Athens like a cancer. At other festivals also, such as the Choës, the happy Festival of the Pitchers, when the new wine was dedicated, money was in later times distributed among the people. It was no wonder that the Athenians were attached to their gods, who gave them food and money. But when they congratulated themselves on being the most god-fearing of all men because they celebrated more numerous and more splendid festivals than others, they failed to see that the cult of the gods only served them as an excuse for sunning themselves in the might and prosperity of their state. The state religion understood nothing of the lesson of modesty and self-effacement which Apollo had once impressed upon the poor man from Hermione.

The festivals of the gods served the state as an occasion not only for manifesting its wealth but also for bestowing with the greatest possible publicity the marks of its honour and favour. At the greatest festivals decrees of honour were proclaimed and wreaths conferred upon deserving men both within and without the city. In Athens this was done especially in the presence of the audience assembled in the theatre at the great Dionysia. Here it was the custom of the Athenian state, during its days of prosperity, to have a play performed designed to remind the vast audience of the greatness and power of Athens. The surplus of the state income was carried across the orchestra, talent by talent, in the sight of the representatives of the allied states, who had had to contribute to the total. Then the sons of those who had fallen in battle were paraded ; they had been brought up at the expense of the state and now, having grown up, they received armour from the state so that they might follow in their fathers' footsteps, and were sent out into life. It was a lesson in citizenship.

Athens made use of her great festivals, moreover, to assert the unity of its empire, and this in a manner which to some extent reminds us of the unifying of Attica by means of the cults, although it failed to have the same success, more particularly because of the emphasis laid on the subordinate position of the allies under the ruling state. At the great Dionysia the allies brought to Athens the tax imposed upon them ; the period of taxation was four years, from one celebration of the great Panathenaea to the next. In an inscription which has been preserved the Ionian city of Erythrae is instructed to send a sacrificial animal of a certain value to the great Panathenaea, and any inhabitants of the city who may be present at the festival are assured that they shall have the flesh divided amongst them. When the colony of Brea in Thrace was founded, it was required to bring an ox and a suit of armour to the great Panathenaea, and a phallus to the great Dionysia. It must have been a common custom for allies and colonies thus to contribute to the splendour of the festival, and we can therefore imagine how large a procession of sacrificial animals must, in the palmy days of Athens, have made its way through the town up to the city goddess on the Acropolis.

The great festivals, to which people gathered from all quarters, also provided a suitable opportunity for international transactions and the proclamation of international agreements. At the same time foreigners were given a healthy lesson in the greatness of Athens. In the treaty with the city of Methone in Macedonia it is stipulated that if Methone and the Macedonian king Perdiccas cannot come to terms, each must send an embassy to the great Dionysia to negotiate. When Athens and Sparta made an alliance in the year 421 B. C., it was determined that this should be annually renewed by the sending of embassies to Athens at the great Dionysia and to Sparta at the Hyacinthia.

Our account has chiefly been limited to Athens because little is known concerning other cities. But it may be mentioned that in the document relating to the colony which the Hypocnemidian Locrians founded at Naupactus, it was decreed that a colonist who happened to be on a visit to the mother-city might sacrifice there if he wished, and should obtain his share of the victim. It was laid down in the arbitration between Cnossus and Tylissus in Crete that the Cnossians at a common sacrifice to Hera should present gifts of hospitality to those who sacrificed.

Festivals which are really of purely political significance became more and more common as time went on. The first example is the Eleutheria (Feast of Liberty) at Plataeae, quinquennial games which by a common decision of the Greeks had been founded in memory of those who had fallen in the battle at that place. In name they were dedicated to Zeus Eleutherios. Festivals with the same name were afterwards instituted at several places ; they were especially appropriate where it was desired to commemorate the overthrow of a tyrant. After their victory at Leuctra the Boeotians founded in the neighbouring town of Lebadeia a festival which was called the Basileia after Zeus Basileus. Thanks to numerous inscriptions the founding of the Soteria (Festival of Deliverance) at Delphi is well known ; it was instituted when the Aetolians had succeeded in driving back the Celtic hordes. In other towns also festivals of this name were instituted for the same reason. The diffusion and popularity of the festival afford a good criterion of the power of the Aetolian League. At Eretria in the year 308 it was decided that the citizens in the Dionysos procession should be crowned with ivy because the Macedonian garrison had left the town on the date of the festival and released it from their dominion. All these are purely patriotic festivals which are only in form associated with the cult. An opportunity was soon found in them to display loyalty and submission to the political authorities. A number of festivals were instituted in honour of the Hellenistic rulers, their governors, and the Roman proconsuls, and they bear their names, for instance, the Philadelpheia, the Sylleia, the Mukieia, &c. They endured precisely as long as political circumstances allowed.

Differences of character and of power in the states caused differences in their festivals. The most vigorous manifestation of this political religion is to be seen in democratic and imperially expansive Athens during her period of greatness. In the more loosely organized Peloponnesian League there was no place for it : there, every city had more or less to shift for itself. Sparta laid special emphasis upon the education and the hardening of the young. This tendency appears also in her festivals, the Gymnopaedia and the well-known scourging at the altar of Artemis Orthia, and it was not neglected in other quarters. With the dwindling of political power the school festivals came to fill an important place in the festival calendar of the Greek cities. School pupils took part in the festival processions and athletic contests filled the same place as the games and athletics in our modern schools. Contests and games were associated with all the major festivals, and they were the principal incident of the great international festivals. This is not the place to describe the agonistic contests, nor yet the Olympic and the other great national games. Their importance as an ideal bond of unity between the Grecian tribes split up into their minor states is too well known to need remark.

Instead, another side of the festivals which has received less attention may perhaps deserve a word or two. A festival brought the people together, and it therefore provided the very best of opportunities for any one who had anything to offer or to sell to the public. The very needs which the festival created must have attracted merchants there. Others undertook to amuse the public. *Panegyris* means both ' festival ' and ' market '. The connexion between religious festival, market, and popular amusement is natural, and persisted until Puritanism discovered that it was unseemly to serve God with worldly joys and business. Antiquity was naïve enough never to see this. In Athens we hear of a fair at the Choës (the Pitcher-feast) and at one of the minor festivals, the Diasia. The reason for the importance of the island of Delos lay in the trade which was carried on there at the great Feast of Apollo. Strabo speaks of the festival as though it were a fair, and so it seems to have been even at the time when the hymn to Delian Apollo was composed. At the Olympic games, too, a great fair was naturally held. Several inscriptions mention special measures which were taken with a view to attracting the people to the fairs at the great festivals ; the suspension of the ordinary municipal toll upon articles brought into the city was a favourite method. But we also find it mentioned upon one occasion that the money-changers took the opportunity of a festival to raise the rate of exchange.

The merchants ran up simple shelters and huts to protect themselves and their wares. The great crowds of people assembled at a festival also needed a roof over their heads, especially when the place for the festival did not lie in the vicinity of a town where they could obtain a lodging. A circle was drawn in the sand (at least at the Isthmian games) in order to mark out the spot as appropriated for this purpose. Then, as at the modern Greek popular festivals, there speedily arose a kind of camp, in which natives of the same town had common quarters. When the towns of Teos and Lebedos were politically united, it was ordained that the inhabitants of these two towns should camp together at the common Ionian festival at Panionion. Splendid tents were erected for festival banquets ; Euripides makes Ion fetch textile fabrics for a tent of this kind at Delphi out of the god's own treasure-chamber. Moreover, there were also inns upon the spot, in which the festival could be celebrated with food and drink. A motley crowd of people and a general air of entirely worldly festivity was the result, which was certainly not without its perils and its shadier side. In one inscription women are forbidden to enter the encampment—this may be due to the fact that women were excluded from this particular cult—but some at least of the festivals provided women with the only opportunity they had of leaving their homes and taking part in public life. So it was in Athens and in Ionia ; in the rest of Greece they enjoyed greater freedom. The cult insisted upon their inclusion even in certain nocturnal festivals. But the incitements of the festival atmosphere and the darkness had their perils ; the violation of a maiden during a nocturnal festival is a stock motif both of the myths and of comedy.

The Puritans were not wrong. Religion runs a serious risk of being profaned and materialized by all such festivity and merry-making. But these are things which man needs in every age. They have survived the fall of the old religion and still exist under similar forms in the Greece of to-day.

In later antiquity the civic religion was a shell without a kernel ; religious feeling had turned elsewhere. Of the ancient festivals nothing was left but the outward show, the agonistic contests with their excesses, and the distribution of food, oil, and money, on which wealthy citizens were driven by ambition to waste their riches.

In his description of the patriotic religion of Athens Wide represents the state as its source and says : [1]

' By the state is understood all the spiritual and material blessings which the state can give—the personal liberty and independence of the Attic citizen and all the political privileges which fall to him as a member of the sovereign people, the blessings of peace and the honourable combat for his native land, the daily bread which the state gives even to the poor and fatherless, his share in the splendid and joyous state festivals and his participation in all the wonderful benefits of culture offered him in science, literature, and art in the intellectual centre of the contemporary world. All these blessings descended from the divinity immanent in the state. . . . It is curious that this religious emotion was not associated with the goddess of city and citadel, Athena, as might have been expected.'

But if one had asked a simple Athenian citizen what he thought of all these privileges, he would no doubt have answered that they came from the state gods and in particular from Athena, who of course obtained her share of the tribute of the allies. Unconsciously, however, his idea may have been more as Wide represents it. His patriotism, involving a self-esteem which was not without its justification, told him that it was the citizens of Athens, and among them himself, that had created the glories of the Attic state. It is true that this conception is supported by a feeling akin to the religious, but whether it can really be called a religious attitude does not seem to me so certain. Then as now a politico-social ideal put itself forward as a rival to religion. It was supported by faith and hope, the fundamental forces of religion, but these cannot with their full power and enthusiasm be directed upon more than one object. The stronger the political and social hope and faith became, the more the religious hope and faith dwindled. But the rivalry was not so open as it is to-day ; it was only latent, for this political ideal had laid hold of the religion and bound it to the service of the state.

[1] Wide, *op. cit.*, p. 227.

It is no wonder that the Athenian citizens clung to the religion which gave them so many privileges, and that they maintained the state cult and religious tradition. When the age of enlightenment began to direct its unaccommodating, intellectual criticism even against cults and gods, religious prosecutions began. This new curiosity, this disposition to discuss, arose among the highly educated, who exalted themselves above the crowd ; it was therefore regarded with suspicion from the outset by the democratic public. And when it was directed against the gods, who provided for the people so many delights, that was the crowning offence. But the power of the state could not shield and preserve the religion from which a political ideal had ousted the spirit. A religion of such a kind is an empty shell with no power of resistance ; it can withstand neither blows from without nor rationalistic criticism. With the collapse of the Greek states the state religion also fell. Of genuine religion there remained, as far as the old Greek religion was concerned, only the mere traffic with the gods induced by habit, and the simple cults at country springs and trees. However, this fundamentally irreligious state religion was not without its positive effect upon the religion of Greece. It lived and breathed in particularism, and the gods too became more particularist than ever. Many-headed polytheism prevailed.

VIII

THE RELIGION OF THE CULTURED CLASSES AND THE RELIGION OF THE PEASANTS

THE intellectual development of Greece brought the defects of her gods and of her religion into the open. The archaic period was a time of great and multifarious movements, some of which continued their development while others died away. It was then that the prophetic figure of Xenophanes appeared. He taught of a god who was not like men either in form or ideas, and he attacked the cult of images and the mythology as it was represented by Homer and Hesiod. But we possess too little of Xenophanes to know whether his single god was a real deity or only a philosophic principle, and whether Xenophanes himself is merely to be included among the philosophers or was also a religious reformer. It is in Herakleitos that we find the saying which is most clearly directed against the outward forms of the cult. ' They purify themselves vainly ', he says, ' by defiling themselves with blood, as if a man who had stepped into mud should wash his feet with mud. He would be thought mad, if any one saw him doing that. And they pray to these images, as if one should talk to a house, not knowing what gods and heroes are.' It is not clear what position these teachers took up in regard to the ancestral religion, whether by their criticism they meant to overthrow it, or whether they held to its old foundations and only meant to purify it by a radical reform. For the moment these sayings provoked little response ; that was to come later.

In Ionia the Homeric anthropomorphism had broken down the belief in the supernatural and paved the way for an explanation of Nature based on natural causes. Thus arose the first science, the Ionian natural philosophy, which sought to explain how the world had originated and had become regulated. The cosmogony had the same end in view. The difference between its mythical and religious explanation and the profane explanation of natural philosophy was not strikingly apparent. The myths of the cosmogony to a great extent served to disguise a development of thought which proceeded without reference to religion, while natural philosophy took the cosmogony as its starting-point and often employed mythical names for its principles. Nevertheless the chief distinction, the fundamental difference between the two, must not on this account be glossed over; on the one hand the world is regarded as a creation of the gods, and on the other as the result of natural causes, from which any supernatural, and therefore any divine, influence is excluded. This is expressed in cautious but decided terms by Hippocrates, the most distinguished representative of the art of medicine, whose great advance towards a rational science falls within the fifth century. He will not believe that ' the sacred disease ' (epilepsy) has, any more than other diseases, a divine origin. All diseases, he says, have their natural causes; all are in an equal degree both divine and human. Just as Homer regarded the actions of men from two contradictory points of view and ascribed them either to men themselves or to the intervention of higher powers, so also the origin and order of the world might be ascribed either to natural causes or to the gods. The two points of view are parallel and facultative; men adopted one view or the other according to circumstances and natural tendency. Just as rudimentary religion can allow contradictory elements to remain alongside of one another without any sense of incongruity, so it was also at first in this case. But it was only a matter of time before increasing habits of reflection would lead to the discovery of the fundamental contradiction, and the conflict would become apparent.[1]

Conditions of a kind to bring about this conflict were developed in Athens towards the end of the fifth century. Ionia was politically powerless, and natural philosophy there belonged to a limited circle. It was transplanted to Athens, the intellectual centre of Greece, where the intellectual conflicts awoke an echo in the minds of the citizens who determined the destinies of their city. The state had established control over religion and driven the true religious spirit out of it, but nevertheless preserved it as an expression of political ideals and of patriotism. During the Peloponnesian war, when Athens was struggling for her existence, she was more than usually sensitive to anything which might imperil her well-being, at the hands of the gods no less than in other ways. The greatest danger came from the mighty intellectual awakening, the period of enlightenment, brought about by the work of the sophists. They did not, like the philosophers, appeal to a limited circle, nor work, as they did, principally through their writings, but came forward as teachers of the young, and the young flocked to their lectures and discussions in order to learn how best to make their way in the state. This was indispensable learning for any one with ambitions in democratic Athens, where Power was acquired by the ability to speak and discuss. All the questions of the day were drawn into the discussions, not excepting the natural philosophers' explanations of the phenomena of the universe. What had formerly been an esoteric science now formed a part of general culture. Thus the explanations of the natural

[1] Fragments of the earlier philosophers in Diels, *Fragmenta der Vorsokratiker*. For the contact of philosophy with the religion see E. Zeller, *Die Philosophie der Griechen* ; O. Gilbert, *Griechische Religionsphilosophie* ; P. Decharme, *La critique des traditions religieuses chez les Grecs*. One special and important side is treated by A. B. Drachmann, *Atheism in Pagan Antiquity*.

philosophers stood out in opposition to the religious ideas, and the conflict became real.

To the mass of the people the new ideas penetrated only in a fragmentary and distorted form ; the nature of the case made this inevitable. Aristophanes' comedy, *The Clouds*, furnishes an illustration, though a highly coloured one, of the popular conception. The cosmogony proper is conspicuous by its absence ; there the points of conflict were not prominent. The philosophical explanation of the meteorological phenomena—rain, thunder, and so on—was set in the foreground, because this was in direct opposition to the popular belief in the weather-god Zeus as their cause. Accordingly a philosophical *primum mobile*, Rotation (Δῖνος), which dethroned Zeus, was also brought forward. It is significant that to this was attached the ethical polemic against the gods, which placed the higher moral demands in antagonism to popular belief. Zeus does not strike perjurers with his lightning, but he strikes the tops of the mountains, tall trees, and his own temples. Some years earlier a spokesman of the official religion in the popular assembly of Athens succeeded in carrying a resolution directed against ' those who did not believe in the divine, and promulgated doctrines about the phenomena of the heavens ' The prosecution of Anaxagoras was based upon a charge of atheism, because he declared the sun to be a glowing mass and the moon a lump of earth no bigger than the Peloponnese. In the above phrase ' the phenomena of the heavens ' (τὰ μετάρσια) are included not only the celestial but also the atmospheric phenomena. There was in fact less danger of a conflict, unless it was deliberately sought, in regard to the former than in regard to the latter. The divinity of the rivers was not diminished by the fact that they were treated as a material substance, that water was fetched from them or people bathed in them ; they belonged in spite of this to the most ardently worshipped of the gods. Just as little need it detract from the divinity of the sun that it should be regarded as a glowing mass ; besides, the sun-god was principally a mythical figure, who had a very unimportant cult. It becomes apparent that it was not the idea in itself that conflicted with religion ; the crime consisted in the novelty of the theory and in the application made of it.

In later times the divinity of the heavenly bodies assumes ever-increasing importance. According to a passage in Plato the heavenly bodies were the first gods of the Greeks, just as they were still worshipped by foreign peoples. One of his successors, Xenocrates, wrote a book about the nature of the gods, in which he dealt with the eight gods of the heavenly bodies and called them the Olympian divinities. The phenomena of the heavens are always adduced as a main source of the belief in gods. But this belief is not of popular origin. Of the Greek natural sciences astronomy was that which had developed farthest and was studied most eagerly ; this is the true reason why the heavenly bodies became involved in the discussion of religious and scientific questions and occupied a prominent place therein. Their cult only attained popular significance when astrology under Oriental influence pressed forward into a position of prominence ; philosophy had prepared the way by impressing upon the mind of the public, and more particularly of the educated public, the idea of the special claim of the heavenly bodies to divinity.

The statement that the sun was a glowing mass and the moon a lump of earth could not, as we have said, form a very serious point of dispute. The cause of conflict lay rather in what was implied, that they were nothing more than this, that the criticism of the sophists would recognize nothing but what was taught directly by reason and the senses. We here penetrate to the very core of the principle which animated the teaching of the sophists. There is nothing in the world which cannot be erected into a problem

for logical disputation, where the answer depends upon skill
in dialectic and the art of words. Ratiocination and logical
proof are referred to as the highest court of appeal. Dialectic
knows no other conditions; it respects neither political,
ethical, nor religious values, but tests and dissects them all
in its claim for the higher and better rights of reason.
Religion and its ideas were exposed, no less than the state
and its institutions, to this sort of discussion, which took up
the ideas already thrown out by certain philosophers. One
of the most distinguished of the sophists, Protagoras, pro-
pounds the existence of the gods as a problem for discussion. He begins his book about the gods with the words :
' Concerning the gods I cannot know for certain whether
they exist or not, nor what they are like in form. There
are many things that hinder certainty—the obscurity of the
matter and the shortness of man's life.' The meaning of the
last clause is disputed, but the main point is that Protagoras
represents the existence of the gods as a matter for discussion. This no religion can tolerate without abandoning
its most important position. It was a perfectly sound
instinct of self-defence that led to the prosecution of
Protagoras for atheism, even though he never appeared as
a challenger of popular religion.

A central point in the discussion of the sophists with
regard to the phenomena of human life was whether these
were grounded in Nature or in law (convention), $\nu\acute{o}\mu\varphi$ $\mathring{\eta}$
$\phi\acute{v}\sigma\epsilon\iota$. We are accustomed to translate $\nu\acute{o}\mu os$ by ' law', but
this translation involves a misinterpretation of the sense.
By ' law ' we denote both that which is enacted and that
which is necessitated, and we include in the latter physical
necessity ; the word $\nu\acute{o}\mu os$ involved for the Greeks the idea
of an enactment which is the decree of some one, whether
man or god, and is therefore not the result of physical
necessity. This sense of the word is better expressed by
' convention ', but on the other hand the latter translation

does not convey the idea of compulsion and command which underlies νόμος. In order to understand the discussion we must clearly distinguish the things contrasted : natural necessity and the work of man. Law and custom, the state and its institutions, do not proceed from natural necessity but are the work of man; they are imposed upon the individual by the majority. The consequence is that the individual who does not think them right is not morally bound by them. The same point of view was applied to religion, closely associated as it was with the state. The differences between the cults and gods of different states showed that religion was founded not in Nature but in convention. There is, it is said later, one god according to Nature, but many according to law and custom. The logical consequence here also is that the gods are the work of man. With that idea religion was overthrown.

How far this rationalistic criticism of religion proceeded is shown in an interesting fragment of a drama, the *Sisyphos*, the author of which was one of the best-known followers of the sophists, the tyrant Critias. We are there told that men first lived like wild beasts, without law and order ; force decided everything. Afterwards laws were made and punishments instituted so that justice might rule instead of force, but then men did wrong in secret. Thereupon some wise and far-seeing thinker invented the gods, who hear and see everything, in order that men should not dare to commit crime even in secret, and set those gods in the region where the phenomena that men fear most are manifested—thunder and the heavenly bodies. The tendency of this teaching is clear. The sun is called ' the bright molten mass of the star of day ', and of the wise man in question it is said that ' he veiled the truth with false tale '. This platitude was afterwards repeated to satiety, but it must have made an enormous impression when it was first uttered. Its origin in the discussion about the state and its institutions is evident.　Religion according to this theory is but a complement to the state, a secret police-force which maintains the legal conventions, and has been so cunningly instituted that none can escape it.

This was, however, far from being the only explanation of the origin of religion and the gods which was put forward in sophistical discussion.　As the sophists by virtue of their interest in the art of exposition laid the foundations of linguistic research, so they also deserve the credit of having founded the science of religion.　The honour is not diminished by the fact that they built upon still earlier foundations. What certain gods signified, in terms of natural phenomena, was shown by linguistic usage as clearly as could be desired, for instance, when Homer says that the Achaeans held the flesh of the sacrificial victim on a spit over Hephaistos, or when the oracle answered the Athenians before the Persian war : ' O, Salamis, thou shalt destroy many sons of women, either when Demeter is scattered or when she is gathered.'　So again Dionysos could mean ' wine ' and Aphrodite ' love '.　In the tragic writers linguistic usage goes still farther, in connexion with the Homeric conception of the *daimones* which we have previously discussed ; almost every phenomenon or mental quality is described by them as a ' god '—Happiness, Wealth, the recognition of friends, Discretion, Reason, Jealousy, even an excellent meal—sometimes the god is given a definite name, as when Euripides says that all folly among men is called Aphrodite.　This mode of expression suggested that the origin of the gods might be sought also in the phenomena of mental and emotional life.

The sophists' interest in language readily led them to indulge in etymological theories.　They had ancient authority for so doing, for there were already etymological myths. Hesiod's story of the rising of Aphrodite from the foam of the sea is probably due to the fact that in her name was

recognized the word ἀφρός, ' foam ' ; the other name of
Delphi, Pytho, is derived by the Homeric hymn from
πύθεσθαι, ' to rot ', because the body of the slain dragon
rotted in the sun, and by Sophocles from πυθέσθαι, ' to
inquire ', because men sought the oracle's advice. The
Ionians eagerly adopted this rationalistic method of explanation. The legend that Cyrus was suckled by a bitch is
explained by Herodotus thus, that his foster-mother's name
was Spako, a Persian word corresponding to the Greek Kyno,
' bitch '. Plato's *Cratylus* is full of the wildest etymological
guesses. He seldom hits upon a correct or at least a reasonable one, as he does when he derives Pluto from πλοῦτος,
' wealth ', or explains Hades as ' the invisible one ', ἀειδής ;
usually it is merely an arbitrary juggling with sounds and
letters. Hera is explained as the air (ἀήρ), Hephaistos as the
light (φάος), and Dionysos is the giver of wine (Διδ-οίνυσος).
The etymologies are used to support explanations derived
from other quarters. Plato was not the first to play in this
manner with the names of gods.

Much more important, however, was the method of
explaining the myths which was developed in connexion with
the interpretation of Homer, already a school-book among
the Grecian people. The first commentator on Homer of
whom we know anything was Theagenes of Rhegium, who
lived in the time of Cambyses. It is said of him that he
interpreted the war between the gods in the twenty-second
book of the *Iliad* as a contest between the elements, the wet
and the dry, the hot and the cold, the light and the heavy.
Apollo, Helios, and Hephaistos represented fire, Poseidon
and Scamandros water, Artemis the moon, Hera the air,
Athena Reason, Aphrodite Lust, Hermes Discretion. At
first sight Theagenes seems to exemplify all the modes of
interpretation which have been mentioned in this chapter,
but it is probable that he did not seek to interpret the
significance of the gods in general, but only in this particular

passage, that is to say, his purpose was not to explain the origin of the gods but only to give an allegorical explanation of Homer's account of their appearance in the struggle. The respect in which Homer was held caused men to seek a deeper meaning and a hidden wisdom in the apparently absurd and indecent fables which occur in the poems. Anaxagoras' pupil, Metrodorus of Lampsacus, declares that Homer treats of virtue and justice. He goes the whole way, and not only means that Homer uses the gods as an allegorical disguise for his wisdom, but says in so many words that the gods are not what those who built temples to them thought them to be, but represent natural substances and arrangements of the elements. He explains Agamemnon as the ether ; our source adds that it would be just as easy to explain Hektor and Achilles, Paris and Helen allegorically and to deny that they ever existed. He was right ; Metrodorus was a worthy predecessor of modern cosmic mythology.

The foundation was already laid for the interpretations by which the age of enlightenment was able to explain away the gods. Euripides combines several such explanations in his last tragedy the *Bacchae*. The myth that the infant Dionysos was sewn into the thigh of Zeus has a physical and etymological origin :

> When Zeus . . .
> . . . bare the babe to Olympus, Hera then
> Fain would have cast his godhead out of heaven.
> Zeus with a God's wit framed his counterplot.
> A fragment from the earth-enfolding ether
> He brake, and wrought to a hostage, setting so
> Dionysus safe from Hera's spite. In time
> Men told how he was nursed in Zeus's thigh.
> Changing the name, they wrought a myth thereof,
> Because the God was hostage once to Hera.

In the preceding verses he seems to say that the godhead of Demeter is due to the fact that she is the Earth, which nourishes men, and that of Dionysos to the invention of wine. It is related of Prodicus, who is the author of the

well-known allegorical myth of the Choice of Herakles, that
he declared that the men of olden times considered as gods
all things that were useful to them in their lives, such as
the sun and the moon, rivers and springs, meadows and
fruits, just as the Egyptians regarded the Nile as a god ;
and accordingly bread was regarded as Demeter, wine as
Dionysos, water as Poseidon, fire as Hephaistos, and so on.
This is the old naturalistic explanation to which the very
nature of the gods seemed to point, but it is characteristic
of the sophists' attitude of mind that they appeal to utility
as the reason for the origin of ideas about the gods. In the
hands of the sophists these explanations became something
more and something other than they had been before, since
their purpose was to explain the convention by which men
had made gods for themselves. If the attempt was successful, or if at least their theories gained an appearance of
probability, then the conclusion lay ready to hand, whether
it was expressed or not. Religion and the gods were
proved to be the work of man, and a delusion.

Our knowledge of the period is unfortunately fragmentary
and scanty, otherwise we should certainly hear more of the
attacks upon the religion. The criticism of its outward
forms, which had already begun and was afterwards continued with great vigour, cannot have been silenced. The
falling esteem in which the purificatory ceremonies were
held is reflected in the rising demand for purity of heart
and intention rather than purity of the hands. Socrates'
pupil, Antisthenes, taught, as Xenophanes had done, that
God was one, that he could not be recognized in an image or
seen with the human eye, and was not like any mortal man.
This is an instance of the common method by which a
higher conception of religion and gods was set up in opposition to the gods of popular belief and of the official religion,
and the shortcomings of the latter were then measured
by the standard of this higher conception. This is what

Socrates does in Aristophanes. In the sphere of ethics Euripides has summed up the reasoning in the well-known sentence : ' If gods do anything base, they are no gods.' With this saying the gods of Greek mythology were doomed. They could not be quit of the myths. This criticism was no attempt to purify the popular and mythological ideas about the gods, like that of Pindar and perhaps of Xenophanes. It was not that the way was being prepared for a higher conception of the gods ; the old gods were undermined without any new and better gods being put in their stead.

Belief in the oracle had already begun to waver, as we can see from Herodotus and Sophocles. Herodotus criticizes the oracle ; Sophocles holds fast to Delphi but rejects the private oracles. Even the reputation of Delphi rapidly declined, and by the end of the century the oracle had already scant authority. Lysander turned to the oracle of Zeus-Ammon in the great oasis, which was at a greater distance and was therefore regarded with more respect. There is a significant story about Anaxagoras. A prodigy, a ram with a single horn in the middle of his forehead, was brought to Pericles. The seer Lampon interpreted this to mean that of the two political rivals, Pericles and Thucydides, that one would conquer to whom the omen had been brought. But Anaxagoras had the animal's skull cut in two and showed that the brain did not fill it in the usual way, but was egg-shaped and was concentrated towards the root of the single horn. Even the omen was due to natural causes !

Religion had no bid to make in its own defence. It was bound to the state and was incapable of any exaltation or purer conception. The same criticism attacked with similar weapons and method as well state and society as religion. The criticism of the age of enlightenment came from the upper and educated classes. It was therefore quite naturally suspect to the popular democracy whose interests were bound up with the existing form and religion of the state, and which felt its own foundations shaking. The popular suspicion of the over-curiosity of the sophists was given inimitable and not easily translatable expression in Kleon's words in Thucydides: 'A slow wit combined with steady judgement will come to more good than an undisciplined cleverness.' His bitter opponent, Aristophanes, agrees with him on that point. The official religion was merely a target for criticism and had for its defence nothing but the legal and other machinery of state—a very poor defence in a case of this kind. It was used, however. The religious prosecutions show what the average citizen of Athens thought about the criticism. They continued into the fourth century. The prosecution of Socrates was one of the first acts of the restored democracy after the expulsion of the thirty tyrants. After him various philosophers were accused of atheism. The accusation of Aristotle had a political motive in the hatred of Alexander, but no such motive was present in the cases of Stilpo the Megarian, Bion the Cynic, or Theodoros the Cyrenaean.

In the following century, the third, the religious prosecutions ceased, although such scepticism as that of Carneades might just as well have led to prosecution as the criticisms of Protagoras. The religious indifference which was the result of the undermining work of the critics had seized upon the whole people, even the masses. At the time of the Peloponnesian war men committed sacrilege, mutilated images as did Alkibiades, or polluted them as did Kinesias, under the dangerous attraction of the forbidden and with something of the perverse feeling which actuates those who celebrate the Black Mass. Somewhat later, in Xenophon, we hear of a young man, Aristodemus, who does not sacrifice to the gods, does not seek the oracle's advice, and mocks those who do so. Here is something which is more dangerous to religion than sacrilege—pure indifference. Aristodemus seems to have belonged to a type not unusual in his day;

it was soon to become still more common. The treatment of atheists which Plato recommends in the work of his old age, *The Laws*, is significant. They are to be shut up and admonished—by the pastor, we are almost tempted to add ; but if they persist, they are to be punished with death. Demosthenes certainly has the names of the gods on his lips, like every one else, but he is fundamentally irreligious, throws the blame for the failure of his policy upon Tyche, and accuses the Delphian oracle of serving Philip's ends. At the end of the century the Athenians did homage to Demetrius Poliorketes, who delivered them from the despotic rule of his namesake, the philosopher. They were not content with deifying him, but also showed their contempt for the old gods. ' Either they are far away or have no ears, or else do not exist or care not a whit about us,' such was their song in honour of Demetrius. Notwithstanding all the flattery bestowed upon Demetrius, the old religion must have fallen very low before such words could be uttered at a public ceremony. In some cases blasphemy was a fashionable craze. Philip V's admiral Dikaearchus used to raise altars and sacrifice to Impiety and Lawlessness. Agathocles mockingly justified his raid upon Corcyra and Ithaca by referring to the mythological stories of the deeds of Odysseus in Sicily.

The art of the period still bears its silent but eloquent testimony. For Praxiteles, indeed even for Alcamenes, the image of a god is not an object to be approached by the artist with reverence, but an occasion for the solving of an artistic problem. In the Hera and Aphrodite of Alcamenes the problem of the clothing is of more interest than the goddess herself. In the Hermes and Cnidian Aphrodite of Praxiteles there is not a spark of anything religious except the beauty, and in the Apollo Sauroktonos a genuine cult-motif is playfully dissipated We can understand that if a real cult-image was needed, it was necessary to go back to an earlier style, as Kephisodotus did in his Eirene with Ploutos. The Cnidian Demeter is the most deeply moving work of antiquity, but it is the purely human feeling in the sorrowing mother which grips us. When artists became conscious of the lack of religious impulse, they knew no better than to substitute theatrical effect for calm, inward dignity. Leochares began the process, if the Belvedere Apollo and its counterpart, the Artemis of Versailles, are correctly ascribed to him, and the sculptors of the Hellenistic period continued it, with still bolder methods. The Zeus from Otricoli may stand as an example for all the rest.

However, it was not only the growing religious indifference which crippled the power of resistance of the old religion : the impotence of the state contributed to the process. Greece was first broken up in a war in which every state fought against its neighbour, and then passed under a foreign yoke. After her last convulsion in the Chremonidean war, Athens lost every vestige of political independence, and soon her trade and industry also died away. The state had no longer anything to offer to its citizens, and they on their side had no reason to plead the cause of the state gods. With the dwindling of political power the religion attached to the state declined also.

The philosophical attempts at explaining the origin of religion and of the gods were allowed to continue in peace. They have henceforth greater interest for the science of religion than for its history. We have already seen that practically all the tendencies which have helped to shape the modern science of religion had already appeared in antiquity, but for the sake of completeness it may also be mentioned that the historical school, which derives the ideas about the gods from one particular country, was not wanting either. It was represented, for instance, by Herodotus, who is of opinion that the Greek gods came from Egypt. The origin of the gods in natural phenomena was too obvious not to be followed up. It has already been mentioned that the heavenly bodies came more and more into the foreground. Aristotle refers on the one hand to the sun, moon, and stars, whose regular movements seemed to betray their divine origin, and on the other to certain special mental phenomena —enthusiasm in the antique, religious sense, dreams and prophecies, as to the fulfilment of which there could sometimes be no doubt. The inclusion of the mental phenomena is a great step in advance, yet it led to nothing more than the defence of the belief in the supernatural, for which purpose it was adopted by the later Stoics. Allegorical interpretation played a far more important part, and above all with the Stoics. We still possess a compendium of Stoic theology in Cornutus' summary of the mythology, to which too little attention has been paid. The interpretations were all the bolder since Stoic philosophy was now also looked for in the myths. For instance, Homer's story of how Hera was fettered by Hephaistos and liberated is said to show that the order of the universe depends upon the balance of the elements ; when Zeus hangs her suspended in the air, this points to the origin and succession of the elements, and the tug of war between Zeus and the other gods represents the ordering of the spheres of the universe. The lameness of Hephaistos shows the difference between heavenly and earthly fire ; earthly fire must be fed with wood, just as the lame man needs a staff for his support. Hephaistos was hurled from heaven to earth : men lit the first fire from a flash of lightning—and so on.

This kind of interpretation of the myths was merely an intellectual amusement, the arbitrary character of which was only too obvious and easy to attack. Plato in one place expresses himself quite disrespectfully about it, but in another passage he calls mythology an investigation into the past. This was a point of view from which the full consequences were not extracted until the Hellenistic period, but it was perceptible to the Greeks from the beginning. Mythology was the earliest history, and pedigrees were traced back to the time of the myths. But soon it became a question where the conception of the myths as history was to stop. It could not reasonably be extended to anything which was of such a character that it could not be adapted to history as men usually conceived it. And so the necessity of choosing among the myths presented itself, of rejecting some and accepting others. But another device was also practicable, namely, to touch up the myths so that they might look like historically credible narratives. Those who did this thought that they were freeing the historical kernel from its mythical shell. Hecataeus of Miletus, who lived during the period of the Persian wars, is the most distinguished representative of this tendency. His interpretation of the Herakles and Kerberos myth was that Kerberos was a dangerous serpent who lived in a cave near Taenarum and was therefore called the hound of Hades. Geryon was an ancient king of Epirus, who owned great herds of cattle, part of which were stolen and carried off by Herakles. The interpretation of the myths as history involved also the necessity of adjusting the chronological relations between the mythical events. A chronology had to be created for the whole mythical period. The epochal year became that of the fall of Troy. From this starting-point the mythology and genealogy were arranged in chronological order, not without great difficulties.

Although there was a difference in the cult and in popular conception between gods and heroes who were dead men, they had the mythology in common. If the historical method was pushed to extremes, it was bound to include the gods also, and the process was assisted by the fact that certain myths spoke of some gods as having died and been buried, for instance, Zeus in Crete, and Dionysos at Delphi. The cult which during the Hellenistic period was addressed to rulers and other distinguished personages helped to obliterate the distinction between gods and men. Total disregard of the distinction was a bold but natural sequel, as is proved by the success which attended the attempt. The method is associated with the name of Euhemerus, although it is uncertain to what extent this mediocre writer was the originator of it. He had predecessors, the most remarkable of whom, Hecataeus, was from Alexandria, and it seems certain that the native Egyptian practice of representing the gods as ancient kings is an important source of euhemerism. The fact that it was popularized as a story of travel contributed very largely to its success. On an island in the ocean opposite Arabia Euhemerus professed to have seen in a temple of Zeus a golden pillar, upon which the actions of the gods were recorded in the form of a family and dynastic chronicle. After Ouranos and Kronos Zeus came into power. He lived on a mountain, called the throne of Ouranos, as a judge and the promoter of useful inventions ; at intervals he made a progress through the world and caused temples to be built and cults to be founded to himself ; finally he died and was buried in Crete. Other myths were treated with even less respect. Kadmos was made a cook in the kitchens of the king of Sidon, and was said to have escaped to Thebes along with his flute-player, the girl Harmonia.

It was a bold step to regard even the divine myths as distorted history, but it was a logical conclusion which the age found striking. Euhemerus' book was one of the very first to be translated into Latin, and that by the poet Ennius. His popularity is shown still better by the great abuse showered upon him ; he was placed first among the atheists of antiquity and, indeed, not without justice. The allegorical and physical explanation left, as we shall see, some room for the gods, but the historical explanation, which made them men who by might and cunning had forced their way to divine worship, like the Hellenistic rulers, deprived them altogether of their divine character. Nor did the majority of writers venture to be equally consistent. Diodorus, who included the myths in his history, only applies the euhemeristic method of interpretation to the demi-gods Herakles, Aristaios, and the Dioskouroi, and also to Dionysos, because the latter's victorious march through the world was described after the pattern of Alexander's marches. The Christian polemic against the heathen gods found ready-made and convenient weapons in the arsenal of Euhemerus.

Diodorus favours a kindred theory which makes the gods the authors of the advances in culture ; heurematography, the referring of inventions to certain persons, is a well-known literary *genre* in antiquity. Poseidon becomes the lord of the ocean because he was the first to teach men to build ships and navigate the seas. Hades rules in the lower world because he invented burial-rites and funeral customs. Apollo invented the bow, the lyre, and medicine ; Hephaistos the art of the smith ; Dionysos vine-growing and the preparation of wine ; Demeter agriculture. In reality these inventors of the arts and benefits of civilization, although they have a certain connexion with the mythological culture-heroes, are not a whit better than the princes of Euhemerus, and are the children of the same spirit as they.

If we sum up all the points and methods of attack we find that not one stone was left upon another in the edifice of the old religion. It became a total ruin in the Hellenistic period. The gods were explained away as the vesture in which human imagination and human limitations had clothed physical and mental phenomena, where they were not identified with ancient rulers and inventors of the same order as those so frequently met with in the Hellenistic period. The cult of images was attacked with eloquent arguments which were retailed by the Cynics to the people. The central rite of the cult, the animal-sacrifice, was rejected by Theophrastus on grounds which made a wide appeal. He demanded respect for animal as well as human life, measured the value of the offering not by its size but by the frame of mind of the giver, and stigmatized the animal-sacrifice as a late degradation of the rite, the ancient gifts of the fruits of the earth testifying to a more pious disposition of mind. Purifications ceased to play a part except in the mechanical cult and in the conventicles. The soothsayer's art decayed, and the oracles were silenced. Philosophy respected the heavenly bodies; they became visible gods, but without any cult. The perception of law and order in the course of the universe laid a seed which came to fruit in astrology and then first acquired a religious value of a quite special and oppressive character.

The anthropomorphic gods had lost their power over the minds of the educated, who devoted themselves instead to the art of living. To pilot mankind through the surges of life was now the main task of the philosophers; they became shepherds and confessors of souls. Both the Stoic self-sufficiency and the Epicurean quietism were objective methods of viewing the course of the world, and in this respect they resembled the philosophy of the Seven Sages. But neither had anything to say as to the source from which the events of human life proceeded. These were more varying and more irrational than ever, and man cannot help inquiring into the power which rules his fate, even if he thinks he can defy it or is indifferent to it. The conception of cause does not suffice even in our day, and still less could it satisfy antiquity, since it was only with the victory of the astrological philosophy that it was first rigorously formulated.

Here was an opportunity for the old belief in ' power ' to emerge again, provided only that it could be clothed in a dress adapted to the age. We have met it in Homer as the *daimon*, and in later times as ' the divine ' or ' the *daemonistic*'.[1] The tragic poets prefer to use the word *daimon* as a term for a single event of deep significance, but elsewhere in post-Homeric literature it is more customary to employ it to mean ' fate ' in general, the continuous chain of events. Theognis says that many have a weak understanding but a good *daimon*, and in Pindar we read that the mind of Zeus animates the *daimon* of dear friends. The new age is distinguished from the old by its spirit of conscious individualism, its egocentric point of view. Every man sought his own ; his particular fate was the thing that interested him most. In accordance with this tendency the idea of the *daimon* underwent a change which had some connexion with sayings of earlier philosophers. We find in Herakleitos that character is the *daimon* of man, and in Epicharmus that manners are a good *daimon* in some, an evil one in others. The *daimon* is located in the heart of every individual man. The Homeric idea that the destinies of men were determined from birth had an even wider vogue, for fatalism found a favourable soil in the remarkable vicissitudes of the Hellenistic period. Every man has his fate, his own series of events ; this is regarded as a separate *daimon*, which accompanies him. The idea is already found in Plato, where he says that man after death is led to judgement by the *daimon* who has had him in charge during life, but it was not fully and clearly worked out until later. One example only need be given, the well-known passage from Menander. ' A *daimon* stands by every man, straightway from his birth, to guide him into the mysteries of life, a good *daimon*, for one must not imagine that there is an evil *daimon* injuring good life, but everything divine is utterly good.' The theory that Menander rejects was the commonly received opinion ; Socrates' pupil, Eucleides, had already assumed that every man had a twofold *daimon*. Philosophy had taught that

---

[1] K. Lehrs, *Gott, Götter und Dämon* (*Populäre Aufsätze*, 2nd ed., pp. 143 et seq.).

God was good, but since events were sometimes good and sometimes bad, men had to split up the *daimon* into one which sent good and another which sent evil. The evil *daimon* has been powerfully described in the vision of Brutus before the battle of Philippi, and in the vision of Cassius in Athens, during his flight after the battle of Actium. The good *daimon* became a protecting spirit, an expression of the conviction that man is under higher protection, and among the Stoics it was identified with the divine spark in man ; the description of Epictetus is well known.

The idea of *daimones* comes from an attitude towards man's lot in life very similar to that which Homer expresses by the words αἶσα and μοῖρα. Of these two words the first had vanished from common use, and Moira had been personified and made anthropomorphic, and was therefore out of the reckoning. The *daimon* was split up and divided, so that every individual man had two *daimones* of his own. The general idea of the uniform ' power ' from which events proceed craved better expression, and the language had it ready to hand. Τύχη, that which τυγχάνει, 'happens', is not very different in sense from the Homeric πότμος and μοῖρα, except that for us at least, though doubtless not for the Homeric man, it brings out more clearly the element of the accidental. This development was a matter of time. Tyche was once upon the way to being mythologized like Moira. The twelfth Olympic of Pindar is a hymn to Tyche the Deliverer, daughter of Zeus Eleutherios ; in another place the poet calls her one of the Moirai, stronger than her sisters. Alcman said that she was sister to Eunomia and Peitho and daughter to Prometheus. But the word remained in current use and the mythologizing was not achieved. Tyche remained the irrational in life, not only good fortune, ἀγαθὴ τύχη, but also the *tyche* which crosses men's plans,[1] as for instance in Demosthenes where he excuses himself for

---

[1] Lehrs, *Dämon und Tyche, op. cit.*, pp. 175 et seq.

the miscarriage of his political schemes, and in almost every second line of comedy. She is blind, she sports with man, she upsets all his calculations, she is envious ; the old idea of the envy of the gods passes over entirely to her ; but she also throws good fortune and success upon the lap of the sleeper. A satirical picture represented an Athenian general, Timotheus, the son of Conon, sleeping, while Tyche caught the cities in her net for him. Tyche's marked characteristic is that she comes independently of man's actions or deserts. It is significant that Timoleon established a cult to Automatia, ' that which comes of itself', a still more precise expression of the favourite idea of the age.

Tyche and the *daimon* were combined. Everything happens to men in accordance with Tyche and the *daimon*, says Diagoras. Agathe Tyche and Agathos Daimon are placed side by side in inscriptions and reliefs. Both to some extent received cults ; Tyche was represented and received a cult as the protecting goddess of a city, for instance, the Tyche of Antioch, but these are only feeble efforts which cannot conceal the fact that Tyche is nothing but an expression for the belief in irrational contingency, at most for undeserved success, an obviously non-religious idea which the dying Greek religion could not mould into its own forms, as it had done with Moira. If it ever does assume an externally religious shape, the disguise is as transparent as possible and deceives no one.

The ancient gods were tottering ; they received fresh comrades who at one and the same time superseded and still further depreciated them. Men began to worship personages in authority.[1] In opposition to the uncompromising condemnation of the cult of men in earlier times, attempts are now made to arrive at an understanding of it and of its

[1] E. Kornemann, *Ueber die antiken Herrscherkulte* (*Klio*, i, 1901, pp. 51 et seq.) ; J. Kaerst, *Geschichte der hellenistischen Zeit*, ii. 1, pp. 374 et seq.

possible origins in Greek religion. It is true that the Greeks had been accustomed to worship mortal men, but not until after their death. For a living man it would offer little attraction to be worshipped under the forms of the cult of the heroes and the dead, and this was only done exceptionally. Tribes were, indeed, named after princes as formerly they had been after heroes ; but this only shows that the sense of the old distinction had been lost. Festivals and contests were held both in honour of the gods, the heroes, and of human rulers. The forms of the cult of living men were in general not those of the cult of heroes ; sacrifices of blood (σφάγια) were not offered to the former, but altars were raised and burnt-offerings made upon them just as to the gods.

The first man to receive divine worship was Lysander, the conqueror of Athens. The cities raised altars and sacrificed to him as to a god, and sang hymns in his honour. The Samians changed the name of their principal festival, the Heraea, into the Lysandreia. The beginning of the hymn that was sung in his honour has been preserved ; it describes him not as a god but as the Spartan commander-in-chief ; as to his formal association with a cult we know nothing, but it is doubtless to be presumed that a certain moderation was still observed. The praise of Lysander might have been associated with a divine cult without his actual deification. The political festivals treated above (pp. 257 et seq.) afford examples of an association of this kind.

When Athens, a hundred years later, celebrated Demetrius Poliorketes, an immense step forward had been taken. Demetrius and his father Antigonus were hailed as saviour-gods, and the first archon became their priest. They were represented in company with the gods in the texture of the mantle which was offered to Athena at the Panathenaea. The spot where Demetrius stepped out of his chariot was declared sacred and was made the site of an altar to Demetrius Kataibates. The two were to be received with *theoxenia* (divine banquets), like Demeter and Dionysos. Instead of envoys, *theoroi* were sent to them as to festivals of the gods. Two new *phylai* were instituted, which were called after them. The Dionysia were rebaptized the Demetria, and the name of the month Munychion was altered to Demetrion ; the last day of every month was called Demetrias. Further, his two mistresses were worshipped as Leaina and Lamia Aphrodite, and altars were raised, and a hero-cult offered, to his favourites. There was to be some distinction of rank, however.

This is a transference of all the forms of a divine cult to a mortal man. It is significant that Lysander was the first to be the object of such a cult, contemporaneously with the emerging of individualism and the dissolution of the state ideal. Criticism and the course of events had overthrown the gods, or at least the unreflecting belief in them, and the compelling power of the state, which had kept the individual in his place, had fallen to pieces. There was no longer any limit to man's aspirations. That which, with mingled envy and horror, the Greeks had seen long ago in the tyrant, man the equal of the gods, now presented itself once more with redoubled force. The old barrier was pulled down, it was no longer felt to be insolence (ὕβρις) to raise oneself above the level of ordinary men. To the new rulers such a position was conceded, and by that very fact they approximated to the gods. The individual, who had renounced both the submission to the gods imposed by belief and the submission to the state imposed by the law, was driven by the compulsion of events and of life to bow to men. He knew no better than to transfer to their honour the forms wherewith the gods, as protectors of his state and his life, had previously been worshipped. The origin of the cult of rulers has been sought in state policy.[1] The correct view is rather that the

[1] Ed. Meyer, *Alexander der Grosse und die absolute Monarchie* (*Kleine Schriften*, i, pp. 283 et seq.).

cult of men did not originate as a measure of state policy—
it should be remembered how powerless even the strongest
state is to impose an entirely new form of religion—but was
adopted and regulated by the state to serve political ends.
Even the divine position of the Oriental kings only exercised
an indirect influence. The origin of the cult of men in
Greece is to be sought in the convulsions of the dying
religion.

Plutarch relates that when the Panathenian mantle with
the representation of Demetrius was carried in the festival
procession through the city, it was torn in two by a gust of
wind, and that the poisonous hemlock, which was not found
elsewhere in the country, grew up around the altars of the
new gods. At the Dionysia, renamed the Demetria, a night-
frost occurred—something quite unique in Athens at that
time of the year—which destroyed the corn and damaged
fig-trees and vineyards. The gods had not yet forgotten
their ancient ways of showing their wrath at human impiety,
and there were still men who saw and believed this. The
words of the comic poet, Philippides, seem almost to belong
to another age : ' To transfer to men the honour due to the
gods is to dissolve the democracy.' Yet he was right, except
that this was but a symptom ; the foundations had long ago
been withdrawn both from democracy and its gods. Even
Polybius, who is anything but religious, agrees that the
unhappy end of the blasphemer Dicaearchus was a just
punishment both from gods and from men. Unbelief and
blasphemy are infectious, but a time-honoured faith, however deep its decay, has so firm a hold upon mankind that it
cannot be expelled without leaving behind it secret mis-
givings in time of trouble, and these, too, are infectious.

The best evidence for the existence of this curiously
mingled state of mind is afforded by the philosophers.
Their rational explanations of the origin of the belief in gods
—φυσικὸς λόγος it is called by the Stoics—proved the

most effective instrument for undermining that belief ; when it is a question of building up of their philosophical systems the gods have to be content with whatever place therein may be available, if there was any at all. But when faced directly with the question : ' Do the gods of popular belief exist or not ? ' the philosophers refused to commit themselves. In such a case they preferred to call in the evidence *ex consensu gentium*. What all men believe without exception—for there is no people which does not know some gods—cannot be a pure delusion. And to this was added the belief in dreams. It was impossible to get away from the idea of a higher inspiration in dreams. Whence did it come ? Democritus declared dream-images to be real images which penetrated through the pores of the body ; and therefore he had also to grant real existence to the gods who appeared in dreams. Aristotle says that the belief in gods belongs both to Greeks and to barbarians, and he introduces it into his state on the score of utility ; his ideas were circumscribed by the city-state. Epicurus, who is praised by Lucretius with genuinely religious feeling because he delivered mankind from a harmful conception of the gods and of punishment in the lower world, and who is opposed to all forms of cult and to the belief in providence, nevertheless concludes by granting the existence of the gods on the grounds of the same evidence ; he merely relegates them to an eternal, passive state of blessedness at an inaccessible distance.

Philosophy peeped out at its back-door upon the ancient gods, and soon the door was left wide open. Plato supplied the means. He had incidentally described the *daimones* as intermediate beings, acting as a connecting link between gods and men. This suggestion was taken up by one of his successors, Xenocrates, and developed into a system. Xenocrates certainly spoke of the eight gods of the heavenly bodies as the Olympian, that is to say, the true deities, but on the other hand it was clear to him that the divine extended through the whole of Nature. Even in the elements he found divine powers, to which, like Prodicus, he assigned names of gods. The power in the air is Hera, that in the water Poseidon, that in the earth Demeter, and so on. In the lower, mundane sphere prevails a mingling of good and evil, of things profitable and injurious. This cannot be due to the gods, for they do not enter into direct communication with men but only work through the agency of the *daimones*. The *daimones* stand midway between divine completeness and human incompleteness. There are both good and evil *daimones* ; therefore there may be cults of a gloomy or offensive nature.

The Stoics had from the beginning no love for the popular religion, and a handsome anthology could be compiled out of their attacks upon the outward forms of the cult— temples, images of gods, myths, and prayers. In the full and genuine sense they recognized only one god, that first prin- ciple which Cleanthes in his magnificent hymn calls ' Zeus who interpenetrates all '. But experience shows that pantheism can thrive side by side with the most unlimited polytheism, so that the attacks of the Stoics upon the popular religion became less and less serious and passed into something akin to recognition. In addition to the one, uncreated, and eternal God, they recognized the created and perishable deities ; they distinguished between the divine power as a unity and the special manifestations and expres- sions of that power. Thus first of all they naturally recog- nized as gods the stars ; further, they recognized the years, seasons, and months ; and finally the elements, air, water, earth, and fire in its lower form. The heroes of old time, the benefactors of humanity, were also deemed worthy of worship. To these were added personifications of human qualities and mental states, and lastly the *daimones*. The soul, and above all its reasoning part, was of divine origin ;

it was regarded as man's protecting *daimon*. Besides the human soul and the gods of the firmament, other souls endowed with reason, that is, *daimones*, must necessarily exist, for the completeness of the universe demanded it. There was therefore plenty of room for the gods of popular belief. Their lack of morals was not difficult to explain, for among the *daimones* were harmful malicious spirits. All this was wrapped up in the allegorical interpretation of myths as in a protecting mantle. Soothsaying also found its justification. It was regarded as a proof of the existence of the gods and of providence, and the Stoics managed to explain prophecies based on the flight of birds and the entrails of sacrificial victims by the sympathy which binds together everything in the universe. Dreams and inspired prophecies became a testimony to the divine origin of the human soul.

It has been said that the *daimon* theory offered the only possibility of solving the problem presented by the popular beliefs of antiquity, if the two propositions were to be maintained that popular belief and cult rested upon a foundation of reality, and that moral perfection was an essential element in the conception of a god. This is true, but the consequences of the solution must also be considered. It involved a depreciation of the gods, who were degraded to the second rank of divinities. The highest principle became the only real god ; this appears most clearly in the so-called Zeus of the Stoics. This god, who was nothing but a philosophical principle, could not be a refuge to which man might turn in his contrition, his hour of need, or his minor troubles ; he could not, to use the language of the official religion, become a cult-god. The gods were driven from the high road and were reintroduced along by-paths. Those which had been and still were cult-gods were stamped as belonging to a secondary class, as is evident from the name bestowed upon them, *daimones*, as philosophy understood it. Their finite character and incompleteness were stressed ; their power was limited, they became links in the chain of the universe. Herein was shown the antagonism between philosophy and the unreflecting religious sense, which may tolerate many contradictions and imperfections in its gods but, when it turns to them, lets all these defects fall into the background and forgets them. The assumption of evil spirits explained the coming of evil from above, but by this assumption the morality of the gods was also stigmatized. The incompatibility of the old ideas about the gods with a higher conception of gods and the divine was in fact demonstrated with complete success. Christianity, which taught of one, almighty, just, and merciful God, had merely to accept this doctrine, and accepted it eagerly. The issue was already decided before the battle was begun.

Unbelief is seldom unaccompanied by some feeling of uneasiness. There is so much in heaven and earth that philosophy, and still more the plain man, has never dreamed of : doubt comes upon him whether his simple everyday materialism will see him through. The inherited ideas of something supernatural, of gods, will not let him go. In times of need and misfortune, when he is abandoned by men, he shrinks back from the empty void he has created. This fundamental religious feeling was more tenacious than popular unbelief or philosophical enlightenment. But it did not benefit the ancient gods, for they were worn out.

A vacuum was therefore created, and a vacuum must be filled. Superstition flourished in the irreligious period ; we meet superstitious people in Plato, in Theophrastus, in comedy. But this did not satisfy, and man craved for gods in which he could believe. Foreign gods poured into the vacuum with fresh vigour. The immigration began earlier than is usually supposed ; Bendis and the Great Mother came to Athens as early as the fifth century. Plato speaks of Tyrrhenian and Cyprian gods. There was only one

Greek god who had a vogue during this period, and that was Asklepios. His shrine at Epidaurus became world-renowned and there were many other centres of his cult. At Epidaurus we find a characteristic blend of the crudest miracle-cures, such as appealed to the masses, with a recognition of the individual need of divine solicitude for man's distress and infirmities. In this very fact is seen the most striking contrast with the state-cult of an earlier age. It was the individual that turned to Asklepios; he gathered adherents from all quarters into his halls. His worship gave scope for warm and sincere feeling, but it was at the same time a clear and pronounced expression of the egoism of the age—both aspects are seen in Aristides the rhetorician ; it was devoid of any very high religious value or any deep moral and religious foundation.

Apart from this, it was only the mysteries that managed to survive the crisis without surrendering. The Eleusinian mysteries, by virtue of their freedom from dogma and the appeal which they made to the depths of the human heart, were able to follow the tendencies of the age ; but of them too we hear very little until, in the time of the emperors, they once more came to fill an important position in pagan religion. More is heard of the Dionysiac mysteries. Evidence of their extension in Italy is afforded by the well-known resolution of the senate by which they were suppressed. In Egypt they were regulated by Ptolemy Philopator.[1] Their popularity under the Empire was due to their connexion with the belief in immortality ; it is significant that the child Dionysos is so often represented upon sarcophagi. Orphicism too awoke to new life and finally entered as an important element into the syncretistic religion.

The old cult lived on by force of tradition as an empty

---

[1] According to a papyrus most recently dealt with by P. Roussel, *Compte-rendu de l'Académie des Inscriptions*, 1919, pp. 237 et seq., and C. Cichorius, *Römische Studien*, pp. 21 et seq.

shell without a kernel. Sometimes it sought its salvation in the adoption of modern forms and ideas, sometimes in association with foreign gods. There are a number of examples of this to which comparatively little attention has been paid. The impressiveness of the cult was increased by better lighting,[1] which became possible through the use of many lamps instead of the old torches. Archaeological discoveries show that lamps were first used in the cult shortly before the conclusion of the Hellenistic period, and thereafter became more and more common ; in late classical times they were among the most common instruments of the cult. It is significant.that in the Dionysiac mysteries the awakening of the god was accompanied by the tones of the water-organ.[2] The new theories about the special divinity of the heavenly bodies made their way into the ancient festivals. The old agrarian festival of the Skiro- phoria was ascribed to Helios and the Horai ; these divinities are entirely in keeping with the Stoic doctrine. Calculation by stars and seasons, which had hitherto been only a profane reckoning of time, now came into sacral use. Cleidemus already calls the old festival of the Proērosia the Proarcturia, i. e. the festival held before the rising of Arcturus. At Olympia the so-called Basilai offered a sacrifice upon the Hill of Kronos at the spring equinox, and this is a date which can only be determined by quite advanced astronomical observation.

At Tithorea in Boeotia an ancient festival, which seems to have belonged to Artemis Laphria, had in the time of Pausanias been transferred to Isis. Attempts were made to introduce the fashionable mysticism of the period into the old customs and myths. The ordinary wedding was made into a mystic ceremony ; the mystic fan was carried

[1] Examples collected by the present writer, in *Götting. Gelehrter Anzeiger*, 1916, pp. 50 et seq.

[2] *Jahreshefte des österreichischen archäologischen Instituts*, vii, 1904, p. 92, et seq., lines 24 et seq.

round to the accompaniment of the mystical formula : ' I have escaped the evil and found the better.' The favourite idea of the age, the suffering of the god, was looked for in the ordinary agricultural labours. Thus the treading of the grapes in the wine-press was interpreted as the dismembering of Dionysos, and the festival of the grapeharvest accordingly acquired a mystical Dionysiac character. An attempt seems to have been made to introduce the same idea into the corn-harvest, to judge by the verse : ' When the young men cut off Demeter's limbs.' Only Demeter and Dionysos afforded an opportunity for this idea, and hence the importance which the cults of these deities continued to possess. The old cult was brought into a theological system and was at the same time developed and refashioned in the spirit of that system. This theologizing tendency has ancient roots and was encouraged even during the Empire by men like Apollonius of Tyana and those who thought with him ; neo-Platonism erected it into a comprehensive system. We have only room here for an illustration or two. In earlier times weddings were celebrated on the luckiest day of the month, the day of full moon ; when the neo-Platonists substituted for this the day of the conjunction of sun and moon, astronomical considerations were clearly involved. Of a similar character is the distinction which was established between the cult of the gods and that of the heroes and the dead. The morning belonged to the former, the afternoon and night to the latter ; a strict distinction was made between the altar upon which offerings were dedicated to the gods and the *eschara* on which offerings were made to the heroes.

Notwithstanding the scepticism of the Hellenistic period, interest in the ancient religion and its forms increased, but it was an historical interest with a romantic and sentimental background, such as is usually found in an age which is weary of its culture. The myths were the earliest history, and the first historians related mythological events. This tendency was repressed by Thucydides and kindred spirits, but in the fourth century it again became prominent, in direct association, as it would seem, with knowledge of religious traditions and the sacral laws. The so-called Attidographers, who dealt with the early history of Athens, originated among the guardians of the national cults ; their work must be regarded as an attempt to defend the threatened old religion. The earliest of them, Cleidemus, was an exegete, and both he and Autocleides wrote works in which the sacred laws were interpreted. At a later date the ancestral maxims of the Eupatridae and the Eumol- pidae were collected. The need of records was felt ; it is a sign of the times that oral tradition should no longer be regarded as possessing sufficient authority. The political upheavals, moreover, sometimes involved the necessity of regulating the official cult. In such a case advantage was taken of the sacral knowledge possessed by certain Attic families. Methapus the Lycomid organized the mysteries of the Great Goddess at Andania after the liberation of Messenia, and the Kabir mysteries at Thebes. Timotheus the Eumolpid was a kind of minister of public worship to Ptolemy I, helping him to found a branch of the Eleusinian cult and to establish the cult of the new national god, Serapis. A glance at the titles of the works dealing with these subjects is instructive. They include writings on the interpretation of the sacred tradition, and, in particular, numerous works on the festivals, as well as on sacrifices, mysteries, oracles, temples, days, months (i.e. the sacral calendar), families, and the epithets and epiphanies of the gods.

These works form the proper literature of the cult,[1] but the numerous local historians and antiquaries also took pleasure in dealing with subjects of this kind. This branch

[1] A. Tresp, *Die griechischen Kultschriftsteller*, *RGVVV*, xv. 1.

of literature was in fact diligently cultivated throughout Greece. After the cities had lost their political independence and importance, local patriotism, which was not yet extinct, found here a field for its energies. Antiquarian interest and lore took a prominent place. Inscriptions and archives were used, and to this habit the learned Polemon owed his nickname of 'the inscription-picker' (στηλοκόπας). An extremely interesting example is the temple-chronicle of Athena Lindia, which was drawn up by a certain Timachidas and carved in stone in the year 99 B.C. ; the inscription, which contains an account of notable votive offerings, as well as an enumeration of epiphanies of the goddess and other noteworthy events which had taken place in the temple, has recently been discovered. From the Tauric Chersonnese we have a decree of honour in favour of a local historian Syriscus, who described among other things the epiphanies of Athena, goddess of the city.[1] The work of these writers may be compared to that of modern investigators of local history and tradition. There was a good deal of dilettantism about it, but it was supported by glowing enthusiasm and a lively interest in the native city, its traditions and its honourable past. With the exception of a few fragments all this voluminous literature is lost, but it has left traces in Alexandrian poetry. The cultivated and exquisite taste of these writers delighted in tracing out remote and forgotten myths and religious customs. The most interesting representative of this branch of poetry is Callimachus ; and Lycophron speaks oracularly in riddles. Callimachus, for instance, in his elegy of Acontius and Cydippe, mentions a curious custom of Naxos according to which the bride before marriage had to sleep with a boy whose father and mother were both alive. He composed

---

[1] C. Blinkenberg, *Die lindische Tempelchronik* (Lietzmann's *Kleine Texte*, no. 131). Syriskos: *Sammlung der griechischen Dialektinschriften*, iii. 1, no. 3086, and *Klio*, xvi, 1919, pp. 203 et seq.

a whole poetical work, *Aitia,* dealing with curious customs of the cult. A fragment recently discovered begins with some valuable information in regard to two Attic festivals ; it breaks off just where the poet passes over to his real subject, a custom observed in the cult of Peleus on the island of Icus.[1]

The interest in the old sacral customs and traditions of the cities was largely increased as a result of this lively literary activity. Men took a greater pride in these matters as the sphere of their political ambitions became more limited. Evidence of this is furnished by Pausanias' description of Greece, which has collected and preserved for us relics of an important branch of literature, and is also to some extent based upon his own travels. Coins of the time of the Empire were often stamped with representations of works of art, famous images, temples, and even scenes from the cult and the myths, and are thus a valuable source for the study of ancient art and for the history of religion. The tendency was particularly strong during the second century A. D., when the romantic and antiquarian interest became a fashion. It was favoured to a high degree by the emperor Hadrian, who overwhelmed Greece with benefactions and himself shared the tastes of the age. This was the last blazing up of the fire before it was finally extinguished.

The world of culture was shaken to its very foundations by the religious crisis, and the population of the cities also became involved in its after-effects ; the bankruptcy of the state religion deprived men of faith in their gods and made them turn instead to gross superstition and to the new and vigorous deities introduced from abroad. But among the simple and peaceful country-folk the rudimentary cult still lived on, in which men worshipped with untroubled faith and confidence the gods of their native districts. These were not so much the great deities whose names resound in

[1] M. P. Nilsson, *Eranos,* xv, 1915, p. 181.

mythology as all the minor local gods dwelling in rivers, springs, caves, and so on. I have already pointed out (p. 118) to how great an extent a classical landscape was dotted with these little centres of cult, and the pictures to which I referred belong precisely to the Hellenistic period and the beginning of the Empire.

Pausanias takes a special interest in curiosities of the cult ; in this he is a child of his age. It is certainly doubtful how much he himself has seen and how much he has taken from books, but there is no doubt as to the conclusion to be drawn from his work : the more distant and the less influenced by culture the district is, the more numerous will be the remnants of its old special cults and gods. The enclosed valleys of Arcadia, with their little unimportant towns which at that time rather deserved the name of villages, formed a veritable museum of religious curiosities. The conditions for the preservation of the local forms of worship were more favourable there than anywhere else. Archaeology has naturally little to contribute to our knowledge of these minor cults. The tiny shrines are difficult to find and do not yield much to research. Most of them have no doubt altogether disappeared, together with their votive offerings, which would be of a most perishable nature. Nevertheless, examples are not entirely wanting. On Mount Parnes, in Attica, there is a cave where, as the finds show, a cult was carried on from prehistoric down to Christian times ; it is called the ' Cave of Lamps ' from the quantity of late antique lamps found there. It was dedicated to the nymphs.[1]

In late classical times Greece was a poor and insignificant country. The great battles between Paganism and Christianity were fought out in more important provinces of the Empire. There, in the country districts, we hear of the stubborn resistance of Paganism, finally compelling its

[1] *EA*, 1906, pp. 99 et seq.

conqueror to make far-reaching concessions ; but as to Greece itself our sources are silent. Our method must therefore be indirect, at the conclusion as it was at the beginning, when we sought to investigate the earliest stages of the Greek religion. We must go to the popular beliefs of modern Greece and see what is still left in them of the old religion.[1]

Pagan gods have disguised themselves in Christian dress. Instead of Zeus, Saint Elijah lives upon the mountain tops, Kosmas and Damianos have succeeded the Dioskouroi. The old forms have proved still more stubborn than their contents. An ancient Greek would feel at home at a modern Greek *panegyris* or popular festival, usually held in honour of some saint. Miracle-cures are wrought at Tenos as formerly at Epidaurus ; men lie down to sleep in the church in order to be cured by an apparition in a dream. Such evidence, which is often obscure and disputed, is not the only evidence ; there are customs and ideas which without any pretence at disguise have persisted until our own day. In Cyprus gardens of Adonis are still planted in potsherds and baskets, are watered, and allowed to wither away. It is true that they are brought to the church to be blessed, but this is only an external adaptation of the custom to the new cult. In Macedonia the boys still march round at the beginning of spring bearing an image of a swallow, the herald of the season, and sing a song and collect gifts ; similar practices were observed in antiquity in Rhodes and at Colophon. The *panspermia*, a mixture of all kinds of fruits, was often found in the ancient Greek cult, either in the cult of the dead at the general Feast of Souls, or at festivals held for the protection of the standing crops and growing fruit. In modern Greece it is just as common and makes

[1] C. Wachsmuth, *Das alte Griechanland im neuen*, 1864 ; B. Schmidt, *Das Volksleben der Neugriechen und das klassische Altertum*, 1871 ; J. C. Lawson, *Modern Greek Folk-lore and Ancient Greek Religion* ; G. F. Abbot, *Macedonian Folk-lore*.

its appearance on the same occasions. It has different names ; in some cases the old term is preserved, but most frequently it is called κόλλυβα, from the boiled grains of wheat which form one of its principal ingredients. It has its established place in the cult of the dead, being found at the banquets which are held at least on the third, the ninth, and the fortieth days after the funeral and on its anniversary, just as in classical times. Part of it is carried out to the grave, and libations of water, sometimes of wine, are offered. It is also found at the general Feast of Souls from which the Saturday before Whitsun takes its name of ' the Sabbath of souls '. At the festival of harvest all kinds of fruits are brought to the church, are blessed by the priest in the course of the mass, and then part of them are strewn before the altar and the rest distributed with good wishes among the congregation. At Arachova, near ancient Delphi, where the *panspermia* has kept its old name, the women on a day in late autumn stew fruits of every kind in a pot ; the members of the family eat of them, and it is recognized that this is done to promote the fertility of the year that is to come. In the mystery cult the *panspermia*, in which wine and oil were included, was placed in a special kind of vessel, consisting of smaller vessels secured upon a common base, and to this lights were fitted. This curious implement can be traced back to prehistoric times, and a similar vessel is still occasionally used in the Greek church.[1]

The ancient gods were the first to disappear before the new doctrines, but their traces have not been entirely obliterated. When the Greek peasant says : ' God is raining ', ' God is sifting ' (when it is hailing), or ' God is shoeing his horse ' (when it thunders), this idea of God as the immediate cause of the phenomena of the weather undoubtedly recalls the ancient weather-god, Zeus. Still clearer traces are found in folk-lore. Lenormant has recorded at Eleusis a story which

[1] S. Xanthoudides, *Cretan Kernoi*, BSA, xii, 1906, pp. 20 et seq.

tells, in the style of the modern folk-tale, of Demeter's sorrow and search for her lost daughter. We have several versions of the legend of St. Dionysius, who, when on the way to Naxos, found the tender vine-plant and hid it first in a bird's leg, then, when it grew bigger and bigger, in a lion's leg, and finally in the leg of an ass. But there is always the possibility that these legends have been scattered afresh among the people as a result of learned tradition, which has never been entirely interrupted in Greece. We cannot be sure that they are genuine folk-tales, and least of all, unfortunately, in the case of the first of the above.

The smaller, rustic divinities proved to be ineradicable. The nymphs are just as popular in the Greece of to-day as they were in classical times, only they are all called by the name of the water-nymphs, *Neraids*. Sometimes they are called simply ' the maidens ' or ' the mistresses ' (κυράδες). They are represented as slender and dazzingly beautiful young girls, but sometimes it is said that they have animal's feet. They live not only in the water but everywhere, on mountains and plains, in woods and valleys. Place-names such as ' Cave of the Neraids ', ' the Neraids' Spring ', are common. Like the nymphs of Calypso, they have learned the art of weaving, but above all else they still delight in music and the dance. They have a queen, who is called ' the Great Mistress ' or ' the Queen of the Mountains ' ; in Aetolia she is said to hunt or to dwell among the mountains. The development is now at the stage at which Artemis once appeared as the mistress of the nymphs. Sometimes we hear of a queen of the sea-shore, who stands up to her waist in the water, and, like the Sirens, sings passionate love-songs to those who pass by. It is no doubt the same being that is called the Lamia of the sea. Lamia has kept her old name ; she destroys infant children ; like Empusa or Onoskelis in classical times, she has a leg of copper or an animal's leg. The *neraids* are not seldom malicious and cruel. The madman has exposed himself to the wrath of the *neraids* and become possessed with them, just as in antiquity. Popular legend tells of men who have won a *neraid* as a bride ; but they have had to take possession of her by force and hold her even though like Thetis she transforms herself into a lion, a snake, or fire. The marriage does not last long ; the husband commits some indiscretion and the *neraid* thereupon vanishes. About a century ago, it is said, offerings to the *neraids* used to be placed at cross-roads ; in Athens the offering was brought to a rocky cavern at the foot of the hill Mouseion.

The Moirai are living figures in the popular belief of modern Greece. They are present at the cradle of the new-born child on the third night after birth, and they apportion its lot in life ; sometimes we hear of a good and an evil Moira. Moira, Tyche, and Charos are sometimes mentioned as the dealers of fate ; Charos here represents what Homer calls the *moira* of death. The Moirai receive offerings. In Macedonia a table with bread, salt, and a few coins on it stands before the image of the Holy Virgin for the first three nights after the birth of a child. On the third night, when the Moirai are expected, a table is placed at the baby's pillow bearing a mirror and a honey cake baked by a girl whose father and mother are both alive. Formerly girls who wished to marry used to bring to the Moirai offerings of cakes and honey. The Moirai have here evidently succeeded the nymphs, whose cult was often carried on in a cave.

The god of death, Charos or Charondas, bears an ancient name but his character is entirely changed. Only seldom do we hear of the custom of placing a coin in the mouth of the dead man. Charos is the strong and cruel robber, who mercilessly snatches men away from their life in the light of day. He subdues his victims by force, wrestling with the strong, and running races with the swift. He is most frequently represented riding on a black horse, armed with sword or bow. It is said that he drives the young men in front of him, drags the old men after him, and strings up the infants on the pommel of his saddle. Death is often conceived as a marriage with Charos. The kingdom of the dead is the lower world, the underworld, the place from which none returns. Legend tells of many who tried to force their way into it but became its prey. A flight of steps leads down to it. It is a dark and dismal place, covered with spiders' webs, where day never dawns, no cock ever crows, water does not run, and grass will not grow. The hungry may not eat, the thirsty may not drink, the young men are deprived of their weapons, and the maidens of their jewels, little children even of their shirts. But there are also less gloomy conceptions. Now and again we hear of the garden of Charos, where maidens dance and young men sing and play. But in its emptiness and dreariness the kingdom of the dead for modern Greeks is Homer's realm of the dead. The Christian doctrine of heaven and hell is known, but it is a remarkable fact that the conception of Homer has been so strongly impressed upon the mind of the people that neither mythology nor Christianity has been able to uproot it.

NOTES AND CORRECTIONS (TO THE TEXT)

p. 10, n. 1. Add J. D. S. Pendlebury, *The Archaeology of Crete*, 1939.

p. 11. It is now established that the language of the Hittites was fundamentally Indo-European but very much mixed up with native languages. They took over gods of the country, e.g. Teshub, and were deeply affected by the Babylonian culture. Their influence hardly reached the western coast of Asia Minor; see D. G. Hogarth, *Hittite Seals*, p. 1.

p. 13. The most important of the new finds is a small sanctuary at Gazi between Knossos and Tylissos with five idols and implements from the latest Minoan age, *AJA*, xl, 1936, p. 371; Marinatos, *EA*, 1937, p. 278. Other similar idols were found at Karphi in eastern Crete. They are described but briefly, *AJA*, xli, 1937, p. 628. They are interesting because they belong to the protogeometric age. The Minoan tradition is still to be traced in the sanctuary at Dreros from the end of the Geometric age, Marinatos, *Bull. corr. hell.*, lx, 1936, pp. 214 et seqq.; summary, *JHS*, lvi, 1936, p. 152.

p. 13, l. 32. Idols were not laid down in tombs during the great age of Minoan civilization; they are abundant in Mycenaean tombs, especially the chamber tombs.

p. 15, ll. 26 et seqq. I tried, *Min.-Myc. Rel.*, p. 373, to show that the paintings of the H. Triada sarcophagus represent the cult of a deceased deified man.

p. 17. A. W. Persson, 'The Religion of Greece in Prehistoric Times', *Sather Classical Lectures*, vol. xvii, 1942, the last comprehensive treatment of Minoan religion and its offshoots, puts the vegetation cycle into the foreground.

p. 20, ll. 22 et seqq. Evans, *The Palace of Minos*, i, p. 19, proves that this daemon is an adaptation of the Egyptian Hippopotamus goddess Ta-urt.

p. 22, n. 1. Add my *Homer and Mycenae*, pp. 71 et seqq.

p. 23. I have not discussed the so-called Ring of Nestor, published by Evans, *JHS*, xlv, 1925, pp. 1 et seqq., because it is very suspect; see my *Min.-Myc Rel.*, pp. 549 et seqq., especially

p. 554. The famous treasure from Thisbe, published by Evans, *loc. cit.*, is also open to very grave doubts; see my note, *Gesch. d. griech. Rel.*, i, p. 263, n. 1.

p. 23, n. 4. The cave at Amnisos was explored by Marinatos; see his reports in the *Praktika* of the Archaeological Society in Athens, 1929, 1933, &c. Remains were found from the neolithic down to the Roman age. In historical times it was dedicated to Ilithyia who in origin was probably a Minoan goddess; see pp. 23 and 30.

p. 30, n. 3. K. Kourouniotis, 'Das eleusinische Heiligtum', *ARW*, xxxii, 1935, pp. 52 et seqq.; cf. *ibid.*, p. 112.

p. 37, nn. 1 and 2. See now Ch. Picard et J. Replat, 'L'Artémision délien et les deux tombeaux des vierges hyperboréennes', *Bull. corr. hell.*, xlviii, 1924, pp. 247 et seqq.

p. 38. The new excavations on Ithaca, *BSA*, xxxiii, 1932–3, and xxxv, 1934–5, have not brought anything which upsets this opinion.

p. 40. At Messenian Pylos Professor Blegen made the astonishing discovery of a hoard of inscribed clay tablets, *AJA*, xlii, 1939, p. 557.

p. 41, l. 17 et seq. The myth of Athamas belongs to Mt. Laphystion between Orchomenos and Coronea; see my *Myc. Origin of Greek Myth.*, p. 135.

p. 41, ll. 28 et seqq. A Danish expedition has excavated the Greek town of Calydon with the temple of Artemis Laphria, but the Mycenaean site higher up on a hill where remains of walls and Mycenaean sherds are found is left unexplored.

p. 47, ll. 10 et seqq. See now L. Radermacher, *Mythos und Sage bei den Griechen*, 1938; interesting but not wholly satisfactory.

p. 61, n. 1. The equating of names mentioned in the Hittite tables with those of Greek mythical kings is inadmissible, that of Ahhijava with the empire of the Achaeans probable but contested. F. Schachermeyer, *Hethiter und Achäer*, 1935, supports the identity of the country of the Achaeans, *viz.* Ahhijava, with the realm of the king of Mycenae in a lengthy and circumspect treatment. E. Cavaignac, *Bull. corr. hell.*, lxx, 1946, pp. 58 et seqq., advances the identification with Crete.

p. 63, l. 13. Pausanias, x. 1. 6; l. 21, Plutarch, *mul. virt.*, p. 244 B et seq.

p. 81, l. 33. The word φῶς, 'light', is hardly used by pagan writers in this sense, although light played a great role in magical rites. Words of a more concrete significance are common, πνοή, πνεῦμα, 'blowing', 'breathing', ἀπόρροια, 'efflux'. See my *Greek Piety*, p. 107.

p. 83, ll. 23 et seqq. *Syll. inscr. graec.*, 3 ed., Nos. 982, 983, &c.

p. 85, ll. 17 et seqq. Cynaetha, Polyb., iv. 21. 8 et seq.; Argos, Plutarch, *praec. ger. rei p.*, p. 814 B.

p. 86. The text refers to Tzetzes' account of the usage at Colophon; in other cities the *pharmakos* was driven out like the scapegoat; see my *Gesch. d. griech. Religion*, i, pp. 97 et seqq.

p. 89, l. 6 et seq. *Iliad*, iii, v. 299; p. 89, n. 1. Add L. Deubner, *Attische Feste*, 1932.

p. 94, ll. 17 et seqq. The interpretation of the scourging of the Spartan boys given in the text is open to grave doubts; see my *Gesch. d. griech. Rel.*, i, pp. 458 et seqq.

p. 99, l. 7. Aristotle, *Ethica Nicom.*, p. 1160 [a].

p. 99. On burial and cremation see H. L. Lorimer, 'Pulvis et umbra', *JHS*, liii, 1933, pp. 161 et seqq.

p. 101, ll. 12 et seqq. The statement that bones from other graves were brought up when the place of the shaft-graves at Mycenae was levelled is not correct. These human remains belong to graves from the Middle Helladic cemetery on the same site.

p. 111, l. 8. Something more ought to have been said of the Nymphs. For they were extremely popular and much venerated; see my *Greek Popular Religion*, p. 13.

p. 119, l. 7. Strabo, viii, p. 343.

p. 122, l. 17. Hesiod, *Op. et di.*, vv. 465 et seqq.

p. 125, l. 27. Sophocles, *Antigone*, v. 487.

p. 126, l. 24. Herodotus, v. 66.

p. 129, ll. 16 et seqq. See my paper, 'Vater Zeus', *ARw*, xxxv, 1938, pp. 156 et seqq.

p. 132, n. 2. See my *Gesch. d. griech. Religion*, i, pp. 527 et seqq. Here I add only that Professor Hrozný, 'Les quatre autels "hittites" hiéroglyphiques d'Emri Ghazi et d'Eski Kisla', *Archiv Orientalní*, viii, 1936, p. 171, reads the name of a god *Apulunas*, protector of the gateways.

p. 134, n. 1. Add M. P. Nilsson, *Homer and Mycenae.*

p. 137, ll. 15 et seqq. *Iliad*, xxii, vv. 512 et seqq.

p. 138, l. 4. *Iliad*, xxiii, vv. 103 et seqq.; l. 18, *Odyssey*, xi, vv. 489 et seqq.

p. 141, l. 5. *Iliad*, xxiii, v. 34.

p. 142, ll. 8 et seqq. *Iliad*, iii, v. 278; resp. xix, vv. 259 et seqq.

p. 146, ll. 15 et seqq. But see now my *Mycenean Origin of Greek Mythology*, pp. 223 et seqq.

p. 146, l. 24. The world 'chivalry' is apt to be misunderstood. The State of the gods is created after the pattern of the Mycenaean feudal society; see my *Myc. Origin of Greek Myth.*, p. 221.

p. 150, l. 12. *Iliad*, xvi, vv. 514 et seqq.

p. 170, l. 14 et seq. *Iliad*, xxiv, v. 49.

p. 178, l. 17. *Iliad*, v. vv. 149 et seqq.; l. 20, *ibid.* xii, vv. 243 et seqq.

p. 181, n. 1. Add H. W. Parke, *A History of the Delphic Oracle.*

p. 182, ll. 25 et seqq. Hesiod, *Op. et di.*, v. 209, resp. 174 and 270.

p. 190, l. 16. Demonax; Herodotus, iv. 161; Diodorus, viii. 40; *Oxyrh. Pap.*, xi, No. 1367.

p. 194, ll. 23 et seqq. Kleomedes Pausanias, vi. 9. 6 et seqq.; Plutarch, *Cimon*, 19; Agylla Herodotus, i. 167.

p. 196, ll. 30 et seqq. The killing of the metragyrt happened not about 430 B.C. but in the end of the sixth century, for the temple of the Great Mother was built at this time. There were other plagues than the famous one of 430 B.C.

p. 198, l. 29. Glaukos: Herodotus, vi. 86.

p. 206, l. 24. Lycurgus, *Iliad*, vi, vv. 136 et seqq.

p. 207. See the introduction to E. R. Dodds's edition of the *Bacchae.*

p. 209, ll. 24 et seqq. Plutarch, *de Iside et Os.*, pp. 364 E et seqq.

p. 214, ll. 1 et seqq. The 'Rhapsodic Theogony' is, according to the now prevalent opinion, composed at a late date but may have incorporated earlier elements.

p. 215, ll. 25 et seqq. It is uncertain when 'Time' was put at the head of the Orphic cosmogony and likewise if he derives from Zervanistic speculations.

p. 218, l. 27. Aristophanes, *Frogs*, vv. 145 et seqq.

p. 221, l. 30. It is doubtful if the texts of the gold leaves mentioned can be said to be Orphic in the strict sense.

p. 225, n. 1. Add J. Adam, *The Religious Teachers of Greece*.

p. 226, ll. 9 et seqq. Pindar, *Pythians*, iii, vv. 59 et seqq. and 81 et seqq.

p. 237, ll. 16 et seqq. The religious means employed for uniting Salamis with Athens are very illuminating; see my paper 'The New Inscription of the Salaminioi', *Amer. Journ. of Philol.*, lix, 1938, pp. 385 et seqq.

p. 246, l. 15. Aristotle, *Politics*, vi. 4, p. 1319 B.

p. 263, ll. 13 et seqq. Herakleitos fr. 5 Diels.

p. 267, ll. 7 et seqq. The proof of the divinity of the Heavenly Bodies was found in their regular motions and the purposeful structure of the Universe as opposed to the arbitrariness and incalculability of the old gods. See my paper 'The Origin of Belief among the Greeks in the Divinity of the Heavenly Bodies', *Harvard Theol. Rev.*, xxxiii, 1940, pp. 1 et seqq.

p. 269, ll. 18 et seqq. Critias, *Sisyphos*, in Nauck, *Fragm. tragic. graec.*, 2 ed., p. 771.

p. 272, ll. 24 et seqq. Euripides, *Bacchae*, v. 288.

p. 275, l. 4. Thucydides, iii. 37.

p. 283, ll. 27 et seqq. Menander, fr. 550 Kock.

p. 288, l. 21. Philippides, fr. 25 Kock.

p. 296, l. 23. It is not correct to say that Timotheos founded a branch of the Eleusinian mysteries in Alexandria; they could not be transplanted. He founded a cult of Demeter borrowing, as others did, from the Eleusinian cult.

p. 301, ll. 34 et seqq. See A. B. Cook, *Zeus*, i, p. 173, n. 1. B. Schmidt, 'Demeter in Eleusis und Herr François Lenormant', *Rhein. Museum*, xxxi, 1876, pp. 273 et seqq., proved that the tale is a fake.

INDEX